A GROWING CONCERN

An Autobiography by

NIGEL BROACKES

WEIDENFELD AND NICOLSON
LONDON

First published by
Weidenfeld and Nicolson
91 Clapham High Street, London SW4

Copyright © 1979 by Nigel Broackes

ISBN 0 297 77654 1

Printed by Willmer Brothers Limited,
Rock Ferry, Merseyside

Contents

Contents

Illustrations

Preface

I have chosen at the age of forty-four, perhaps half-way through a normal business life, to write this autobiography because I enjoy writing and I want to record my experiences at a time when people can still remember what things were like when they took place.

This is not a company history or a business manual, and I have minimized the technical and numerical references – these things are available elsewhere, in any case. The book is a subjective account of how I recall the events and surrounding circumstances of childhood, adolescence, and the creation of a large business. The story deals more with takeovers and personalities than it does with management and administration because the day-by-day details, though engrossing, have less place in my recollection of what influenced me and contributed to the generation of Trafalgar as it is today.

Many doors have closed since the commercial events of the last twenty years took place. Others will open, but, I fear, less readily. It will be clear from the book that I have enjoyed all the experiences immensely, though I worry more than I used to about the future – less about Trafalgar's than about the will and resolution of the free world to grow in the way that is indispensable to the social and economic fabric which has developed during the last few decades.

1

Childhood

I was an only child, as were both my parents, so I was also an only grandchild. I was born on 21 July 1934 at Wakefield in Yorkshire, where my mother's parents lived. Grandfather Tansley was spare, quiet, amiable and placid, the most successful of a family of eight children from Leeds, and largely educated by his own efforts: when he matriculated at the age of thirteen he was earning enough as a violinist to pay for his continuing education. He then qualified as a civil engineer and spent the rest of his working life with Green's Economisers in Wakefield. An economiser is a large and complicated piece of plant used to recover unconsumed fuel in the exhaust gases of power stations, and the Green family had developed considerable wealth from the world-wide sale of their equipment.

Granny Tansley was a clergyman's daughter and her father was Rector of the West Riding Asylum for many years. She was always a beautiful woman and was devoted to her husband. They had a happy life together and played a large part in mine until their deaths in the 1960s. Grandfather Tansley retired as Green's chief engineer in 1939 at what was then the most respectable salary of £1,000 a year, but he had only a small, fixed pension. As he lived to be ninety-four it is not surprising that what must at first have seemed adequate savings for retirement proved insufficient. I was impressed by the kindly and paternal way in which Green's gave him what he needed without question or argument as the cost of living began to rise throughout the 1950s.

I was told that the Broackes family originated from Russia, moved in the sixteenth century to Holland and settled as farmers at Yatton in Somerset soon after. Grandfather Broackes started his adult life as a schoolmaster and then crossed the Bristol Channel to Cardiff in search of a commercial career. He was something of a property developer, and he was a member of the Territorial Army, becoming a lieutenant-colonel during the First World War. Later he became an ardent convert to the Baptist Church, even going so far as to prohibit assignment of his tenancies to Roman Catholics. But his main career was in coal, and this led him to the Richard Thomas Group and ultimately to the West Yorkshire Collieries where, by the time of his retirement in the mid-1930s, he was in a most prosperous position: as my mother recalls, £15,000 per annum, Daimler and chauffeur, and three domestic servants provided by the company. Later speculations greatly reduced his fortune, particularly support for the financier Jimmy White, who subsequently went to prison.

He retired with his wife to the Marine Hotel in Porthcawl, where we used to spend short holidays, and sometimes he would come on his own to stay with us at Bingley in Yorkshire. He was a stern and autocratic man, and perhaps a little eccentric. He was fastidious about food and would always arrive to stay bearing his own fish – not fish he had caught, but a fish he preferred. I remember once at Sunday lunch he opened the window, seized an unsatisfactory joint of lamb by the bone and flung it into the garden. And I am told that at dinner parties, including his own, he would rise at 9.15, briskly bid good night to whoever was there, and go to bed. His authority appealed to me, and he seemed kinder to me than to other people. He was the only commercially-minded man I was to meet for many years, and consequently the only one who could answer the kind of questions that interested me. For example, 'What is paint, grandfather?' produced without hesitation a full description of the product, its manufacture, and the nature and sources of the raw materials needed to make it. His wife I remember only as a small, slender, silver-haired figure with a Pekingese dog.

My mother had been to Leeds College of Art and had then become a successful commercial artist; indeed, before their marriage, she was earning more than my father. They got on well together, but he discouraged her from her career after they were married.

My father was an extremely tough man, and I suspect that he had been driven by my grandfather to what, for him, was not the most satisfactory career. He was educated at Repton when the headmaster was Lord Fisher, later Archbishop of Canterbury. After this he went to Peterhouse, Cambridge, where he qualified in law and became quite a distinguished athlete. He was a double blue, two halves and a whole, in the long jump, the 440 yards and boxing. He clearly was not an academic, but I have the impression that he was more sensitive and shy than his achievements would indicate. After Cambridge and a spell in France working as a lumberjack (for further toughness rather than for better French) he returned to Yorkshire where a major argument with my grandfather concerned his desire to become a professional boxer. He was still required to call his father 'Sir' at that time, and the arguments culminated in estrangement when, out shooting with my grandfather, he refused to carry a guest's guns. This resulted in the termination of what had been a most generous allowance of £800 per annum.

He became a partner in the solicitors Wetherhead & Butcher, who had an excellent practice in Bingley and a good reputation throughout the West Riding of Yorkshire; but he probably never earned as much as his former allowance. We lived in a moderate terrace of modern houses called Villa Road; we had one employee, a sickly girl called Amy, who looked after me as well as the washing and cleaning. Our car was a green 4½-litre Bentley with a collapsible roof and a broad, brown-leather strap over the bonnet. Our friends tended to be enthusiastic sportsmen, county cricketers and the like. My father would spend at least thirty minutes a day doing vigorous and taxing exercises, and at weekends he would take solitary walks on Ilkley Moor lasting anything up to eight hours at a time. As war approached he would carry a revolver with him on these long walks for target practice in remote places.

We returned to Bingley after my birth, and I have only the most vague and indistinct recollection of a handful of minor events during the years before the war. An early tendency to kleptomania was arrested when my mother discovered after a shopping expedition that I had pocketed a tube of toothpaste and a number of fishes' eyes, surreptitiously popped from their carcasses on the fishmonger's slab. Subsequently I was punished more severely for a more serious crime: dismantling our wind-up HMV gramophone. This must have taken me an hour or two, and I remember being confident of my ability to reassemble it until I found I could not possibly get the spring back into its case. My mother was distressed to discover the mess, and at this point my father returned from his office; he was angered by what he saw, and I was beaten.

A further exasperation for him must have been to be asked by my mother immediately after the punishment to repair an electric plug on the landing outside my room, where the Hoover had failed to perform that morning. He approached it with the screwdriver I had used in my earlier work, there was a vivid flash of blue light, and he fell backwards down the stairs. Occasionally today I have comparable experiences of retribution, and at the time the event may have given me an inverted appreciation of conventional moral values.

I remember a day of beagling when my mother and I followed (by eye, from a central point) the hunters who, on foot, followed the hounds who, in turn, chased a hare which led them all cunningly in a broad circle round our vantage point before disappearing. My father was one of the energetic hunters. On the whole the pre-war years at Bingley were happy, although I disliked learning and can recall devastating languor in the early afternoons at school and total boredom with the alphabet.

My father was passionately pro-Churchill long before Munich, and as a result he joined the Royal Artillery early in 1939. Thereafter we travelled round the country following him as best we could from place to place, in a series of furnished rooms and hotels, but it was only at Wincanton in Somerset that I can remember seeing him in the company of his colleagues: even a boy of seven could tell that he was treated with unqualified admiration and respect. He must have been a very good regimental officer.

Whilst we were in the West Country I was sent to a series of dame schools, where I struggled with boring work and arithmetic. The standard of teaching was poor, discipline was

Dickensian and usually administered with an ebony rod across the palm of the hand. But I enjoyed the interiors of the strange private house where these lessons took place. Excellent Victorian mahogany furniture, glass domes on every table and mantelpiece under which perched strange birds, seashells, dried flowers and porcelain, and drab brown and maroon carpets with curtains of high quality dating from the previous century. These confronted uninspiring paintings, engravings and strange forms of marine life embalmed in clear bottles of alcohol.

In 1942 my mother and I moved to Porlock in Somerset, and by this time my father's location was secret. I learned later that he was in the Isle of Wight training Canadian anti-tank gunners for commando operations and particularly for marine assault. The last time I saw him was just before the raid on Dieppe, when he joined us for forty-eight hours' leave and was understandably tired and tense. On this occasion he carried out his target practice in the garden and I was greatly impressed to watch him pin a playing-card to a tree, retire fifteen paces and systematically shoot out six pips with a ·45 revolver.

On Christmas Day 1942 my mother received a telegram and told me that she must leave at once to see my father who was in hospital in Kent. I was sent to stay at a large house nearby and I remember feeling bewildered, rather than worried or lonely. On New Year's Day the house seemed strangely calm, and after lunch I was taken by a very pleasant woman to a small room with a fire. 'I want you to sit down and be very brave. Daddy's been taken to heaven.' My small world disintegrated; I could not comprehend, but I recognized that a totally unbelievable disaster had occurred. We had not been very close, and I had not seen much of him, but he was the pivot around which my life revolved.

My father had developed peritonitis and died in hospital on 1 January 1943 at the age of thirty-eight, leaving a total estate amounting to just £38. I suppose that his pay as a major was no more than £40 per month; I received his penknife and, later, his signet ring. The British Legion paid for my mother's case against the War Office to secure a widow's pension, but we failed to prove that death was the result of a war injury.

My mother must have been devastated by this tragedy, but her responses were sound and practical. Grandfather Broackes died a few months later and his widow offered financial support if we would go to live with her, but not otherwise. My mother declined, preferring to live on a £4-a-week pension from the British Legion. Granny Broackes lived for another year and left her money, £4,000 or so, in trust for me until the age of twenty-one. Her husband had left about £28,000 initially for his widow, but with provision for an income for my mother pending remarriage, and the capital in trust to be released to me at the age of twenty-one. In the meantime, income was provided for my 'education, benefit and maintenance'. It will be appreciated that this money was of decisive importance to us and that the figures were perhaps five times more significant then than they would be today, due to inflation; in the case of school fees, indeed, the factor must be nearly ten times the war-time level.

By this time I was, so far as I know, the last remaining male Broackes. My mother a few years ago endeavoured through the Genealogical Society to trace the family history: the line through the eighteenth century was clear, but became dispersed and indistinct subsequently. One, I remember, died of cancer of the penis; some could only sign their names with Xs (which had not been the case previously); and the only one to achieve distinction was the founder of the Military Police, apparently the first man to rise from the ranks to become a general in the British Army. My grandfather had a brother, but we never met; I have twice met an airline hostess on British Airways flights to Nice whose maiden name was Broackes, and a cousin named Pat Batchelor, née Broackes, now lives in retirement with her husband near Cheltenham and takes our younger son Simon out for the day from his prep school at Oxford several times a term. My wife also was an only child, but we now have three children and perhaps something more cohesive will follow.

At present, apart from my own achievements, the only record of the family is a tablet in the Church at Yatton which reads:

HERE LIE THE REMAINS OF
RICHARD BROACKES (Yeoman)
and his wife HANNAH of this Parish
also THOMAS their son
died 24th June 1806 aged 74
also EDWARD BROACKES
of the parish of KINGSTON SEYMOUR
died 5th July 1820 aged 81
and his wife ANN
died 27th June 1831 aged 84

AND IN MEMORY OF THOSE WHO WERE WARDENS OF
THIS CHURCH

THOMAS BROACKES	1694
EDWARD	1712
JOHN	1717
EDWARD	1718
THOMAS	1719
RICHARD	1739

AND BURIED NEAR HERE

2

School

A year after my father's death I was at prep school and I remember toiling up a steep, snow-covered hill, one of a long line of boys carrying wood for the fires. I felt flushed and breathless and had a sharp pain in my chest. I reported this to Matron and was put to bed with assumed measles. Brambletye School had been evacuated from East Grinstead to Lee Abbey at Lynton in Devon early in the war and occupied a fine former hotel beautifully sited in an isolated position at the end of the Valley of Rocks overlooking the sea, two or three miles from Lynton, and twenty miles or so from Porlock, where by now we lived. I was sent to Brambletye soon after my father's death, and at this stage my attitude towards the school was neutral, rather than hostile, and later I came to enjoy it very much.

I had been sickly and listless for many months and rather welcomed the idea of a few days in bed with a recognized conventional illness. The doctor came that afternoon, confirmed that I was one of several boys who had measles, and set off on his return journey to Lynton, saying that the snow by now was so heavy that the Valley, our only access, would soon become impassable. The diagnosis of measles was correct, but incomplete; the pain became sharper, and I fell asleep during the late afternoon. When I awoke to bright sunshine and was offered a plate of Spam by Sister I was bewildered, particularly by the light of early afternoon, as I felt as if I had slept for only a few minutes.

In fact I had been unconscious for three days with a temperature rising to 108°. Penicillin was not available at that time; they could not get an ambulance through the Valley; and my life was probably saved by a drug called M & B, then a relative novelty. As well as measles, I had pleurisy and pneumonia, and the nastiest part of the subsequent treatment was to find myself encased with hot poultices round the chest. I was ill for several more weeks and arose to convalesce during one of those marvellous periods of early spring warmth and sunshine that represent, for me, the best four or five days of any year of English weather. A cloud had lifted, the boil had burst, so to speak, and my spirits began to revive after a year's despair following my father's death.

I had no school work to do, but I was expected to rest frequently; otherwise I was free to wander through the grounds and to discover what a beautiful place it was. Lee Abbey marks the western boundary of the country described in *Lorna Doone*, with Lovers' Leap at its extremity, a balustraded grotto a hundred feet or more above the sea, and no more than five minutes' walk from the school past a fine cedar of Lebanon and through a corridor of rhododendrons.

I was released before the end of term to join my mother for further convalescence at a small hotel near Teignmouth on the south coast of Devon. The climate was bland and rather enervating, the trees and flowers semi-tropical, and the atmosphere like a small Torquay or an even smaller Bournemouth. It was here that I first found books on elementary electrics and electronics and confidently embarked on a hobby that was to enthral me for the next six or seven years. I also developed an early interest in explosives.

The Porlock chemist had been co-operative in supplying saltpetre, charcoal and sulphur for simple gunpowder experiments, but wisely refused hydrochloric and nitric acid when I wanted to graduate to nitro-glycerine and gun-cotton. I determined to see what could be done with glycerine alone, and at first produced nothing more than a feeble flame, even with gunpowder as a detonator. Then I selected a used Sparklet bulb (a small cylinder of carbon dioxide used to make domestic soda water), filled it carefully with my ingredients, and tried to set it off. I had sealed it with a nail, hoping that impact would cause it to explode. This didn't work, nor did heating the container with other chemicals, so I took it to our living room, where my mother was sitting and writing a letter. I quietly placed it among the glowing coals of our small fire, and withdrew. After a few minutes there was a report – more of a sharp thud than a bang – and I returned to the room, which was filled with smoke. My mother was agitatedly beating the cushions against one another because, although the explosion was small, it had propelled the contents of the fireplace across the room and lumps of burning coal had punctured the upholstered furniture, where they smouldered within. The contents of the room had to be taken into the fresh air for these incendiaries to be identified, and some of the furniture was damaged beyond repair. My mother's response to the incident was restrained, and soon I found myself back at Brambletye.

After an ear operation at Wincanton I was warned never to dive or to swim under water, and after my more serious illness I was advised that my heart would be weak. Neither of these incidents seem to have left any sustained impairment, but the latter gave me an easy alibi for a while from games. I am the opposite to my father and have no interest in games or sport of any kind, even today. But I became unusually strong. In the past I had avoided rather than resisted bullies, but now I found I could wrestle with the more aggressive and physically self-confident boys and beat them. The turning-point occurred in public when for some reason a larger boy threw me to the ground and sat on my chest; without thought or difficulty I flicked my right knee round his throat and shot his head back to the ground with a force that stunned him. I became known as 'Beefy', and had no further trouble.

By this time my mother had taken a job working for the American Broadcasting Service in Europe; the pay was good and they released her during the school holidays. We went to St Mawes for the summer of 1944 and stayed at Mrs Tiddy's guest-house. Most of the other guests were in St Mawes to fish or to sail, and the 'life and soul of the party' was a group captain with a clipped moustache named F. R. Gibson Craig Alford, whose friends called him Alf. He must then have been in his late forties and was full of *bonhomie* and jollity to a degree that might have become slightly oppressive over any long period of time; I detected in his wife's demeanour certain subtle traces that this was indeed the case. She was attractive and effective in a quietly feminine way and quite obviously, though I could not have defined it at the time, of a higher class and culture than the rest of us.

More than two-thirds of every year I spent, of course, at school; but as nothing of great interest happened there during the year, let me pursue for a moment the story of Uncle Alf, as he was to become – for not long after the sudden death of the lady we had met at St Mawes – his third wife – he became my stepfather.

He was born in Canada and his mother was German. His father, who lived by this time a happy, hermit-like existence in a wooden bungalow beside the sea further up the estuary from St Mawes, was reputed to be an illegitimate son of the Victorian artist W. P. Frith. He had spent his life as a journalist; his biggest 'scoop' had been the San Francisco earthquake of 1906, for he happened to be staying there at the time whilst working for *The Times*. My stepfather came to Europe in the First World War with the Canadian Black Watch, and he earned the Military Cross leading a group of motor cycle-mounted machine-gunners in one of the numerous engagements in which he took part. Later in the war he joined the Royal Flying Corps, and in due course was given a regular commission in the Royal Air Force, as it became. He served for some time afterwards with Rolls-Royce armoured cars in Iraq and for several years before the Second World War he was with the aircraft carrier HMS *Hermes* in China. By the time of the war in 1939 he was too old for an active role, and promotion to a more senior rank eluded him, so he was appointed commanding officer of various training establishments, concluding with Jerby in the Isle of Man. He was awarded the OBE, but it puzzled me at the time that he had not got further with his career, for few of his friends and contemporaries were less than air commodores, and several were air marshals. I am sure he was a good CO, but I came to understand later why he really would not have been suited for higher rank. Although others with less merit may have got further in various branches of the forces, I think in his case his extreme extrovertness may have raised ineradicable reservations in high places. Life for him in the RAF came to an abrupt end over a trivial and well-intentioned offence: he obtained illicitly a flyer's sheepskin coat and gave it to one of his sons, both of whom were in the Royal Navy. A court martial followed, and he lost his job, though he kept his rank and pension.

The wife we had met was called Binks, and she was the widow of a former racing-car driver named Lucy, who, in turn, was the father of her daughter Josephine. Binks had a large property in Scotland where later we went to live for some years. Her maiden name had been Gibson Craig, and the family had lived at Riccarton for several centuries before we arrived there; but by that time the fortune and the title had become separated, and the former was in trust entirely for Josephine at the age of twenty-five. Mr Lucy had become Gibson Craig Lucy just as my stepfather was to adopt a triple-barrelled name, and this can sometimes be material in terms of Scottish inheritances – though in Uncle Alf's case it yielded very little. His first marriage, like his third, had been to an heiress, but somehow he failed throughout his life quite to 'get it together'.

His first wife was Rosie, a Tankerville Chamberlayne, whose family lived at Cranberry in Hampshire and owned many marvellous paintings as well as much land and, at one time, a lot of the waterfront at Southampton. I do not know what led to the divorce, for she never married again, but they had three children: Ian, Mark and Iris. The boys were sent to Dartmouth and spent the war at sea. Ian married Jackie, sixteen at the time, during the latter part of the war. They were both most kind to me during the early years of my mother's new marriage, and my wife and I see them regularly today. Mark was cast in a more sombre role, for I cannot believe that my stepfather was not indulging in some elementary dynastic intrigue when it was decided at the end of the war that Mark should marry Josephine, then a plump and beautiful young WAAF. The marriage was not a success.

I was back at school when my mother wrote to announce her marriage plans; I felt it was more her business than mine and I replied affirmatively. Around this time VE Day was declared and we had a whole holiday and took to the surrounding hills with picnics. Nothing much else happened at school, and the summer holidays resumed at St Mawes, where my stepfather had a red sailing boat called *Siskin*, a 16-foot half-decked one-design which he had bought before the war from Frank Perkins, the St Mawes boatbuilder. I remember being cold, cramped and bored during long days at sea. Josephine arrived later, and we spent happier times in her short blunt-ended dinghy called *Pook*, which had only a single sail and nearly drowned us both on one occasion when suddenly the skies turned dark and an evil and unexpected wind drove us towards ugly rocks some hundreds of yards from the coast facing our temporary seaside home. We were rescued by a motor boat which must have been despatched by my stepfather. The summer holidays finished in style at North Row, just behind Park Lane, where my mother now had a flat above an antique shop.

In the meantime Brambletye had returned to East Grinstead, to several hundred agreeable acres and a large, well-built house which was constructed around 1900 for Barney Barnarto, the South African millionaire who had been an acquaintance of Rhodes. The school was requisitioned during the war for service purposes, and the grounds were still rich with military relics. The swimming pool was inches deep with detonators, and we found unexploded hand grenades, ·5-inch Browning ammunition, and many other riveting articles in the grounds. By this time I was growing up, and led my own gang of embryo gangsters. My undoing was to discover an incendiary bomb not far from the school. Clearly it was German, for we had an ARP poster which illustrated it and gave a sectional drawing showing how it was made. It should, of course, have been handed in to the authorities, but my friends and I preferred to take it to the basement of the school to what was called the underground gym, and to dismantle it.

The first thing to do was to remove the high-explosive section, which I did, and I set it aside at a safe distance. The next step was to unscrew the detonating mechanism, which contained a delayed-action device. When this was completed a small, round, pink cap was disclosed, rather like the percussion cap in a child's toy gun. I will never forget, and I can still see in slow motion, my friend Raikes taking the canister from me, reaching for a screwdriver with his right hand, and striking the cap. The bomb must have been made of some kind of magnesium alloy, for it exploded like a firework, but went on and on. . . . Raikes had damaged his eyes and went to the sanatorium; the underground gym was filled with

smoke and light, and I withdrew to the top of the flight of
stairs which led through our boots and tuck-box room to the
fresh air. Nothing of the kind had happened to the school
throughout the war and as masters and boys hurried back
and forth with fire-fighting apparatus, I adopted a detached
demeanour and briefly behaved as if I had no connection
with the event. But when confronted I confessed, and it was
expected that I would be expelled. The fire was extinguished
and the damage was slight. The headmaster, Mr Blencowe,
was away at the time and his assistant, an excellent schoolmaster named H. V. Jones, placed me in suspense rather than
on probation. When the headmaster returned he gave me
thirteen strokes with a dog whip. The whip had a semi-rigid
structure and a heavy spherical tip. Each stroke bruised or
drew blood from my naked body and the tip whipped round
to my groin. Raikes recovered and I was told later that the
only reason I had not been expelled was because I took the
punishment silently. This event left no resentment, and by
now I was more concerned with my next school and the Common Entrance exam.

Brambletye was an excellent example of what a prep school
should be: academic standards were not of the highest, games
and athletics were not of dominant importance, much pride
was felt in the place, and we developed all our individualities
within the context of a limited, but complex, society and in
agreeable surroundings.

My father had wanted for me a sort of Outward Bound
education, tough self-reliance and lots of activity in the fresh
air. My mother sought something different and wanted me
to go to Stowe. Mr Blencowe told her that Stowe's entry
standards might be beyond me, but they could certainly get
me into Eton in the event of exam problems.

I was released from school for a day to visit Stowe with my
mother; we took a train to Bletchley, and then a taxi to the
school. I was overwhelmed by the landscape and by the size
and extent of the buildings. We ascended a broad flight of
steps and then were taken down to the headmaster's study.
J. F. Roxburgh was already a legendary figure: he was slim
with well-brushed silver hair, immaculately dressed, and wore
spectacles in a fine metal frame. His manner was urbane and

authoritative, and he quickly put us both at our ease. I liked it and said I wanted to go there. J.F., as the headmaster was always referred to, placed his hand firmly on my shoulder and said he had no doubt my Common Entrance result would be sufficient. He shook my mother's hand and we set off in a taxi for the station along a fine, straight avenue of trees.

Before going to Stowe I spent a summer holiday in Scotland with my mother and stepfather. He was in the curious role of being a former proprietress's widowed husband who had a personal bequest of only £250 a year, but was manager of four thousand acres of excellent land near Edinburgh until Josephine reached the age of twenty-five. Levels of staffing and nourishment were gradually to decline over the years, but began at a higher level than I had ever known. It was a strange situation which I can best describe with mixed metaphors: my stepfather was Toad of Toad Hall and I was perfectly well aware that we were cuckoos in someone else's nest.

I came to enjoy more and more the sensation of being isolated in close proximity to a large city, a preference I have retained. We were isolated geographically, surrounded by much private woodland and several farms, and we were insulated economically and socially from what was a grim period for much of the British middle class.

The early post-war period was in many ways one of greater discomfort domestically than the war had been. Ration allowances were reduced, fuel was short, goods in the shops were sparse and shoddy, and Aneurin Bevan questioned how this could happen to an island built on coal and surrounded by fish. Perhaps there were two answers: firstly, that our doctrinaire Socialist Government was unfit for its very demanding task, and, secondly, that the alternative, the Conservatives, consisted of and were supported by a different category of people, men and women who had on the whole been closer to the major burdens and stress of the war and were exhausted – mentally and physically. I hope I have made this point in a non-partisan manner, for it springs from observation rather than emotion. Many of our best young men, destined to lead in peace-time, had been lost in the war. Just as in the 1914–18 war, it had been inevitable that the best were in the jobs with the shortest expectation of life. Labour had some outstanding men, but their party's previous record in office had been dismal. I make the point at this early stage in my book because it was already part of any small boy's experience to hear his parents and their friends talk interminably of their dismay that a disloyal electorate had preferred Labour to Winston Churchill. Many thought Britain was finished, but they were wrong; perhaps they meant that things would never again be as they were before the war.

I was thirteen when I went to Stowe, and for the first two years must have been a colourless and undistinguished pupil in all principal respects: school work, games and spare-time activities. I loathed games by now, particularly cricket, and my house, Chatham, was not distinguished at cricket or rugger, though we had one or two good players. It must have been for lack of prospects that later on I was appointed to lead our rugger fifteen in the house competition; we had better players, but perhaps they were committed to play for the school. I was under sixteen at the time, slow but fairly strong, and I was determined that we would win. We did, and it was the first time Chatham had won this particular cup for many years. The triumph, such as it was, was one of planning and organization, sustained over a period of eight or ten weeks. Although I was never a good player, I thought it unfair not to be awarded my house colours for the success. Later on in life I found from time to time that I reproduced such periods of sustained, but restricted, endeavour – and to good effect. And I must admit that recognition pleases me.

My housekeeper at Stowe, Mr MacDonald, was an admirable man, but we never understood one another, and he must have been taken aback, to say the least, when a few years ago he learned that I had become a governor of the school. Certainly it was at Stowe that I found myself to be ambitious, and it was there also that I found I could be effective. I was there at the end of J.F.'s regime, and it was not until Bob Drayson's appointment as headmaster in 1963 that the school recovered its former standards.

I suppose the truth of the matter is that I never got on particularly well with any of the masters who taught me, though I developed good relationships with some of the others. I took the School Certificate examination in June 1949, just before the age of fifteen, and at the end of the previous term most of my reports, and certainly Mr MacDonald's, had predicted poor results or failure. In fact I got six distinctions (equivalent to grade As in the present O Levels): English Language, English Literature, Physics and Chemistry, Elementary and Additional Maths; and credits in French, Divinity and Geography. A hundred boys had taken the exam, and only one did better. The results gratified me, but I felt uncertain about how long I could continue with teachers whom I did not much respect and who evidently had little understanding of me. The next term I chose what was known as Side 5, the mathematics department, for A levels and, in my case, a possible scholarship to Cambridge. I continued with physics and a certain amount of chemistry, and I learned the easy way that I was just good enough at maths to be aware that of all subjects it was only worth pursuing beyond a certain point if one was quite exceptionally good, which I was not. The tutor for Side 5 was Freddy Archer, a clever, eccentric man of some economic independence who had been at Stowe almost since its foundation. My wife and I saw him a few years ago, some time after his retirement, and he said to her, 'Nigel really could have done rather well if he'd worked harder.'

In terms of my hobby I had progressed through crystal sets to thermionic valves, and by the age of twelve was making small mains-powered radio receivers which were sold to friends for £4 or £6, at a 100 per cent profit. The components were war-surplus goods, bought very cheaply, mainly in Lisle Street behind Leicester Square; and the circuits were developed from *Wireless World* and other periodicals to produce what were called super-heterodyne receivers of completely adequate quality by the standards of the time. I had a fair understanding of the basic mathematics and physics of this field, and I progressed to make a primitive television set, which never worked very well, partly because the government-surplus, cathode-ray tubes had been made for radar, and left a 'trace' after each image, i.e. a lingering green shadow of the previous picture. I even managed with a friend to reproduce Baird's early scan-ning disc transmitter, but only to the point of sending and receiving simple patterns, letters of the alphabet, and so on. The school was not greatly involved with such things, but the master mainly concerned was Mr Llowarch, the science tutor. The school was to produce Bizet's opera *Carmen*, and I proposed to Mr Llowarch that I should record it, at the science department's expense, on a fairly primitive twin-table machine that had been given to the school by a benefactor. The plan was to sell the resultant records to parents, and the money required was for the cost of making the metal matrices to press the records. The recordings were really rather good, and the profit would have been entirely for the science department; but unwisely I had allowed people to play the original shellac discs on their gramophones to solicit orders before the matrices were made. The immediate result was a large number of enthusiastic orders; but the consquence was several hundred 78 rpm pressings, made against firm orders, which sounded dreadful and must have caused embarrassment to Mr Llowarch, who by this time had adopted the project as his own. I had come top in physics and chemistry, but in subsequent terms was placed in lower sets. I complained to Mr Llowarch and then to my tutor Freddy Archer, and Freddy complained to Mr Llowarch. But all to no avail, and this contributed to a growing disenchantment with school.

At this point it must be made clear that in the meantime the whole tone of the establishment had deteriorated. Great men, when they die in service or when they retire, generally leave behind a vacuum; and their successor, almost regardless of his qualities, has an exceptionally hard task to follow – Trafalgar repeatedly took over good businesses that were enfeebled at a comparable moment in their histories. In the case of Stowe, there was a double blow: a year after J.F.'s retirement his successor, E. V. Reynolds, had a serious mountaineering accident, cracked his skull, and was not to return to complete good health for several years. He was replaced by a man named Crichton-Miller, not a good choice.

At sixteen I became restless and rather disgruntled. Looking back, I suppose I had by then done quite reasonably well: I was a house monitor and a school prefect at a relatively young age; as work became more difficult I found myself better

at it; and I suppose I was quite generally admired and respected by my peers – I even won a house popularity contest
on a points system. But by this time I knew perfectly well, and
some of my immediate superiors must have suspected, that
I simply was not the type of conventional young man to serve,
lead and take responsibility within their closed community. I
hope I am not arrogant, but certainly by this time I was proud,
and prepared only to judge people and issues by my own
standards, without reference to or respect for the customs and
values of the small world in which I happened to find myself
at the time. I had no secret doubts or fears, and I felt the first
stirrings of self-confidence and ambition on a scale to which
my present environment was irrelevant rather than restrictive.
I was non-conventional rather than un-conventional, and
merely marking time in terms of the wider boundaries of my
life. But in terms of my school career, a crisis was developing.

Obviously motor vehicles were not allowed to the boys; but
I kept a 500 cc Triumph motor bike at the nearby Silverstone
race-track. I had bought it for £30 from a steward, and I
remember the feel and smell of it well. It had no silencer (just
a megaphone exhaust) and I never knew how fast it went, for
neither had it a speedometer. It was certainly very powerful,
and I drove once to Southampton in less than two hours. Obviously, again, alcohol was not allowed; but I kept some and
would sell gin diluted with orange juice to boys at parties
after school plays and the like. Smoking was another offence,
a serious matter at Stowe, where in the main building sound
insulation between floors is generally of straw. And so on. . . .
I was never caught and indicted for any specific offence, but
gradually the authorities must have become aware of an ac-
cumulation of suspicion covering quite a wide field. It must
have been in September or October 1950 that the authorities
decided to act, and at this moment there was no headmaster at
all.

A month or two earlier I had been on a motoring trip to
France with two other boys and a master who owned a
pleasant, pre war, drophead car. The holiday had not been a
success because, following an incident at an hotel a few miles
south of Bordeaux, I left, and returned to England by train.
On the first day of the next term one of my former companions

reproached me for having spoiled their holiday, and, in confidence, I explained to him the reason, which he had not
known before. He foolishly repeated it to the authorities and
there followed, simultaneously with the enquiries into the
term-time matters I mentioned a moment ago, an investigation
concerning the holiday incident. The pursuit of all this was
not in firm or competent hands, and the various issues became
inextricably involved with each another, as I fed into the
maelstrom my resentment concerning Mr Llowarch, mislead-
ing school reports, and even the absence of house colours for
leading Chatham at rugger! At this point I should mention
that later in the previous holidays I had had an accident with
my motor cycle which resulted in mild concussion; I had
abandoned all ideas of a scholarship to Cambridge and I
wanted to leave school; and in the meantime I had given up
maths in favour of English. I was in a troublesome and mis-
chievous mood; I had little to lose and, in any case, I wanted
to start my adult life. But first I wanted to express my various
resentments, and to gratify them by winning a conclusive victory in this curious and convoluted situation which I had done
much to create. Before I describe the conclusion let me make
it clear (if anyone doubts it) that the fault for part of this
muddle was mine, and that I had stirred it up deliberately in
an adolescent fit of discontent: I was sick and tired of
authority exercised by older boys and by adults whom I had
ceased to respect. And perhaps I felt a sense of juvenile be-
trayal to discover their frailty for the first time.

I wrote a long letter to my stepfather in which I did my best
to describe the entire situation; he replied robustly and without
question that he supported my proposal that, if I was expelled,
we would sue and expose the seamier side of the story together
with the more straightforward issues which ineptly had been
allowed to become involved with the latter. I declared all
this, and it produced a solution within the day: I would cease
to be a monitor and a prefect forthwith, but would be re-
appointed to both offices on the last day of term, whereupon
I would leave. Most boys left at eighteen and then joined the
armed forces for National Service, but I was sixteen and I
wanted to do a job first.

For the rest of this last term I had a curious, detached role, for the terms of the settlement were quite widely known, and during this time I enjoyed the condition I deplore in others: authority without responsibility. Mr MacDonald told me at the end of term that I really did not have to leave at all, but I replied that I preferred to. Stowe was going through a bad patch, and it happened to coincide with one of mine. In any case, I had already arranged my first job.

3

In the City

My parents, my stepfather and our friends and relations were people with military, artistic or professional backgrounds. Only grandfather Broackes had been a businessman, and it was this more comprehensive area of life that I wanted to find out about. I felt a compelling curiosity to discover areas that none but grandfather Broackes had understood.

David Stewart had been a friend of mine at Stowe, and his father was a director of the Lloyd's underwriting agency Stewart & Hughman. David and I were in the same form for mathematics, and he wanted to try for a Cambridge scholarship (he got an exhibition), whereas his father would have preferred him to leave school and join the firm. Conversely, I wanted to give up school and to start work, so when David told me of his difficulty I asked if I could see his father. The interview took place and I was offered a job, which I accepted gratefully, not knowing at the time that quite by chance I had chosen a place uniquely appropriate to my desire to begin to educate myself commercially before joining the army. I had left Stowe in December 1950 and arranged to join Stewart & Hughman at the end of January.

I have explained that none of my family or their friends had any commercial knowledge, experience, or connections whatsoever – we were completely naïve in this respect. What I needed was a job in a well-positioned office in the City where the transactions were large, but the office was small enough for a young man to get a clear impression of everything that went on. Stewart & Hughman were ideal for this, and my job was a cross between office boy, messenger, clerk and general dogsbody for E. J. Stewart, David's father. At that time the total staff amounted to eighty people or so, divided between Asia House, where I started, and the main Lloyd's building on the other side of Lime Street. The firm's underwriting name is A. B. Stewart and Others – E.J. was A.B.'s younger brother; we were leading underwriters for several classes of business, with six or seven active syndicates, about a hundred and twenty names (individual investors who were members of our syndicate) and a significant role in the marine, non-marine and aviation markets. The staff was small, but at that time we had a larger premium income than the Eagle Star Insurance Company, and never less than £15 million of cash and securities awaiting payment of claims and distributions to our members.

Accounting in those days was assisted by Hollerith cards, and my first job each day was to sort out a large bundle recording the previous day's business: each card was the size of an elongated postcard and gave details of the broker, the risk, the premium and the shares taken by our various syndicates. I would index these under the brokers' names, and soon knew the name of every broker, just as years before I had learned (as a punishment) the names of all the books of the Bible. The office manager, Mr Dale, was imaginative in setting me the widest possible variety of tasks, and these tended more to be matters of statistics and underwriting records rather than straightforward accountancy – though I remember at quite an early stage being able to make a helpful suggestion when the auditors were having difficulty with the books: a Canadian dollar account had been recorded entirely in that currency and translated into sterling at the rate ruling at the year's end, whereas, as I pointed out, our books would only balance if one took the actual rates ruling at the time of each transaction into or out of the currency. An elementary point, and one which interested me.

A.B. was a leading personality at Lloyd's, but not universally popular. He had started there as a manager during the First World War and took over the firm soon afterwards, when the former owners no longer had male heirs. The directors, of course, were all members of Lloyd's, as were the senior staff (the firm would lend them the necessary capital), and the firm made its money from fees and profit shares charged to the members. I saw quite a lot of the private records of individual names, and quickly developed a new awareness of private wealth on a scale that would have been inconceivable to me a few months earlier. I handled some of A.B.'s personal investment records and saw for the first time the great mass of savings that could have been accumulated purely from a very large income during the twenty low-tax years between the wars. One of my confidential tasks was to assist Mr Dale in maintaining a precious little book: this was A.B.'s personal summary of all our business. It was no larger than a pocket diary, and we wrote it up every week in seven or eight different colours of ink.

E.J.'s work was mainly concerned with investment, and he was assisted in this by a kindly, middle-aged man who shared his office and whom he always addressed as Sibbering, never by his Christian name. I would be given cheques, contract notes, share transfers and so on, to be delivered by hand to banks and brokers all over the City. On each occasion E.J. took the trouble to explain precisely the transaction to which the documents related and, of course, I learned a lot of the City's geography on my errands.

My salary was £220 per annum and I had another £250 per annum from my grandfather's trust. I first lived in a furnished room in a house behind Ladbroke Grove, where the weekly charge of £4 included a cooked breakfast and dinner, and we were all fed in a dining room in the basement; the other occupants were single people who were much older than me, and most had been there for many years. There was a solicitor's managing clerk, a mysterious foreign doctor, a lady widowed in the war, and so on. None of them became friends, with me or with each other; it is hard to visualize their lives then, and even harder to imagine what became of them all – for today the equivalent charge must be at least £10 per night, and the place was not particularly attractive. I generally had enough money to go home at weekends, but I had to count it in terms of pennies. I travelled to the office by underground from Notting Hill to the Bank, and initially the cost was 6d. On the return journey it was possible to trudge up the emergency staircase at Notting Hill, and I always did so: if a ticket-collector was at the top, one handed over one's ticket, but otherwise one walked out into the fresh air and the ticket could be used again the next day. These economies were significant to me at the time.

Another friend from Stowe was Rupert Chetwynd, and he persuaded me that Chelsea would be preferable to Notting Hill. Rupert's mother, Bridget, was then social editress of the *Tatler*; she was a talented writer living in Selword Terrace with many friends from pre- and post-war Bohemia. She had what might be termed 'personal problems', and I remember her once picking up a ball of wool from the floor of her sitting room with a hypodermic needle – she would write her dreams in pencil on the walls of the room and had not long to live. Rupert's father was a dapper, ageless major in the Grenadiers, who later occupied an office in a building of ours in Whitehall from which we took my company's name – Trafalgar House. If I knew, I would not say this: but as I do not know, let me state my assumption that for Major Chetwynd to be in that office running something related to Rubber Improvement conveyed an image reminiscent of John le Carré's twilight world of fading post-war espionage and counter-espionage.

Rupert had a girl-friend called Charlotte, whose mother, Isobel Strachey, had a house at 49 Oakley Street, with a room to let in the basement. Isobel shared a bedroom on the ground floor with her daughter; they kept a fine double reception room on the first floor, and the upper part of the house was let to Mark Bonham Carter, who sometimes would have remarkably distinguished visitors during the afternoon. I took the basement room at three guineas a week, which included breakfast, but not dinner. Isobel wrote a book called *Quick Bright Things* in which Charlotte and I were the leading characters. Charlotte married the publisher Anthony Blond, but later she died. Rupert subsequently established a major advertising business.

At this stage I spent a total of only eight months in London, punctuated by a third-class, student-fare visit to Biarritz with my former school-friend Jeremy Scott, Charlotte, and Jeremy's girl-friend Shirley Weare. It was not particularly successful, for the sea was cold, Shirley was shy and Charlotte was morose. The only joke I remember was when Charlotte returned late one day for lunch at our small hotel. We discovered that she had somehow injured a finger on a fish hook, but what she said was, 'I'm so sorry to be late; I caught my finger in a fisherman's

fly.' More serious was an event at the Gare du Nord on the way
back, when we were hungry after the overnight train journey
from Biarritz, and had insufficient money left for breakfast: we
had a good meal at an outside table by the station café, and as
our train to Calais began to draw away from the platform, we
ran for it, leaving all we had on the table. We must all have been
sixteen at the time.

Generally I would go back to our new house at Bursledon
for my short weekends. One notable exception was when
another old Stoic, Jimmy Hartley, asked me to stay at his
mother's house at Whiteleafe between Purley and Croydon.
Pre-war weekends must have been like that. It was not on the
Cliveden scale, but as well as a pleasant house and a nice
big garden there were guest cottages in the grounds, a swimming pool and a tennis court. I am one of the few people I
know who met the late Dr Stephen Ward. He was there, handsome and charming, with a most beautiful blonde girl called
Vicci Martin, who was to die later in a car smash near Maiden-
head. I emerged with a young lady named Judy Elder, with
whom I was on close terms for the next few months.

After this came the army, and I must restore a sense of
proportion to my story by explaining that throughout this
time in London I worked extremely hard and took my job
most seriously. Readers will not be interested in the technicalities of my early work, so all I need say is that I learned
a lot concerning business in general, not just about Lloyd's
in particular, and was most grateful to the Stewart family
and their staff. In those days we worked a full five days per
week plus most Saturday mornings. I enjoyed it, and may have
learned even more than I was taught.

I found time during my working hours to establish a grey-
hound-racing syndicate. There must then have been twenty
dog-tracks around London, with racing two or three evenings
a week, six dogs in every race and eight races in every meeting.
This lent itself to the simple statistical approach of analysing
the results published every day in the newspapers purely in
terms of trap numbers for each race at each place – without
reference to form or particular dogs. I kept these records on
cards, and they indicated the trap numbers most likely, in
terms of probability (as I thought), to win each race at each

track, that is to say the number of the trap which had not won for the longest time. Each afternoon we would examine the records, and two or three times a week a clear pattern of longest-losing sequences for the largest number of races would emerge and pinpoint the particular track to be visited later in the day. Before embarking on the project with real money, we analysed historical results, and the scheme seemed to be faultless – the technique was for me to go to the chosen track carrying the predetermined sequence of numbers and to bet with increasing stakes to recover any previous losses and, in addition, to win £1 for each member of the syndicate plus an extra £1 for me. I carried a small slide rule to calculate the bets, according to the odds. The point about this story is that we never lost, and only once did I have to stay beyond the third race. My partners included Bob Berry, now a respected underwriter elsewhere, and a very nice man who must have been called 'Rip' Kirby. I do not necessarily commend the scheme to others but, as I said, we never lost: and an extra £6 per week was significant to me.

At Stewart & Hughman we were given luncheon vouchers of 2s 6d and then 3s a day, and this was enough to buy a reasonable, quick meal. Generally I would go to a restaurant by the Monument called Mandy's. One also got coffee and tea breaks, which, strangely enough, were taken outside the office. It was during this leisure time that I came to realize what I wanted to do. I did not want to spend my life at Lloyd's – I wanted to create things, buildings in particular. This was the first year after the war, when licences were given for construction on any scale, and daily I would visit the sites of Fountain House in Fenchurch Street and Bucklesbury House, where the temple of Mithras was discovered. At the time I had no concept of the role of the entrepreneur and the developer, and I just wanted to become the effective cause that made such things happen. I would happily have taken a job with no prospects beyond a salary and a pension in order to be able to do so.

4

On my Own

I wanted to get my military service out of the way as soon as possible so I made the necessary application and was called up in September 1951, two months after my seventeenth birthday. I had a very good time during my two years in the army, whether it was at Mons, in Germany, or on a gunnery course at Lulworth. After my basic training I joined the 3rd the King's Own Hussars, a cavalry regiment, in Germany. There was spaciousness and physical freedom, friendship and liveliness, which I thoroughly enjoyed. To my great surprise, for they had not told me when I joined, Stewart & Hughman kept me on half-pay. This, added to my trust income of £250 a year, plus my pay of £16 a month as a National Service officer, enabled me to move from comfort to a life of relative affluence.

After demobilization I returned to my mother's new studio in Shafto Mews, behind Cadogan Square.

I was by now approaching the age of nineteen and a half, and had the expectation of £30,000 capital in eighteen months' time. This would have produced an income of about £1,500 per annum which, in those days, represented a modest degree of independence; my salary on returning to Lloyd's was £750 per annum; and although an outside name had to show wealth of £75,000 in order to become a member, an employee working there could do so for about £30,000 – with the prospect of profits averaging £6,000 per annum or thereabouts commencing three of four years later. So it was assumed by everyone, including me, that I had made a wise choice and was fortunate to have got my job with Stewart & Hughman in the first place. The prospect was for a total income approaching £10,000 per annum in my mid-twenties and, by the standards and values of the time, that was fairly considerable. So I returned to work in Lime Street with few worries and no doubts about the future.

I retained my earlier dreams about construction and large buildings, but for the time being my practical ambitions were quiescent, and perhaps somewhat stifled by the cosy and relaxed experience of the army and the apparently effortless affluence that was facing me. Few of my friends had comparable prospects in terms of a business career, and fewer still had yet even reached the point of the preliminary apprenticeship that I had started three years earlier.

It is worth taking a moment to summarize the basic workings of Lloyd's. The underwriter is a man who assesses risks and takes on commitments for himself and his syndicate, each member of which has a stated share of the profits or losses that result. The underwriter spends most of his working life in what is known as a box, a structure not unlike a large desk with four men seated one on each side and separated by a central bookshelf giving them all access to the documents and records of their business. In the old room on the west side of Lime Street there must have been more than a hundred of these identical boxes, containing nearly a thousand underwriters and their clerks with anything up to a thousand brokers milling around between them and placing their risks.

The broker works for the insurer on commission, and he carries a slip for each particular transaction which he takes from box to box, where the underwriters decide if they want the risk, and if so what line (percentage) to take. When the slip is 100 per cent subscribed the insurance is complete and results in a cascade of the cards I used to sort out when I first arrived there. Similarly, matters concerning claims and amendments are taken by hand from box to box to be noted and agreed by the underwriter concerned. Premium rates for each risk are settled by negotiation between the broker and the leading underwriter (the man who first commits himself), and the subsequent underwriters then have no choice beyond deciding what, if any, share they want. Obviously great intricacies and finesse are involved in this complex market; it is unique, probably the most efficient in the world, and now occupies a fine new headquarters which was under construction at the time I worked there. Our head underwriter was called Mr Lloyd, and long queues would form at his box, for we were leaders in many fields, and brokers would know that once our name was on their slip, others would follow without difficulty. We would sign 'Tyser', and I came to have restricted signing rights myself – after a warning to beware of the personable broker, evidently in rather a hurry, who thrusts forward a slip and asks the favour of a quick signature to cover what is purely a formality – but is in fact presenting something which calls for consideration at a higher level.

I was set to work at one of our boxes for Mr Elcome, the non-marine underwriter, and spent some of my time in the offices upstairs, producing and examining records. The first few weeks were an exciting challenge, and I probably have an underwriter's temperament – certainly not a broker's; but gradually I began to feel a sense of claustrophobia, which worsened as winter approached. I am not good at sustained routines, and at the same time I began to feel again the restless stirrings and desires for a broader and more creative life. I tried to suppress these emotions, for I felt they were a rational and temporary reaction to such a sharp contrast with the army. That may well have made the problem worse, but, whatever the cause, I became ill: I had flu, I developed a mild anaemia, and it became indisputably clear to me that I could not spend my life working in the airless confines of a small box in a large room, regardless of the financial rewards.

So I left. There were no recriminations, but obviously my mother was disappointed, and adult friends thought it an unaccountably silly thing to do. The year leading up to my twenty-first birthday was an obscure and muddled period, and I will not confuse my narrative by trying to make it seem clearer than it was. At one point I was about to start art lessons at the Sir John Cass College in East London; at another I thought seriously of becoming a geologist.

I moved from Shafto Mews to a flat in Cadogan Square: a short lease of an unconverted house in the Square then cost £2,000 or £3,000, and the Cadogan Estate would, for a few thousand pounds more, offer a new lease of 99 years to an owner who would convert the house into flats. In the case of No. 38 an enigmatic man named Mr Fellows was doing this, with the aid of a single workman. He had started at the top – the fourth floor – and was slowly working downwards – very slowly. The rest of the house was a derelict mess, and Mr

Fellows must have been pleased to be approached by a young man prepared to offer £6 a week for a four-roomed attic with water and electricity, but no lift. I was joined in this enterprise by Rupert Chetwynd, and by Henry Sanford, a few years older and recently MO to the 3rd Hussars. Henry had the largest room, which he shared with Marcelle, a Belgian lady whom he was soon to marry. The arrangement had for me the unique advantage that I was only a hundred yards from my mother's studio, so really I had the best of both worlds.

For some months I did no work at all and then, as spring came, my vitality and imagination began to recover and I used to take long walks through Hyde Park and Kensington Gardens. I shall always be grateful to Mr Seymour Dagne, manager of the Midland Bank Executor and Trustee Company in Bristol. They managed the trust and we would correspond about investments and advances as my majority approached. He agreed that I should buy a second–hand Mk 7 Jaguar which I used as trading stock in a joint venture with an engaging car dealer named Peter Buckley whom I had met in the King's Road. Peter later became insolvent, and I lost my share of the accumulated profits, but my original stake was intact and in the meantime I had learned an enormous amount about the seamier side of what was then the glamour occupation of car dealing. I also got my first introduction to the hire purchase business, and another totally unexpected bonus was that Peter put me in touch with a man he had met in a pub at Little-hampton, Michael Rawlence. I tried to form a property conversion partnership for a house in Pont Street with Simon Gandolfi Hornyold, another, remoter, army friend, but his trustees would not collaborate.

I had by now several minor business interests, none of which led anywhere, but which developed my concentration. I moved to a single room at the back of the ground floor of 38 Cadogan Square, which was still far from complete, but by now also had a third-floor flat occupied by three girls, two of whom I remember: an extrovert Australian with a very good figure named Beverley Waxman, and Jennifer Prestwich, later to marry Michael Boyd Carpenter, who lived next door at No. 40, a somewhat more advanced equivalent to No. 38 in the hands of a strange eccentric called Mr Learmonth, who progressed unaccountably in the letting business to the point of owning the Lime Tree Club in Ebury Street. I was very friendly for a while with Roiseen, a handsome blonde girl who had the first-floor front room of No. 40.

It was in my quiet, well-lit, ground-floor back room that I began again to work. Ideas were germinating all the time and I realized that I needed technical knowledge across a broad front. I bought a manual on company secretarial practice and read it carefully; I bought copies of all the current Landlord and Tenant Acts from the Stationery Office; I bought recent Finance Acts; and I bought the 1948 Companies Act. I spent many hours of quiet concentration learning a little about the law as it was at the time, and even memorizing the numbers of particularly relevant sections. I had for three or four years read the financial daily and weekly papers, and by this time I had little difficulty in reading and understanding balance sheets and accounts.

I found I had quite an easy fluency in a wide range of subjects, and whereas it is customary for a young man to specialize and become an expert in one particular subject, I chose intuitively to go for a broader spectrum altogether. My objective, quite simply, was to know more about law than people who were not lawyers, more about accounts than people who were not accountants, and so on, across the field of business, with some extra emphasis on the numerous professions that relate in some way to property. I did not find this work at all hard. Whilst I enjoyed my temporary, withdrawn, contemplative life, several things began to happen, not in any particular sequence, but obviously related to my becoming twenty-one.

After giving a small party in my flat for perhaps a dozen people, I took my mother on a short holiday to Jersey, where we met Shane Milward, a property developer from before the war, who had been helpful to the D. E. & J. Levy estate agency during the war; my mother introduced me, as a potential client, to David Fremantle, a stockbroker who lived across the road at No. 1 Shafto Mews; and at a party given by my friend Sarah Barnard at her mother's house on Campden Hill I met a young solicitor called John Batt. Of course there were many other events, but this short list gives a few landmarks of greater or lesser relevance to what happened soon afterwards.

The next part of the business story falls into two distinct parallel, but unconnected, sections; with David Fremantle, and through Shane Milward, we laid the foundations of what became Trafalgar; and through John Batt, I pursued for a while quite different commercial things which were absorbing and instructive.

Let me deal first with the matters in which John Batt was instrumental: he introduced me to his friend John Graham, then the manager of Barclays Bank at Hill Road, Wimbledon. We banked with him until he retired a few years ago as manager of their Brook Street branch in Mayfair, when he said to my wife, in a relaxed mood, 'I knew from the start he'd either go to gaol or become the richest man in Europe.' (Both extremes were exaggerations.)

John Batt and I had become friends, and have been ever since. He is a talented and productive man who, apart from his work as a solicitor, had already led his own dance band and had written the signature tune chosen by ITN for the television news. More recently he wrote a weekly serial for television called *The Main Chance*. John's office was opposite the Wimbledon underground station and I would visit him there two or three times a month, sometimes for lunch at the Dog and Fox nearby. I got a clear impression of suburban business life (as opposed to metropolitan life) from these visits and came to be on friendly terms with many people who belonged to this typical infrastructure of local business. Suburban business tends to be parochial and can be small-minded, but it is from studying such a small-scale model of the fabric of commercial life that one learns most readily of all the different trades and professions and how they interrelate to produce a social and economic unit. I had known nothing of these things before. I met the local estate agents, various bank managers, accountants and surveyors, and so on. Later I will describe some of the property schemes I carried out in the area, for they have more place in the general narrative; but at this stage I will start with two ventures that were to be important for two or three years, and then no more. My desire was to be a property developer, but that was not possible for the time being. Arising from my brief experience and observation of car dealing, I had decided to form a hire purchase company and to run it myself. I wanted also to make one or two investments in things run by others, partly for profit but also for the indirect experience. The only sizeable venture in this second category was a tool-making and thermoplastic injection-moulding business.

John Batt had met two potential entrepreneurs named Leslie Herridge and Jack Rashbrook who wanted to set up in business together and were at the time employed by a plastics company at Guildford as tool-room foreman and salesman respectively. John formed for them a company named Tratt Plastics Limited and I agreed to lend money to it, to become a director, and to take 40 per cent of the equity – Leslie and Jack having the other 60 per cent. Business started on a small scale in a barn at Send near Ripley in Surrey with two or three hand-operated, injection-moulding machines and a larger, hydraulically operated machine from R. H. Windsor. Production was mainly of cheap toys for firms in the East End of London, and soon we were employing a dozen men and the plant was working twenty-four hours a day. I would visit the factory for a morning or an afternoon once or twice a month, and it seemed that things were going well. Then there arose the question of expansion and larger premises: Jack thought he could get big orders from Ford for various PVC (soft) car components; Mrs Jonas of Bell Toys and Games (a vigorous business run from a converted church on the fringes of the City) offered a lot more work subject to price and quality; and the Master Vending Machine Company of Wardour Street, which had introduced American ball gum machines to this country, offered contracts for literally millions of plastic charms. I concurred in the expansion plans, and offered to buy the property they wanted, and to rent it to them; this was near Bagshot and consisted of an Edwardian house with an adjacent 2,000 square feet or so of factory which formerly had belonged to the racing driver Bob Cowell before he changed his sex and became Roberta Cowell.

The company took on a lot of new plant, much of it on hire purchase or rental, and before long the place was a hive of in-dustry, with fifty or sixty full-time employees, again working three shifts, often seven days a week, and at one point no fewer than a hundred and eighty outworkers who removed 'sprues' and 'flash' and counted and packed our colossal output of plastic charms – the most successful was a white polythene skeleton who had to have his head tucked between his legs in order to be sufficiently ball-shaped to fit the bubble gum machines. Our tool-making capability was good, and Leslie achieved miracles of tool design and engineering from what really was quite a small plant. With the help of a new member of the management, Michael Thorburn, we got the Ford orders and at one point were making something like 80 per cent of their total UK requirements for flexible, black, plastic 'gaiters' for gear-levers, hand-brakes, and parts of the heating system. They always had other suppliers, but we were cheaper; in addition, we were saturated with orders for toys. My investment and loan capital was now approaching £20,000; bookkeeping was supervised by a chartered accountant from London, and at the time it seemed remarkable that so much had been accomplished with such slender resources – but the débâcle was not far away, and the first balance sheet and profit-and-loss account came as a most disturbing bolt from the blue.

Jack's success as a salesman had been based on price, and very few of his orders were at adequate prices. This had occurred in part because at that time (and for some years to come) there was over-capacity in the industry, because, in turn, it was so easy for someone with too little capital to set up in a barn with his first machine; and we were undercapitalized. The accountancy in terms of book-keeping was in good shape, but in terms of financial analysis it was almost non-existent.

A deteriorating financial position was meticulously recorded in all its details, but it was not understood until too late! Many orders had been taken on the basis of marginal costing (priced on the assumption that overheads were largely already covered by other orders, which they were not) and much overtime and weekend work had been authorized on the assumption that the only related costs were raw materials, labour and electricity, which was not the case. The need for money for all this expansion had led them to offer 3¾ per cent discounts to customers for cash settlements of invoices within seven days – sometimes more than the net profit optimistically expected in the first place. My visits became more frequent, and unrewarding work was eliminated – but then our receipts declined, whereas the demands of creditors, who had supplied the raw materials for the much higher level of production two or three months earlier, did not.

It was nearly twenty years later that Ronald Lyon came to see me (before the collapse of his empire) with what he described as 'a slight cash flow problem' – it was more than that and, like his business, Tratt Plastics was insolvent. I had no more money to invest; I was fully committed elsewhere; and in any case the business was too far gone. There was no alternative to liquidation, and the position was made worse by the failure of some of our debtors. I had to do most of the talking at an angry creditors' meeting because I was the most articulate and had by then the best understanding of what had happened. A committee of creditors was formed and the representative of Monsanto led a faction to seek to make me personally liable on the assumption that I must have known whilst we continued trading that we were already insolvent – but he had a heart attack and died. The largest asset in the liquidation turned out to be the tax loss, and we placed the undertaking in a subsidiary formed for the purpose which was sold free of the liabilities. My investment virtually was wiped out, and this happened at a particularly vulnerable moment, for by this time, as I shall relate, I had been married for more than a year; our first child had been born; and my main business, Southern Counties Discount, was running into difficulties following a substantial fraud by one of our customers. The lessons learned from all this are fairly obvious: there is no substitute for experience, and mine was beginning to accumulate, just as my resources started to decline. And so it was to be with Southern Counties Discount.

David Fremantle, who became my stockbroker, was a friend and neighbour of my mother and stepfather. David then was in his late forties and worked with Montagu Loebl Stanley, having before the war been a friend of Montagu Loebl; David himself, as he would admit, had had little in the way of a career until after the war. His father, still alive at this point in the story, was Admiral Sir Sidney Fremantle, who had commanded our naval forces during the abortive Dardanelles campaign in 1915, and David had been a well-connected, but not very well-off, young man: at one time an insurance broker, a welcome guest in several houses, and perhaps overshadowed by his father – all previous members of the family had been distinguished in the navy since the time of Nelson. David was in the process of making an aggressive play, his takeover, to acquire with friends and clients control of a moribund concern called the Eastern International Rubber and Produce Trust. He had a good following of family and private clients, and together they succeeded in his objective and replaced the former board. The new directors were David, the chairman, Frank Woodward, a former don and senior wrangler at Cambridge, and D'Arcy Biss, a solicitor, then senior partner of Ashurst Morris Crisp & Co., who now is our longest-serving director of Trafalgar and who, at the time, gave me some excellent advice about the Tratt Plastics problem, and offered his bright young assistant Michael Gampell to help – a great kindness. It was unfortunate that at this time misunderstandings developed with David's former firm and also with another supporter, Walter Salamon of Rea Bros, the bankers. David moved on a half-commission basis to a smaller firm of stockbrokers called Arthur B. Winch; and the secretarial and registration work, which Walter had expected to get, was given to Touche, now Touche Ross, Trafalgar's auditors. My friend Douglas Baker then ran their secretarial department and now runs the whole of the much enlarged firm.

David Fremantle and I would meet regularly and I found that he was ambitious. He had done well for his clients and for himself, and was better aware than most other stockbrokers of what was likely to happen in the next few years as the 'cult of the equity' gained wider acceptance. David wanted Eastern International Investment Trust (as by now it was renamed) to make limited investments in service industries – insurance broking, for example; he wanted to invest on a small scale in property development, and he was willing to consider other unquoted investments. In other words, and for £100,000 or so, he wanted the Investment Trust (whose total assets were less than £500,000) to venture into the world beyond conventional Stock Exchange securities, in the hope of producing higher yields and, perhaps, improving capital values.

I had started my hire purchase company in 1955 through

my acquaintance with Peter Buckley, the car dealer, and with the help of Kenneth Kendrick, an accountant who already ran similar companies for the Coleman family, who later became clients of John Batt. I took a room in Ken's Streatham offices at Sunnyhill Road and bought some Roneo office furniture which can still be seen in the Arlington Street offices at Hampton & Sons, the estate agents. Initially the company was called N. B. Finance and the capital was £10,000, all mine. Not long afterwards I was pleased to get from the Registrar of Companies the more impressive name of Southern Counties Discount Limited, and began to attract deposits from private investors. We never advertised for money, it came from friends and through stockbrokers. The business, for which Ken kept the books, took individual hire purchase contracts through a handful of small car dealers and, as happened in the latter stages of Tratt Plastics, I became slightly acquainted with the shades-of-grey world of commissions, discounts and reciprocal favours. People might have thought that a car dealer would prefer to sell for cash rather than credit; it was not generally known that in those days a hire purchase company would pay commission to a dealer of anything up to 40 per cent of the finance charges that would come with the customer's instalments. The arithmetic was elementary – the true rate of percentage return is nearly double the rate stated in a hire purchase contract (if the repayments are re-invested in the same business). At the time money could be borrowed at $6\frac{1}{2}$ per cent or 7 per cent, and the gross return was well over 20 per cent per annum with negligible overheads. The only risks were fraud, or else default in a case where the customer had no money and repossession would not cover the debt.

A regular source of extra revenue came from 'early settlements', where the customer wanted to change his car and first had to settle the hire purchase by reference to the instalments outstanding, rather than in terms of what had been advanced in the first place. I would not want to return to this business (and it has changed in the meantime), but it was profitable and instructive at the time. David put £15,000 of Eastern's money in, so as to own 60 per cent of the then £25,000 capital, and at the same time he began to introduce his clients as depositors; so before long we passed the £100,000 mark in total assets. We developed towards the wholesale business rather than the retail: for example, a young dealer in Luton, named Tony Hill, who wrote his own hire purchase on second-hand cars, would from time to time 'block discount' a bundle of contracts with me for immediate cash, and the customers' instalments would be assigned to Southern Counties Discount. At that time the American process of 'factoring' was unknown in this country, but I developed what we called invoice discounting, where a small manufacturer or supplier would register his sales company at my office, his invoices would be issued on that letter-head, he would get immediate cash from me (subject to a discount) and in due course the debtor's cheque would come straight to SCD's office. By this time I had taken a second-floor office with a flagpole outside over Dr Scholl's shoe shop at 59 Brompton Road; profits were growing rapidly and business looked good. But trouble was on the way.

I had met a tallyman draper called (Percy) Michael Hunt who sold minor articles, mostly clothing, throughout South London on the well-known door-to-door tally basis that the customer paid one shilling in the pound deposit and twenty weekly payments of one shilling for each pound's worth of goods purchased. Mr Hunt would block discount a large bundle of contracts with me every week, but on this occasion the repayments came through the customers' payments to him, and when receipts began to falter I became alarmed. Some time earlier I had engaged a private detective to check a random sample of two or three hundred debtors, to confirm that they existed and acknowledged their debts – which they did. Michael Hunt telephoned to say that he had heard of these enquiries; he understood my concern, but asked me to be patient because he was going through a most trying time caring for his former wife, who lived at Fleet in Hampshire and had undergone a dreadful operation, losing a leg. This was sad news, but I thought it worth confirming the story, so I drove to Fleet and, with some difficulty, found the house of the first Mrs Hunt. She acknowledged who she was, said she hadn't seen her husband for several years, and very evidently was in good health, with both her legs intact. I called in the police, and David Fremantle mentioned this relatively unimportant (to Eastern) incident in his statement with their annual accounts in October 1958.

What he said was to the effect that 'the directors have called
in the police to examine the conduct of a customer of a
subsidiary', but what the *Daily Telegraph* published on its
front page was 'the directors of Eastern International Investment Trust have called in the police to examine the conduct of
their company'. It turned out that the entire Hunt family, including his old father, had spent many hours, every night, for months
on end, forging six copies of every credit sale agreement – which
(Percy) Michael would then discount with six different hire
purchase companies.

A few months later I paced to and fro one morning in the
concourse of the Old Bailey, having been warned by the police
that the case might last for months, for there was a huge number of documents involved, and Mr Hunt intended to plead
not guilty; he paced fro and to, gave me a worried nod, and
returned to earnest conversation with the barristers, solicitors
and plain-clothed policemen who surrounded him. He was persuaded to plead guilty, and I was told I could return to my
office. Later in the day I heard that he had been sent to prison
for eighteen months, and I never heard another word from
him, or about him. All our accumulated profits had been lost,
and much of the original capital. David took me for a sack-
cloth-and-ashes lunch at an ABC café near the Guildhall, and
we each had what appeared to be a baked herring to eat and
a cup of tea to drink: this was a low point for us both, but
I had many more things to worry about, and therefore took
a more philosophical view. The only way to go was forward,
and other, better projects were already in hand. For the most
part these concerned property.

My first property conversion was of two former workmen's
cottages in Markham Street in Chelsea – no damp-proof course
and an earth floor in the basement. The purchase price for the
pair was £7,600, the conversion cost more than it should have
done, and I was lucky to get my money back, after longer than
it should have taken, through sales totalling £15,000. This
was a good example of what not to do – and what not to allow
an architect to do; also when to stop paying the bills, but it
did not teach me anything very positive. The next scheme
went through SCD and was for a single new house in Edge

Street on Campden Hill, and this went like clockwork, selling promptly for £5,000 after site and construction costs of £4,000. At the same time I was doing a part-conversion, part-sale-of-flats project at 11 Rutland Gate, a property seen advertised in the *Estates Gazette* simultaneously by Jane Batt's estate agent cousin, Basil Kelly of Kelly and Adair (later bought by Allsop & Co) and by me.

We bought it for the property company David had formed, Eastern International Property Investments. I had no money at the time, but wanted the activity. The plan was very simple: to modernize and sell a few of the flats to yield more than the original cost of the whole property, retaining an income from the remainder, with the prospect of further capital receipts from their sale in due course. This presented no problem, but was on a small scale.

I used to see Shane Milward from time to time at his house in Wilton Crescent and, although he had plenty of experience as a successful pre-war developer of property, he had not come to terms with post-war conditions, particularly taxation. His connections were good and all sorts of schemes would be offered to him, but in 1956 he had no spare money. One afternoon he asked me if I would be interested in something he had been offered on the corner of Piccadilly and Half Moon Street, a large Victorian block of gentlemen's service apartments, with shops on the ground floor, called Green Park House. The lease had only a year or so to run, but the freeholders would grant a new, longer lease without premium to a developer who would undertake to modernize the flats. The 'fag end' of the old lease was available for £5,000 from a friend of Shane's called Curtis, who doubtless was apprehensive of the terminal dilapidations that otherwise would fall to his account, for he did not want to undertake the conversion. I had no money either, but I told Shane at once that I was sure David would agree to put the project in my hands for Eastern. This was to prove very important.

5

Marriage

Late in 1955 I left Cadogan Square and bought the lease of a better flat on the second floor of 33 Pont Street, from another friend of ours, Marcel Godfrey, a Lloyd's underwriter, who went to live in the country. The lease was for seven or eight years at £350 per annum, and I paid a premium of £300 for it. Henry and Marcelle shared the flat with me for a while, and it was a good arrangement, for they had a large north-facing room in which she could paint; I had a small bedroom in the middle facing the front door, and virtually exclusive use during the day of a bright sitting room at the south end, where I worked, read and made my telephone calls, if I was not at my small office in Streatham. Apart from the plastics business, I had at the time three different categories of commercial activity: the hire purchase business, the property schemes, and the first of a series of company share transactions.

Just after Christmas 1955 I went with my mother and stepfather to a party in the flat opposite their mews which belonged to a convivial grey-haired American called Dennis McEvoy. He always gave excellent parties with plenty of pretty girls, some well known and others just pleasant to look at. On this particular evening I was instantly impressed by an outstandingly beautiful blonde who also was exceedingly well dressed. Her appearance was distinctive, and reminded me of something I could not quite recall; she was friendly and self-assured but seemed scarcely to belong in these surroundings. I was quite unable to place or categorize her, as one can quickly do with most people. Clearly she was more sophisticated than I was, and must have been a little older to have developed such poise. This impression was much reinforced when I found she was willing to talk to me at length and, without being impolite, to the exclusion of the many other interesting and more worldly people who were in the room. This was my first meeting with Joyce, who was to marry me a year later and to whom I have now been married for nearly twenty-three years. I was twenty-one at the time.

She came back with us for supper at the studio after the party, and later we played scrabble (she won by a large margin). I asked her for her phone number and address, which she gave me, but explained that she was leaving for Paris the following morning with a group of friends, and would be away until early in the New Year. As Dennis was our only link, and in the meantime had joined the group going to Paris, I had to contain my impatience for what I thought would be a week. It would be absurd to say that I was in love at this stage, and I think I can best describe my principal emotion as being the most intense feeling of curiosity that I had ever experienced about anyone – or anything, for that matter.

This curiosity was renewed when, a day or two later, I saw her, larger than life, in the Knightsbridge underground station. On one poster she was wearing spectacles for Bateman's, the opticians; and on another, looking at least ten feet tall, she was drinking stout for either Mackeson's or Guinness. I had sent flowers for her return, but they must have been a sorry sight when she got back a week later than planned. I telephoned to suggest a drink at my flat followed by dinner at a local restaurant, and Joyce's attitude was restrained rather than resistant (I learned later that she was not sure who I was). For the first half-hour or so I think we each felt incongruous towards each other and startled to find ourselves alone together. Then the harmony began, and once we began to talk, we could not stop. We drove in my Bentley (1947, 4¼ litre, part of the trading stock) to La Bicyclette in Elizabeth Street, and after a steak and a bottle of burgundy we each knew quite a lot of what there was to know about the other. Her childhood had been confused and unsatisfactory, and her father left home soon after she was born. She had been married very young to a minor film producer called Kenneth Horne; there were no children, and not long after their marriage Kenneth died in a car accident in, of all places, the Brompton Road. She had a little money, but not very much, and earned up to £25 a day at freelance photographic and fashion modelling. The reason she was so well dressed, she explained, was that most of her modelling clothes were specially made for her, and she was generally encouraged by employers to buy them for a fraction of the cost because they had no value otherwise and were too carefully fitted to be suitable for general sale – that is to say, 34-24-34 was far from being a standard size, at least in that price range, and these were the last of the days of real *haute couture* and hand-made fitted clothes. The wardrobe lasted for a few years after our marriage, and was a blessing during a time when in fact we had no money at all and so were anxious to maintain an impression of restrained substance.

During the next year our relationship fluctuated – intermittent at first, then undulating, and sometimes turbulent. At an early point I had a Jaguar XK120 and we went for a few beautiful spring days to Somerset and Devon, visiting Porlock, and many other scenes of my childhood. Generally we would have dinner together in London once or twice a week, or we would go to the pictures, or just for a walk. But she evidently had one or two important choices and decisions to make concerning her future. There was no lack of suitors and some, twice my age, were becoming impatient. She was in no hurry, but they were. So sometimes we would have a row and resolve never to meet again; as others sometimes have trial marriages, we would have trial separations. And then, after a week or sometimes as much as a month, one of us would telephone the other to see how we both were and the answer was always the same – less well than previously, and the affair would resume.

For my twenty-second birthday I had quite a large cocktail party at my new flat in Lennox Gardens where several people, including myself, had too much to drink. I took an Anglo-Indian friend on to dinner at the Pigalle in Piccadilly, where she encountered Mel Torme ('Mountain Greenery' was the song of the day) whom evidently she knew just as well as by now she knew me. I was already in a bad mood regarding several of the male and female friends who had been at my party, not to mention Joyce, who had not; so we left early. My car at the time was a MK7 Jaguar, and we entered Belgrave Square at high speed in second gear. The road surface in those days was based on wooden blocks, the asphalt finish was too thin, and it had begun to rain; I lost control of the car and only a massive cast-iron lamp post stopped us from crashing into the basement area of the nearest house. As it was, the right-hand side of the car was sheered away, and my life was saved by an inch or two as the impact avoided the steering box, which projected beyond the chassis, and otherwise would have driven the steering column straight through the driver and his seat. The wreck was photographed later to illustrate a miraculous escape; all the offside front suspension was torn away. My companion and I were removed unconscious through the roof and I awoke sitting on the front steps of an adjacent house, to be asked by a reporter: 'Who is your companion?' It was only later that she discovered that I had replied, 'I've no idea – I've never seen her before in my life.' The story was on the front page of the *Evening Standard* the next day, but we were both in the Westminster Hospital by then.

The motive for my numerous residential moves was profit plus convenience, and for several years after my marriage we did rather better than live rent-free in the course of up-grading our accommodation. Much the same applied in the case of cars, and despite the problems that were building up elsewhere, the standard of living was high, but by the beginning of December 1956 I was feeling listless and depressed. My relationship with Joyce was at one of its recurrent low points, and had been so for a week or two, but certainly by now I was in love with her, and other companions no longer interested me. I had 'done that bit' and I felt thoroughly fed-up with myself and with my life: all I wanted was Joyce, and only a few days earlier I had done all in my power, through jealousy and unreasoned nastiness, to make that impossible, and she, in turn, had other boy-friends with whom I could hardly expect to compete. One night I had dinner at the Gore Hotel in Queen's Gate with a middle-aged friend I had met at Shafto Mews named Bill Burnside. Bill was a personable and well-dressed man connected with the film industry. Usually he wore either a Brigade tie or an old Etonian tie, though in fact he had been to a grammar school and was never in the army. He had had more than one wealthy wife, he had spent many years in Hollywood, and whatever his personal qualities and defects, he was a wise and experienced observer. I was maudlin and felt ill; I told him my troubles, and half-way through dinner I was sick. Bill took charge at once – perhaps he knew the symptoms better than I did – and after the mess was removed he asked for Joyce's phone number and left me alone for about ten minutes. I then phoned Joyce and arranged to go and see her at once. Her hair was in curlers and she had already embarked on an early night before the phone calls began. This was an important occasion, but not one to be drawn out. I asked her to marry me, she agreed, and we said we would do this at the shortest notice allowed by the Register Office. I left soon afterwards, having arranged a rendezvous for the Passport Office the next day to get her a passport in my name for the honeymoon.

We were married at Wright's Lane a few days later with Bill as best man. We planned to leave that afternoon by train for Southampton and to take the flying boat to Madeira, but the sea was rough, so we had a small party in my flat at Lennox Gardens. We were tired, but the party was enlivened when George Mills, a friend of Joyce's late husband and whose wife Anne was now my secretary, took a phone call from the girl who had been in the Jaguar crash and wanted to know if I was free that night: George explained that I was not.

The next day we went to Southampton, and it was fortunate that once again the flying boat could not take off, for carelessly I had consigned Joyce's luggage to Bournemouth, and it was returned to us just in time, after a night at the Polygon Hotel, for our departure by air on the morning of the third day of our marriage. From Reid's Hotel in Madeira we went on the ss *Venus* to Tenerife, and then to Las Palmas on Grand Canary; we had a good time, but were already good friends and became bored with the place rather than bored with each other, and we wanted to get back. We returned on conventional aeroplanes via Madrid, and the most memorable experiences of these three and a half weeks were the Ritz Hotel in Madrid and, most particularly, the Prado.

For some considerable time my mother's relationship with my stepfather had been deteriorating, and when we returned to London we found she had left him and was living in our flat. Clearly this could not go on for long, so my mother withdrew to remoter accommodation at Aberdeen Park in North-

East London, whilst we took a twenty-one-year lease of 11 Trevor Street, a most attractive little house between Knightsbridge Barracks and Harrods, for a premium of £500 and at a rent of £525 per annum.

Trevor Street was to be the scene of many delights and several disappointments; our first child, Justin, was born there on 26 October 1957, but by this time, of course, the commercial reverses I have described earlier were coming to a head. Already I had more business experience than most young men of my age, and also more responsibilities. The truth of the matter was that my financial resources were exhausted and, although by this time I was well advanced with significant and worthwhile projects for Eastern, I had no money in them. My own net worth had declined to zero, and I did not want to spend my time working exclusively for other people. This, really, was the decisive period of my life, and I had to struggle and fight for my role.

Joyce was quite willing to go back to work, but on her first day with an engagement booked by Michael Sherrard at the nearby Royal Albert Hall, I got flu and our Amazonian-sized nanny left. Clearly it was going to be impossible for Joyce to maintain the professionalism and punctuality required for the job.

At one stage we even invested in some of the bubble gum machines referred to in connection with the plastics business, and Mr Hunt sometimes helped with the collection of huge numbers of pennies from these dispensers on the forecourts of fifty or sixty small shops in South London. This supplemented our income, but when capital was required to get back in to the mainstream of my career, it became necessary to sell the house. This produced a profit of three or four thousand pounds, for Joyce had made the place look marvellous, and values had risen in the meantime. We took a flat on the second floor of Hornton Court, over Chesterton's, the estate agents, in Kensington High Street. On this occasion there was no premium at all, and the rent was less than £600 per annum for four bedrooms, two bathrooms, a nice kitchen and two reception rooms interconnected by a small ante-room. Quite a lot of builder's work was necessary to bring it up to the standard we had achieved at Trevor Street, and even then Joyce felt a powerful longing for the house we had left. Nevertheless, the flat was a good place to spend the next two or three years, because by now I was working very hard and wanted the other parts of my life to be as simple and trouble-free as possible. Apart from holidays, life was work.

Hornton Court was our home at the time of my first investment in Trafalgar, and we were still there, but looking for a house to buy, when the first and all-important deal with the Commercial Union was concluded in 1961. It was a period during which my net worth expanded from nil to something over £100,000, our domestic expenses were small, and our private lives very much wrapped up with ourselves and our son. We saw little of our friends and I was exceedingly busy.

Our first holiday had been a trip to Zermatt: £40 each for two weeks and transport by couchette. Then David asked us down to La Violetta, a house on Cap d'Antibes which he had borrowed from his friend Pat Egan, and again we travelled second class by train; this, incidentally, is the house we were to buy ten years later. We loved the South of France and returned almost every year for periods varying between a long weekend and a month. We would also go sometimes to Majorca, in the days before the package tour infestation of that beautiful island.

6

Central London

I have mentioned the importance of Green Park House, the project introduced by Shane early in 1956 and undertaken by a subsidiary of Eastern. I was not a director of the company in the first place, I had no shares, and I did the job for a fee of a few hundred pounds; but in several widely different respects it marked a pivotal point in my career. Firstly, it was remarkably profitable: for costs of less than £40,000 we produced sales of £75,000 within a year and a half, plus a continuing net income of £5,000 per annum, and this was a vital step in building my reputation. Secondly, it was the occasion of my introduction to Cubitt Nichols, architects and surveyors to the Sutton Estate, and to Horace Wilkinson, who runs the Estate. Thirdly, it was the reason why I took up Peter Buckley's introduction to Michael Rawlence, the estate agent Peter had met in a pub at Littlehampton. This led to Eastern buying a share in Collins & Collins & Rawlence, which initially gave me a West End office, car and secretary, experience of estate agency, and ultimately resulted in Trafalgar's 50 per cent interest in Hampton & Sons. Fourthly, it was my first contact with Trollope & Colls, to whom we gave the building contract and whom we were later to acquire. Fifthly, it established my work in the West End, as distinct from the suburbs. And, finally, though I did not know this at the time, it was my first connection with Victor Matthews, who was then a contracts manager with Trollope & Colls; his last contract before he left them was the war damage repair work then going on at the Naval and Military Club next door to Green Park House.

Neither David Fremantle nor I had any particular connections with the kind of agent we needed for flats and shops in Piccadilly, so I telephoned Michael Rawlence and he came to see me at 33 Pont Street, where I was living at the time. We examined the plans and he gave his views. Mike is tall, slim, good-looking and slightly Irish by temperament, though there is no trace of this in his speech. He must then have been about thirty-five. He had qualified as a chartered surveyor after spending the war in the Irish Guards and had an easy fluency with words, the ability to make people laugh, and an air of firm authority.

Perhaps I should explain at this point the reason why the residue of the lease at Green Park House was available so cheaply: the freeholder was willing to grant a new lease for no consideration apart from a higher ground rent, but only for thirty-five years, so as to be coterminous with the leases of adjacent properties. Most developers at that time would not have thought the conversion expenditure justified on such limited tenure, because it could be tricky to sell this number of luxury flats on short leases, and the technique in any case was new to London. No one had any previous experience to guide him, so the proposition, proved and straightforward today, called for fine judgement in 1956. Mike had confirmed my expectation that Collins & Collins and Rawlence & Squarey, as they were at the time, would be a reasonable choice as selling agents, and I went to his office in Curzon Street one afternoon a few days later to settle the terms of their appointment as sole agents for the sales. Mike introduced a young man called Douglas Porcas as 'the manager of our town residential department', and we set to work. Before long I was to realize that Douglas was not just 'the manager of our town residential department', he was its sole employee: at the end of our meeting I mentioned to Mike the potential interest that David Fremantle had expressed in putting some of Eastern's money into a service industry of some kind and I asked him if he had any ideas. Mike's first response was to say: 'Thank you, Porcas, you can leave us now and I'll see you in the morning.' He then asked me to return to my seat and got us both a large whisky and soda from a cupboard at the far end of the room.

The firm of Collins & Collins and Rawlence & Squarey belonged half to an elderly gentleman, A. P. Saunders, who had formerly owned Collins & Collins and who wanted to retire, and the other half belonged to Rawlence & Squarey of

Salisbury, in which Mike had a share, but not a large one. He could sell his stake in the Salisbury practice, whose partners in any case wanted to relinquish their interest in the London office, and he could then afford to buy half of Collins & Collins and Rawlence & Squarey, but not the other half. I remember that at the time their annual gross fee income was £28,000, they had a staff of twelve or fifteen people including secretaries, and the net profit available for the partners was no more than £7,000 per annum – and even that was before paying rent, because the partners also owned the building, a freehold on the corner of Chesterfield Gardens, from which they received income by letting to others all but the fourth and fifth floors, which accommodated the estate agency. The profit record was poor, but they had good connections and much to look forward to (as usually is the case with estate agents).

I reported to David, a meeting was arranged, and soon it was agreed to proceed, with Mike buying half the business, Eastern buying the other half, and me going to work there. Implementation was slow, because the former owners first wanted us to buy the building, then wanted someone else to do so, and later decided to rent our two floors to us before selling the freehold to a third party as an investment in a year or two's time. Another hold-up concerned the Royal Institution of Chartered Surveyors, which would not (and do not) allow their members either to trade with limited liability or to share their revenues with those who are not members. In this case, Mike was quite happy to put his membership into suspense, and to resume it later if he needed it. (We were to encounter the problem again some years later when we bought Hampton & Sons.)

The name Squarey was dropped, and Collins & Collins & Rawlence was established as a partnership belonging to a limited company. The cost was only a few thousand pounds, and the main interest to me was that I went to work there, leaving my Brompton Road office just at the time it was becoming difficult for me to support it. I was never an active estate agent, but I had helped to set up the deal, and was involved with the subsequent management of the business, which improved steadily to become just the kind of high-yielding, unquoted investment in a service industry that David had sought in the first place. My office was on the top floor; I received a fee of £1,250 per annum from the firm and was free to conduct my other business from their office. I learned a lot at Collins & Collins. I spent a weekend mastering Moore's *Modern Methods of Valuation*, then a standard textbook for chartered surveyors. And I began to learn that sometimes I had a knack of bringing out the best in people: that is to say, that by knowing enough of their work and their latent capabilities, I could lead or influence them to do more inspired work than they were used to, and generally better work than I could have done myself.

Green Park House produced ten self-contained flats, all but two overlooking Green Park, and four shops. The flats were sold without difficulty on thirty-five-year leases, and in my supervisory role I learned a great deal, for I penetrated every aspect – legal, financial, architectural, quantity surveying, marketing and so on, in the most minute detail. Some of the studying I had done in my leisure year began to come in useful. This, and the next three or four years' work, gave me a variety of knowledge and experience that it would be hard for any one individual to accumulate today, for the scale was within the grasp of one young man, but the problems and activity were much the same as on a larger scale, and, above all, the basis was metropolitan. It could not all have happened so effectively from Streatham, or even from the Brompton Road, because the mainstream of money, value and variety is largely restricted to Central London.

The architects came with the scheme, so to speak, because the freeholders wherever possible required this particular firm to be retained for developments on their estate. Cubitt Nichols himself (we were never on Christian-name terms) was a shy, capable man in his late fifties, qualified as a surveyor and as an engineer, as well as being an architect, who then worked from a top floor in Norfolk Street between the Strand and the Embankment. He had two capable assistants, the brothers Peter and Geoffrey Favell, respectively surveyor and architect, plus an office boy and a typist – and that was all. The office contained many black tin trunks, as one still finds occasionally in lawyers' offices: this must have been the filing system, for

most were named 'Sutton Estate', but there were others, dating
from an earlier, more broadly based practice – one, I remember, was marked 'W. H. Smith Esq're'. By this time
the Sutton Estate was virtually their only client, apart from
developers and tenants who were required by the estate to use
them.

Late in the sixteenth century the daughter of Sir Laurence
Poultney, formerly Lord Mayor of London, married a Sutton,
and she brought with her what must have been a large fortune:
today it takes the form of virtually the whole of the freehold
of Piccadilly from Hamilton Place to Bolton Street, the whole
of Sackville Street, other parts of Mayfair behind Piccadilly,
and several acres of Soho; not to mention many thousands of
acres of farmland. All this is managed from a discreet office in
Bolton Street by Horace Wilkinson, who reports to a distinguished board of directors and trustees who, in turn, represent
what must by now be several hundred heirs and beneficiaries.
The family had been one of the more substantial in Britain
for several hundred years, but so far as I know they always kept out of the public eye. The present baronet lives
quietly in the country where, I was told, he enjoys being a special
constable.

My Markham Street experience with a bad builder who had
been slow and expensive made me determined that this time
I would go to the best. This may cost more but the advantages
of individual skills, quality and supervision pay off in performance, flexibility and customer satisfaction. And it was important to make a good impression on the Sutton Estate with my
first job there. So I chose Trollope & Colls for what was only
a £28,000 conversion job. This may have been rather small for
them, but a director, Charles Westerman (Victor Matthews'
old boss) would come to the site meetings and Mr Bradley, the
general foreman, had command of all that went on. The performance was immaculate.

The elementary and obvious objective of property development is to create something that is worth more than it has cost,
and margins tend to be much the same whether a scheme is
large or small. The attraction to me of working in the West
End, and then in the City, was basically that there one finds
the highest values, and consequently the largest profits; also,

of course, I have a very definite interest in buildings themselves, and it is in the areas of highest value that one can build
the best buildings. But, as with other industries, it is hard to
get into Central London development work if one has not
already a proven record of previous competence and success.
My early schemes were residential, not only because the sector
fascinates me, but because major established developers do
not care for it, and so there were more opportunities. Green
Park House was a residential scheme, but it was in the middle
of Piccadilly and the freehold belonged to an estate with much
other property to be redeveloped, mainly commercial. I was
determined to impress the Sutton Estate so as to be considered
for some of their commercial schemes. They are fastidious in
their relationships with developers and highly selective with
regard to whom they allow to operate on the estate. Thus Green
Park House, a textbook example of success on its own small
scale, was directly to lead to office building opportunities where
the figures were very much larger – first ten times, then a
hundred times, and so on.

The reason I have described all this in some detail is to
illustrate the condition I had created for myself in my endeavour to establish a business of high quality at the centre of
things – for I was ambitious, and most particularly for a role in
the West End. The geographical location of C & C & R and the
firm itself increased greatly my ability to meet more people in
the property industry and elsewhere. As I said earlier, it could
not have been done from Streatham or even from the Brompton
Road. Green Park House led to Sackville Street, and as the
former drew towards its successful conclusion there were other,
smaller schemes. Also I did quite a lot of work on examining
companies quoted on the Stock Exchange, nothing at this stage
approaching a takeover, but all profitable and informative, and
thus contributing to what I needed.

I should perhaps explain that the Tratt Plastics and Southern
Counties troubles overlapped the period I am writing about,
and several people knew of one or the other – but no one except
Joyce knew all about both, or realized that at one point my
finances were exhausted. The experience had given me a shock,
and focused my mind and my energies in the knowledge that,
in truth, I must fight for my life to preserve independence,

create a first-class continuing business, and make money. I knew perfectly well that single schemes and one-off speculations were no substitute for the commercial life I wanted to build, and was perilously close to being unable to begin. The basic choice lay between striking out on my own as an independent developer or acquiring a significant share in what was then Eastern International Property Investments. I had not much time to spare, but it was not difficult to be patient, because there was little I could do to accelerate matters in the meantime: property takes patience.

I was helped by the fact that so many people in, or near, 'the establishment' were conditioned by pre-war attitudes and ideas. I felt that I had been lucky to start work in this positive post-war period when relatively few senior people had yet ceased to hanker for 'before the war'. Some were still, of course, war-weary, but many of my own generation felt positive, confident and forward-looking. We were not contaminated by the immediate post-war lethargy, but the fact is, for whatever reason, that most men in positions of authority in those days were unduly influenced by experience of pre-war recession, if not the war itself, and their minds tended to be inflexible. There were great opportunities now for individuals with imagination and breadth of competence, particularly because so much of the economy was still in the hands of highly specialized, but obsolete, people. Much of what I describe in this book will seem straightforward and unsurprising, as it did to me. I was helped by the fact that so many others were retarded in their knowledge and ideas. I had a strong feeling that I was on my own and should not rely too much on conventional wisdom nor on established authority. This reinforced my confidence in my own judgements, which were based on my own observations and analysis.

There were several notable entrepreneurs in the fifties, but they did not seem to relate to conventional social or political life. Felix Fenston was a well-known figure of the day, brilliant entrepreneur or destructive opportunist, according to one's point of view; Harry Hyams was well on the way to becoming another, although not long since he had been an employee of Hampton & Sons. Hyams joined Hampton's in 1945 at the age of seventeen and, after a short interval with Dudley Samuel &

c

Harrison, was the first Hampton's employee ever to be re-engaged. He returned there to work on commercial investments and office lettings, and by the time he finally left in 1958 he travelled with Rolls-Royce and chauffeur, though only ten years earlier he had worked for £6 per week plus 15 per cent of the commission he earned for the firm. Charles Clore was probably the most original and inventive financier of the day, with the detached, cold-blooded perception to realize what a wealth of hidden treasure the British people had deprived themselves of through dividend restraint, high taxation, and superfluous legislation of every kind. These people were original thinkers, and they were bold. There were others, but there is no point in cataloguing a list of names that have no other place in my story. The point I am trying to make is that what looks obvious in retrospect was not so at the time; the general standard of financial sophistication twenty years ago was low and backward.

It is sad that none of this talent could have been positively to more use in the national interest, but I fear that our socio-political system lost its way some time before the First World War. Up to that time social and political power went together; those with authority undertook responsibility, and there was a degree of social mobility that allowed the most able to rise to the top within a generation. Afterwards the aristocrats closed ranks and stepped aside, and two separate streams developed: society, wealthy or aristocratic, or both, went its own way, to little effect (and this cannot just have resulted from the loss of so many in the war), while those seeking power and recognition had an easy road to the top in politics, trade unions, nationalized industries, and even public companies in the private sector, without the need to create very much for this country or for themselves. This was not just a by-product of the Attlee Government; Attlee was a symptom of what had gone wrong much earlier. I am not proposing Clore or Hyams for public office, just lamenting that evidently we have lost the easy interchange of people and ideas that must have been a notable characteristic of an earlier, more successful era.

Today the leaders of the new citadels of power, such as the trade unions, have closed ranks; I regard myself as a patriotic free-thinker, and the benefits are mainly for our customers, employees and shareholders, and for myself. I feel no urge to preach or convert. I observe, and get on with my work.

Against this background let me now explain some of the transactions in the shares of other companies. Just like the unexploded bombs at Brambletye, so there were many unexplored sleepy concerns which had maintained a Rip Van Winkle posture since, during, or even before, the war. I have chosen three to describe: in the first I was largely a passenger, in the second I was becoming an accomplished amateur, and for the third I knew exactly what I was doing, but not necessarily how to get out with a profit. Before the army and before John Graham and Barclays Bank, I banked at Lloyds in Fenchurch Street and asked one day to meet Mr Sartin, the manager: I wanted him to recommend an accountant who would help me with my very simple tax affairs. Mr Sartin introduced me to Stephen Lang of Sutton Russell Lang & Co. of Cannon Street. Stephen's office contained only himself, an articled clerk and a typist, but he had another office in an attic at home in Ealing where he kept twenty-six sets of company books and twenty-six company seals.

In those days, when a company had a rights issue, any shareholder could apply on a special coloured form for 'excess rights', and in any good issue would get a scaled-down allocation worth appreciably more than the cost; the *Financial Times* commented on the procedure after their affiliate Lazard Bros had carried out an underwritten issue at a large discount for Rolls-Royce, and many shareholders, by not taking or selling their rights, missed what might have accrued to them, to the benefit of others; the system was gradually made more fair, and today, of course, the rights are sold by the company for the benefit of shareholders who do not take them up, and if there is a loss, it is borne by the underwriters, who have been paid for this in the first place.

Stephen's set-up was his answer to earlier precautions, for he had a company for each letter of the alphabet; registrars, then resolved to issue only one form per shareholder, could hardly keep track, and the scale of excess rights applications was not related to the size of a holding. In fact current practice favoured small shareholders, and in Stephen's case each of his twenty-six companies held only one share in each of our leading, publicly quoted concerns. He made £10,000 or more a year from this simple process, more than he can have made from his practice. He was a small man of about fifty, and his hobby was to collect vintage Bentleys. In 1956 he suggested to me that I join him in buying shares in Pahi Plantations, a rubber company now with most of its assets in cash. This was an un-exploited 'asset situation'. We spent a few months buying shares at prices which started at $2\frac{1}{2}$d and rose eventually to over 1s before the company was taken over at 2s 6d per share, and we both made several thousand pounds when we sold out our small stake. The situation was elementary and obvious, but few saw the opportunity.

The second case I have chosen to illustrate this type of speculation was Southern Areas Electric, a company based at Guildford, which John Gray, David Fremantle's assistant, had mentioned to me. It was a classic situation of a mini-conglomerate, where the parts were worth more than the whole. We got all the subsidiary accounts from the Companies Office, and these confirmed that at least one individual company in the group was doing better than the group as a whole – the losers could be closed or sold, and the result would be a leaner business making two or three times more money. I did parts of the analysis myself, invested a few thousand pounds, and made a handsome profit when David's friend, Eric Robinson, decided to take the company over.

The third example concerns a company called Whitehall Court, which then owned the block of flats of that name on the Embankment, one or two small hotels, and Hanover Court in Hanover Square. The company had agreed terms for others to redevelop the last-named of these properties, and it seemed that the shares were worth at least twice the current market price. On this occasion I developed with colleagues at C & C & R various techniques to value properties without access to the particulars which owners would keep to them-selves. Douglas Porcas was primarily involved, because he was the residential expert; he, Tony Hinton and George Sibbering were all salaried partners by this time. I bought shares and, disclosing that I had done so, mobilized the resources of the firm to find a substantial client to make a bid for the company.

Property people liked the properties, financial people understood the balance sheet, but neither could comprehend the other, so as a result neither could visualize the company's potential. My new-found experience enabled me to interpret both, but I had not the resources to carry it through. As it was, Walter Flack had an intuitive understanding of the situation and bought Whitehall Court itself for his company, Murrayfield, leaving the directors in peace. Walter was one of the outstanding experts on shopping throughout this country, but he merged first with Jack Cotton, then the enlarged concern merged with Clore to form City Centre Properties, and Walter was soon to die in his bath at Whitehall Court; an unhappy man who, like several others in the property business, had spent the war as an NCO and had done exceedingly well afterwards, up to a point. I sold my shares in Whitehall Court for twice what I had paid for them.

Those are three examples, and there were many more. The easiest was when David, as my stockbroker and friend, telephoned one day to offer to buy me some shares in the South West Africa Company, which he said was soon to be taken over. I did as he suggested, and the bid was announced the next day. Today things are different: there are few undiscovered opportunities of this kind, and the rules prevent some of the procedures I have described; and, of course, you have to be technically involved at the right level to get close to the opportunities in the first place.

I had no losses in this category, but Mike Rawlence became friendly with Frank Cradock through two stockbrokers, Lawrence York and Dominick Sarsfield, and things deteriorated in other areas to the point that Lawrence, who could not conceivably have known what he was doing, was sent to prison, where he died. There were several well-known financial disasters of the day, not least the State Building Society affair and the Jasper Group Scandal. Plenty of people made money in the 1950s, but I must not give the impression that it was effortless or risk-free.

The LCC's 1959 Quinquennial Review (in fact the first since Abercrombie in the early forties and the only one) spelled out an altogether tougher policy to restrict office development in Central London. But they were trying to tackle the wrong problem: traffic congestion and the decline in London's population was not caused by growth of offices but by the lack of industrial employment inside London itself, combined with more affluent office workers expressing their preference to live in the suburbs. The GLC are now struggling to restore some of the depopulation then caused by the LCC. At the time the new restrictions, plus a credit squeeze, caused the amateurs to leave the property industry, believing that the post-war boom was finished – whereas it had hardly begun.

I have mentioned thirty-five-year leases, corporate finance and planning policy, in order to illustrate that, although I was intimately involved and working very hard, and although I had by this time a good following of helpful supporters, I tended to make up my own mind at times when most people were taking a different view, or had no view at all.

We were entering the office development business, but continued at the same time with flats and houses. I enjoyed the residential business, and through new development, renovation or conversion, we gave good value for money. But really it was through the commercial side of the development business that we began to accumulate the capital and reserves that later were to make possible so much growth into quite different sectors of British industry.

In 1958 we bought Westland House, the Collins & Collins freehold in Curzon Street. The price was £86,000, which was its value as an investment, but it had potentially a higher contingent value as a site for redevelopment. Office development in the area was severely restricted by now, and in the case of a building with 'established office use rights', i.e. one that had been so used since 1947, redevelopment was commonly thought to be limited to the existing gross floor area or a plot ratio of 3:5:1, whichever was the lower, and on that basis Westland House had no development value at all.

Mike was friendly with an architect called Guy Morgan, who had three young partners – Bob Chapman, John Taylor and Jane Durham – who were soon to set up on their own as

Chapman, Taylor Partners. They are all friends of mine, and Bob has done much of my work ever since. On this occasion he remarked to me that, of all the developers in London, only Harold (now Lord) Samuel seemed to understand the significance of the Third Schedule of the 1947 Town and Country Planning Act. This Schedule was primarily concerned with the calculation of compensation and betterment levy (by then abolished, of course), but it seemed to mean that if a local authority refused consent to rebuild to the extent of the existing cubic content of a building, plus ten per cent, they would have to pay compensation to the owner, and in the case of a large house in Mayfair with sixteen-foot ceiling heights on the lower floors, the difference would be very large because the new building would have eight-foot six-inch ceilings and far less circulation space. So we took Counsel's opinion, which supported us, and made a planning application for office development to a plot ratio of 5·3 : 1, the maximum in this case under the Third Schedule.

This was a novel and exploratory approach, but one that I already had in mind when we bought the building. I was fairly sure that in due course we would get planning permission for a new office building of a size that otherwise would only have been permitted on a site of nearly twice the area of the site of Westland House, and this would make the property twice as valuable. David and Mike were sceptical at first, but we had nothing to lose but our fees, and as matters progressed Mike began to get very excited, for clearly such a consent would bring a profit of £50,000 at the very least if we resold the building to a developer and moved elsewhere; he was so pleased that he offered to give me a third of his share of the profit if we succeeded, and he did not take offence when I asked him to put this in writing – I drafted the letter and he signed it over a sixpenny stamp.

A few months later we received planning consent, and there was great elation. Negotiations commenced to buy out various tenants and to sell the property to someone with the resources to carry out the redevelopment. It soon became clear that the value was even higher than had been thought, and we were thrilled to get more than £200,000 for it. The money from Mike was very welcome.

This section of my book inevitably seems rambling and disjointed, and so was the period to which it relates. Before I come on to the more direct narrative of the development of Trafalgar I will mention three more property projects to illustrate categories of ownership: one was for me, one was for Eastern, and one for a wider partnership in which I had a share.

Soames House is a fine property on Coombe Hill, near Kingston Hill, then standing in four and a half acres of garden with a lodge. John Graham helped me to buy it, and the plan was very simple: to sell the lodge, to get planning consent and put in roads and sewers for five building plots which would then be sold individually, and to live in the main house which would stand in at a small figure of net cost with an acre and a half of garden. All went well, and the main house still had a high, brick wall to separate it from the former kitchen garden where the sub-division had taken place. The residual net cost of the house was not much over £7,000, and it was certainly worth more than £20,000. But Joyce said she would need at least £60 per week for wages and housekeeping if we lived there, so we sold it, for the commitment was too great at that time.

More straightforward was something for Eastern: Frank Woodward then was a financial adviser to Pitmans College, and they had some surplus land beside their premises at Worcester Road, Wimbledon. We bought the land for £4,000, built a terrace of eight small houses, and sold them satisfactorily.

Buckhurst Park was altogether more complicated and exotic, with over 400 acres of land next to Windsor Forest, a large house complete with contents, a farm, and several smaller houses. It came to me from Boyd Gibbins, whom Joyce had known before her marriage to me, and whom I first met in connection with a property called The Wilderness. Boyd was a splendid character: a robust, rough, tough builder of medium height with a very strong personality. He had taught himself to ride in middle age and kept a polo team; his manner was coarse, but irresistible. Certainly from time to time he made enemies, but he had a very wide circle of friends extending to quite rarefied social levels; he said once to Victor, 'I can tell you and

I both went to the same public school,' – he came from East London and had done extremely well for himself. He died a few years ago and is one of the very few personalities I still remember as if they were in the next room. He was extremely kind to me, and to many others, and on this occasion he did not want the deal, so passed it on to me.

Buckhurst Park had been the luxurious home of Sir Henry Deterding, one of the founders of Shell, and then of the Maharaja of Morvi, who died there. The executors sold the estate lock, stock and barrel to two Indian speculators named Hoon and Kapoor, with the benefit of a mortgage of £50,000 repayable a year later. This should have presented no problem, but the Indians were quarrelsome partners, and whenever one of them wanted to do something, the other would get an injunction to stop him, and by now the money was due.

To cut a long story short, we formed a partnership of Eastern, PIT (a company I will describe later), Mr Hoon and myself; we bought the mortgage from the executors, and we foreclosed. Part of the arrangement was that I had an irrevocable power of attorney from each of the other three partners; this was because everyone was full of ideas and I could not risk a repetition of the previous partnership problems. Collins & Collins did most of the work, and Tony Hinton was the partner in charge. It was marvellous: within sixteen weeks, we had sold the farm to the Crown, completed a four-day auction sale of the contents, sold most of the cottages and small houses, and sold the main house with about thirty-five acres of land to a manufacturer of mackintoshes from the Midlands. This was great business for us all, not least for the estate agency, who sold the house twice more, finally to Peter Palumbo, the polo-playing son of Rudolph. My share of the profit added to the resources I was by now accumulating.

In the last few pages I have described a variety of unrelated transactions which, as well as making money, gave me practical experience at first hand; and this was experience as an entrepreneur, not as an employee or a spectator. So what was it *like*? It was, to me, totally new and fresh – and exciting. I retain the clearest recollection of these and many other 'deals', and it seems to me in retrospect that the sun shone for longer then than it does today! This was a period of apprenticeship, a time to learn and a chance to meet people. Friends, acquaintances and a minor reputation all supported a sense of restless curiosity as ambitions began to crystallize and were nourished by a growing self-confidence.

7

Early Trafalgar

Amidst all this bustle and excitement of the late 1950s I knew that what I really wanted was a permanent stake in a real business. As a preliminary part of my bid for financial renaissance I took for myself a building lease of the bombed site of 55 Great Cumberland Place. This was in 1958; the price was small and the money came from Barclays. The plan was for six new flats and a mews maisonette at the back. Trollope & Colls were the builders and I had the same general foreman as before at Green Park House, Mr Bradley. I told my colleagues why I was doing this on my own, and the point did not escape them.

At the same time Eastern had been offered by the Sutton Estate a building lease of the site of 22–25a Sackville Street and 10–11 Vigo Street. We were hardly qualified for this at the time, for there were twenty or thirty tenants in the perfectly good houses that then stood on the site, the construction cost would be over £200,000, and the Estate would normally have sought a more established developer of proven substance and experience. But they had been trying for years to get this project going, and they wanted to get on with the master plan for both sides of the street, which had been prepared before the war on neo-classical lines by an architect from Norwich named Skipper – who, it was said, had met their chairman on a train. Recent negotiations with the Norwich Union had failed because of rights of light anxieties, and Town Investments (now part of MEPC) had withdrawn on account of general economic conditions at the time.

All the Estate wanted was a fixed ground rent of £6,000 per annum for a 99-year lease, so we had a unique opportunity to move profitably on to a larger scale. But David was apprehensive; he felt that this was too large for Eastern, and that if this rate of growth continued, and was financed with borrowed money, Eastern itself would be in breach of the borrowing and investment limits imposed by its Debenture Trust Deed. The Investment Trust's total assets in 1958 were not much over £1 million, and David wanted to run it in an 'orthodox' manner; that is to say with a wide spread of small investments, most of them conventional quoted securities. The issued capital of the wholly owned property subsidiary, Eastern International Property Investments, was £21,000, and it was established as an investment company; that is to say it was run primarily to create income; there was a parallel dealing subsidiary with a capital of £10,000 called EIT Finance, which was used for trading. So all this was on a rather small scale, even in terms of the standards and values of the time, when someone who had made £100,000 would have been regarded as an outstanding and important person.

David was the only one of us on the board of the Investment Trust and, as its chairman, he devised a scheme, which his colleagues approved, for me to subscribe for new shares in the property company to give me a 51 per cent holding and so relieve the Investment Trust of the requirement to consolidate its figures. At the same time he proposed that my partly completed Great Cumberland Place scheme would be bought by EIT Finance, which would become a subsidiary of the property company. But then an unexpected influence came to bear, and altered everything.

Mike had become friendly with Walter Bull, senior partner of Vigers & Co. and a former president of the RICS. Vigers managed a moderate-sized property company called the Properties Investment Trust, which was an old-established, public company, but a minor one. I never quite understood people's desire for 'shells' – for that is all PIT really was – but a controlling interest was available and David became enthusiastic. 51 per cent could be bought for £160,000, and David, Mike and I were each to take a quarter, with a Wembley solicitor named D. Donald L. Davies taking the last quarter, thus calling for an investment of £40,000 each. I was happy to agree, and even arranged the finance for us all with John Graham at Barclays Bank (Brook Street by now) on the basis of £10,000 cash and a £30,000 overdraft for each of the four individuals.

But there was a snag: it was only at the last minute that I discovered that David assumed that as I was doing PIT, the plan for me to take shares in EIPI had lapsed. That was not how I saw things at all, and led to a nasty, but short, argument; I declared that if I was not to have the EIPI investment, I did not want PIT either, and would leave to make a fresh start on my own. This took place one evening at my office in Curzon Street, and David was angry enough to say that if that was my view, I might as well go at once.

I returned the next morning to collect my papers and to say goodbye to Mike, and found him anxious and concerned; he said he felt he should telephone David, which he did, and it turned out that David in the meantime had made another plan which he wanted to discuss with me at lunch that day. The outcome was this: I was to subscribe £1,500, being two shillings in the pound, for 15,000 new shares in EIPI to be issued to me at par with the balance of £13,500 being payable a year later. This gave me $41\frac{2}{3}$ per cent of the property company's capital, which thus became £36,000; EIT would buy 55 Great Cumberland Place and become a subsidiary of the property company, and I would take no part in PIT. My place in the syndicate would be taken by Charles Widdowes, a retired air commodore, introduced by Donald Davies. David later bought 1,000 of my 15,000 shares at £4 each, and if he had kept them they would be worth nearly £1 million today; not long after, Geoffrey Crowther bought 500 at £11 each. I kept the rest of my holding intact until the late sixties/early seventies, when I sold about half.

I had been extremely lucky, which I realized at the time, and I knew that EIPI had a long way to go. PIT went its own way, and I began to concentrate on my new investment and occupation to the exclusion of everything else. I hope it does not sound sententious to remark that I only began to make real money when I stopped trying. My prime objectives concerned the growth and quality of the business, and I was in no hurry for the financial rewards that I had little doubt would follow. From now on, all that I did was for the company. David was the chairman, I was managing director, and Frank Woodward and D'Arcy Biss completed the board. The accounts for March 1960 show gross assets of £66,124 and pre-tax profits of £10,168 with capital and reserves of £22,887. By March 1964 the figures were £5,891,997, £85,653 and £2,047,039 respectively. The extent of our growing property holdings is illustrated by this extract from our July 1963 prospectus for the public issue (*see Table opposite*).

Geoffrey Crowther bought his £500 shares in EIPI a few years after he joined Eastern International Investment Trust as a non-executive director, purely as a favour to Frank Woodward, a friend from the past, and his name gave lustre to this minor board. Sir Geoffrey (later Lord) Crowther was a highly intelligent man, a distinguished economist, a director of the Commercial Union Assurance Company and of several other important concerns. He had become editor of *The Economist* at the age of twenty-eight and now, in his mid-fifties, was its chairman. He was altogether far more distinguished than the rest of us: a small, stout, egg-shaped man with a kind manner and lively wit. Always in a hurry, he can have given little thought to his appointment to the Eastern board. I would see him only once or twice a year; he was sympathetic about the Southern Counties disaster, though sceptical of our property ventures.

The first Sackville Street scheme had been let cheaply at an early stage to secure temporary finance from Barclays; costs of £220,000 had resulted in a completed value of £325,000, but we had no access to long-term finance. A second section of the street was in prospect, and by now there was no longer an easy market in commercial mortgages, as there had been in the fifties, when margins were good and developers could often mortgage a completed investment for more than it had cost them. We were too small and unknown to support a public debenture issue, so the best alternative was to make some sort of equity-sharing arrangement with an institution which would provide fixed interest finance. This in turn could either be related to separate, individual schemes or to the company as a whole, but neither was particularly easy for a fairly new concern run by a young man of twenty-five. I should explain at this point that obviously our buildings could have been sold as they were completed, producing a high cash flow and large taxable profits; but the whole point of the business in those

A. PROPERTIES HELD AS INVESTMENTS

THE TRAFALGAR PORTFOLIO 1963

Property	Description and Tenure	Terms of Tenants' Leases or Underleases	Estimated Net Annual Current Rental Before Tax	Capital Value in Existing State
			£	£
1. 22–25A, Sackville Street and 10/11, Vigo Street, London, W.1.	Restaurant, Shop, Offices and 6 flats. Leasehold. Held for 99 years from 24th June, 1960 at a ground rent of £6,000 per annum. Building completed in 1962.	Entire building let to Scottish and Newcastle Breweries Ltd. for 42 years from 9th July, 1962 with provision for rent revision at the 21st year. Full repairing and insuring lease.	22,450	324,900
2. Trafalgar House, 9, Whitehall, London, S.W.1.	Offices of approximately 11,000 sq. ft. with three shops below. Leasehold, expiring March, 1980 at rent of £15,100 p.a. About 60–70 years old.	8 Underleases, two expire this year, one in 1966, three in 1967, one in 1968 and the remaining one is for the full term of the head lease. Interior repairing leases. Landlords are responsible for structure and provide services. First floor vacant.	2,170	21,000
3. 120–123, Fenchurch Street, and 1, Fen Court, London, E.C.3.	Office building with bank on part ground floor and basement. Built about 1900 (*a*). 120–123, Fenchurch Street. Leasehold expiring June, 1979 at a ground rent of £2,200 p.a. 1, Fen Court. Leasehold expiring June, 1980 at a ground rent of £375 p.a.	Bank premises of about 2,330 sq. ft. let until 1979. Office premises of about 19,600 sq. ft. let until 1967 with tenants' option to break after March, 1965. Landlords responsible for structural repairs and external decorations only.	26,825	190,000
4. Campden Hill Court, London, W.8.	96 flats and approx. 5,000 sq. ft. of storage accommodation. Freehold. Built late 1890s.	19 leases of flats expire in 1967. 7 expire in 1968 and the remainder at various dates between 1963 and 1966 (*b*). One third of the storage space is let until 1968 at £675 p.a. Interior repairing agreements (58 fair wear and tear) with landlords responsible for structure and services.	40,800	605,000

A. PROPERTIES HELD AS INVESTMENTS

Property	Description and Tenure	Terms of Tenants' Leases or Underleases	Estimated Net Annual Current Rental Before Tax	Capital Value in Existing State
5. 28–112, Iverna Court, London, W.8.	80 flats and 1 suite of offices. Freehold. Built about 1900.	All leases expire in 1963, 1964 and 1965 with the exception of 5 expiring in 1967, 4 in 1968 and the offices in 1966 (b). Interior repairing agreements (53 f. w. & t.) with landlords responsible for structure and services.	21,300	405,000
6. 1–15, Cardinal Mansions, Carlisle Place, 25–52, Morpeth Mansions, Morpeth Terrace, London, S.W.1.	41 flats. Freehold. Built about 1890.	All leases expire in 1963, 1964 and 1965 with the exception of 1 in 1966 and 4 expiring in 1967 (b). Interior repairing agreements (33 f. w. & t.) with landlords responsible for structure and services.	9,550	190,000
7. York Mansions, Prince of Wales Drive, London, S.W.11.	102 flats. Freehold. Built about 1895.	All leases expire in 1963, 1964 and 1965 with the exception of 6 expiring in 1967 and 7 in 1968 (b). Interior repairing agreements (75 f. w. & t.) with landlords responsible for structure and services.	19,900	365,700
8. Rutland Court, London, S.W.7.	39 flats. Freehold. Built about 1902.	6 leases expire in 1967, 6 in 1968 and the remainder at various dates between 1963 and 1966 (b). Interior repairing agreements (24 f. w. & t.) with landlords responsible for structure and services.	19,275	352,000
9. 11, Rutland Gate, London, S.W.7.	Terrace house converted into 7 flats including Mews cottage at rear. Leasehold 63 years unexpired at annual ground rent of £50. Built about 1870.	3 flats have been sold for the full term of the head lease, the lessees being responsible for interior repairs and for a proportion of the structural repair costs. The remainder are let on short terms on interior repairing agreements.	1,340	13,500

	Description		£	£
... London, S.W.5.	...shops and 400 sq. ft. storage space. About 70 years old. Leasehold. 99 years from June, 1962 at £1,500 p.a.	the next three years (c). Interior repairing agreements (30 f.w. & t.) with landlords responsible for structure and services. One shop lease expires in 1964, the other not yet let.		...,000
11. Neale Close, Finchley, London, N.2.	An estate of 8 buildings containing in total 56 flats with a site for possible future development (no planning permission obtained). Freehold. Built about 1930.	31 flats let to controlled tenants. 15 de-controlled and let on 3 year or quarterly agreements, all expiring by end of 1964. 3 under offer and 1 has been sold on long leases at ground rents. 6 vacant. Landlords responsible for structural repairs; where flats sold lessees responsible for proportion (d).	3,450	75,000
12. 33, Gt. Cumberland Place, London, W.1.	House and Mews Cottage built about 1795, recently converted into 9 self-contained flats. Leasehold, expiring March, 1978 at a rent of £350 p.a.	6 flats sold on leases co-terminous with head lease. 3 flats let at rack rents on leases expiring June, 1968. Landlords responsible for structure and services, but all costs recoverable from sub-lessees.	1,535	8,750
13. 55, Gt. Cumberland Place, London, W.1.	7 flats built in 1958. Leasehold expiring March, 2025 at a ground rent of £175 p.a.	6 flats sold on leases co-terminous with head lease. One flat let at rack rent on lease expiring 1967, Landlords responsible for structure and services, but all costs recoverable from sub-lessees.	500	6,375
14. Green Park House, and 90/93, Piccadilly, London, W.1	4 shops and 10 flats. Leasehold. 32 years unexpired at annual rent of £6,850 (e). Built in 1883.	Shop leases expire 1966 to 1979; interior repairing leases. Leases of 7 flats sold for term of head lease. Remainder expire 1964 to 1966. All interior repairing leases. Landlords responsible for structure and services.	1,300	10,000

Total £2,672,225

NOTES.—(a) Although held on two separate leases, the buildings have been combined to form a single building. The office premises comprise most of 120–123, Fenchurch Street and all of 1, Fen Court.

(b) In arriving at the valuations of the properties concerned, it has been assumed that, as flats are vacated, expenditure aggregating approximately £437,100 will be incurred in improvements and in decorations.

(c) Four tenants claim to be rent controlled.

(d) As and when possession of individual flats has been obtained, they have been sold on long leases. This process is likely to continue and the valuation has been made on this assumption.

(e) As from 31st December, 1964, 75 per cent of any increase in shop rents and 52½ per cent of any increase in flat rents are payable to the superior landlord as additional rent.

B. PROPERTIES IN COURSE OF DEVELOPMENT OR HELD FOR DEVELOPMENT IN THE FUTURE.

Property	Description and Tenure	Terms of Existing Tenants' Leases or Underleases	Estimated Net Annual Current Rental Before Tax £	Capital Value in Existing State £
15. 9–15, Sackville Street, London, W.1.	Building in course of erection which will contain about 30,550 sq. ft. and consist of Basement, Ground and five upper floors. Ground and first floor to be used for banking purposes, 2nd–4th floors as offices and 5th floor as flats. Leasehold. Held for 99 years from 25th December, 1961. Ground rent as from 25th December, 1963 £14,500 per annum. (f)	Entire building let to Bank of New South Wales for the entire term of the head lease less 10 days, at an exclusive rent of £60,000 per annum. Rent accrues as from 23rd September, 1963. Provision for rent revision at 21st, 42nd, 63rd and 84th years. Full repairing and insuring lease.	—	506,050
16. 50–52, Curzon Street, 16–22, Half Moon Street, and 29–32, Clarges Street, London, W.1.	Shops, offices, a restaurant, a public house and residential uses including service flats occupying a site of about 13,000 sq. ft. Leasehold. (g)	All underleases expire or are determinable in December, 1963, rents in effect payable to ground landlord.	—	4,040 (Cost)
17. Cleveland House, 19, St. James's Square, and 30–40, King Street, London, S.W.1.	4 shops and a block of offices on basement, ground and six upper floors occupying a site of about 10,000 sq. ft. Freehold (h). Built about 1900.	All leases expire in 1966.	16,400	1,225,000
		Total		£1,735,090

NOTES.—(f) Expenditure to complete the building estimated not to exceed £140,000.

(g) Held under the terms of an agreement providing for the grant of a Lease, after rebuilding, for a term of 99 years from December, 1963 at a rent of one penny per annum for the first two years and thereafter £15,000 per annum with rent reviews in the 23rd, 44th, 65th and 86th years of the term. Planning permission granted for erection of a building comprising basement, car park, shops and licensed premises on the ground floor, showrooms and flats on the first floor, offices and flats on the second, third and fourth floors and flats on the fifth floor.

(h) Planning permission granted for erection of a building comprising sub-basement car park, basement and ground floor shops and showrooms, and offices on first to seventh floors.

C. PROPERTIES HELD UNDER CONTRACT TO PURCHASE.

Property	Description and Tenure	Capital Value of Contrast
18. 47, Berkeley Square and 47, Hay's Mews, London, W.1.	Bank and office premises comprising approximately 9,000 sq. ft. on basement ground and four upper floors. Reconstructed in 1896. Three flats and garage for three cars at rear. Built in 1936. Freehold. Completion of the purchase with vacant possession of the whole is due in April, 1964. No deposit was paid on exchange of contracts, contract price for the freehold, £375,000.	£37,000

SUMMARY:—

		Value as above
Freehold	8 properties	£3,254,700
Leasehold	10 properties	£1,189,615
	Total	£4,444,315

days (things changed later) was to create a growing investment portfolio financed at fixed rates of interest, with other people's money supporting an equity which grew with every deal and did not attract tax if there was not a sale. This, plus growth in rents, was the situation that made property companies a boom sector on the Stock Exchange at the time. Oliver Marriot explains it all in his book *The Property Boom* (1966), where he lists a hundred post-war property millionaires, including me.

The obvious first choice for us was the Commercial Union, particularly as Geoffrey Crowther was a director; but David had tried, and failed, a little earlier. Nevertheless I put it to Geoffrey and he arranged for me to see Leonard Cooper, the secretary of the CU, a company with relatively little property involvement, and whose only developer-connection was with Max (now Lord) Rayne. Leonard agreed to take a fresh look at us in view of the way we were growing. I spent some time with him over the next few weeks, and with Ernest Spiller, then senior partner of Daniel Watney, Eiolart, Inman & Nunn, their property advisers and surveyors. I preferred them to take a direct share interest in the company itself, rather than shares in separate schemes, and so did they, for it seemed reasonably likely that in a few years our company would get a quotation and their fixed-interest advances could themselves become marketable. They agreed to buy 14,000 new shares at £4 each (making our nominal issued capital £50,000) and to lend us £550,000 in the form of first mortgage debentures. I went to Leonard Cooper's office one sunny afternoon in July 1961 to collect the £56,000 cheque for the shares; he was going to join our board as their representative, and just as I was leaving he said, 'By the way, do you put this appointment in the Directory of Directors?' I replied that personally I did, but it was up to him; he thought for a moment, and then said that, as he had done so recently in the case of Westminster & Kensington Freeholds, he would do the same with us. I was astonished to hear that he was a director of W & K, and asked if he could spare a few more minutes. I stayed for nearly an hour.

Some months earlier, following our success with Westland House, Bob Chapman had mentioned to me a block of flats in Knightsbridge called Rutland Court. It was a sound Edwardian building which he thought might lend itself to the Third

Schedule treatment for redevelopment as flats, and I agreed to see what I could do to get the owner's name and find out if it could be bought. I have mentioned when dealing with Whitehall Court that Douglas Porcas and I had developed certain elementary techniques to identify and value properties without the owner's concurrence. On this occasion the first part was easy, for I had only to look up Rutland Court in the telephone directory to find 'see Westminster and Kensington Freeholds Ltd.', where, in turn, all W & K's properties were listed. The company was not well known, so we carried out a company search and found that the company belonged to the North British and Mercantile Insurance Company Limited, to whom I wrote, and got an unhelpful reply. What I did not know was that the CU had recently acquired the North British.

Leonard was frank: W & K had been established in about 1909 by the North British and the Prudential; at that time there was a depression in the property business, and these two insurance companies had formed this joint company to take over and manage a series of properties where they held mortgages that were in default. In due course the North British bought out the Pru, and ever since had run the business as a quiescent, quasi-autonomous, property company. The CU did not much like it, because the commercial buildings were multi-tenanted management situations, and the flats, over a thousand in all, were in poor condition; many were let to friends, and some even to staff, of the North British, at uneconomic rents. The CU were concerned that any criticism of the set-up tended to be taken personally by their new North British colleagues; and they did not want to face the hostility that might occur if hundreds of rents were doubled or trebled to bring them into line with current values. The only sign of life W & K had shown recently was to buy four blocks of flats in Hampstead Garden Suburb, which had merely made their running problems even worse. There was no cause to be harsh to the management of W & K, because they had been trained to do a job that was no longer relevant or worthwhile, and that was not their fault: times had changed, and the old-fashioned, property investment company that purchased completed properties and collected the rents no longer had an effective role to play. This was partly a tax question, which was to become more marked, partly a political matter, for residential property was notoriously tricky and unrewarding, and mainly a function of the market, which reflected these, and many other considerations.

A development company could develop and hold for invest-ment, to considerable effect, and the insurance companies and pension funds did well to buy modern, well-located shops, offices and factories let to single tenants of high repute. But W & K's portfolio was obsolete in all respects and, had it been more attractive, it would already have been absorbed directly into the endowment and pension funds of the insurance com-pany. What this situation demanded was a sale to an entre-preneur who would sort it all out. Leonard admitted that this was now under consideration, and agreed to bear my interest in mind.

I heard from him again in September, and went to see him. He told me that three potential buyers, of which we were one, were to be given two months in which to submit proposals. Only the briefest details of each property would be given, because the existing management was not to be informed or disturbed unless or until a sale was imminent. I do not think our competitors can have penetrated as deeply as we did. In the case of the flats we got access to official records made for rating and Schedule A purposes; so, with the additional know-ledge of the tenure of each block, the accommodation of every flat, and the condition of a random sample visited surreptiti-ously, it was not difficult to put a present value on each build-ing, to estimate the costs of necessary renovation, and to calcu-late what the income should be, compared with what it was at the time. There were ten blocks of flats and three office properties. Of the latter, two were straightforward: 120 Fen-church Street and Trafalgar House in Whitehall; the third, Cleveland House in St James's Square, was more complicated, and the key to the whole affair.

Cleveland House stood next to the The Distillers Company's Adam headquarters and had been built just before 1900 on the site of a well-known private house; it must at one time have been one of the best blocks of flats in London, for there had been only twelve flats, averaging over 5,000 square feet each, and some even had ballrooms. But, as I learned later, it had been requisitioned no less than three times for government offices – in the Boer War, and in both World Wars – and was still leased to the Ministry of Works. This was a potential Westland House on ten times the scale, so Bob Chapman enthusiastically set to work to see just what kind of new office block we might produce on the site. Lord Silkin had been responsible for the 1947 Act and its Third Schedule, and I was told that at that time he occupied a first-floor office in, of all places, Cleveland House, overlooking King Street and the gardens in the square.

I suspected that Sir Keith Joseph, then Minister of Town and County Planning, was thinking of changing the rules. There was no point in not telling Leonard that, properly handled, this one property could be worth as much as the other twelve put together, but speed was desirable, and might be decisive. So, whilst the other calculations and negotiations continued, Bob and I were allowed to meet Mr Wallace, the manager of W & K, and Mr Charlton, the company secretary, on the strict understanding that we were concerned purely with redevelopment propositions and their assessment.

I put in many weeks of extremely hard work on W & K, prepared an illustrated report, and composed a bid which, though unorthodox, was to beat the others. We offered £3,345,000 for the properties (not the company), financed as to £3,335,000 to be left on loan by the CU, £9,000 of preference shares to be subscribed by them, £450 of equity for them and £550 for us. Thus we got 55 per cent of the deal for £550, and the point of the preference shares was to transfer ownership of the properties without paying stamp duty, as £66,900 in cash would have been a strain at the time. Michael Gampell was the solicitor acting for us, and he was an indispensable help in getting the transaction completed by March 1962. A month later a planning consent was issued for Cleveland House to be rebuilt as shops and offices to a plot ratio of 6:3:1. A week later came the announcement that, with immediate effect, the law would be changed. In future the Third Schedule would relate to superficial area rather than to cubic content; so thereafter sixteen-foot ceilings ceased to be relevant. We had bought Cleveland House for £816,000 and the site with planning consent was worth more than £2 million, but first we had to get vacant possession by buying out or rehousing the present occupants.

The Ministry, the main tenant, was slow, but not reluctant, to negotiate; then all we had to do was to rehouse the ground-floor tenants, who included Harveys of Bristol, Wilton's Restaurant, Rigby the gunsmith and O'Dell the optician. As luck would have it Collins & Collins had been retained at this time to handle *The Economist*'s St James's Street scheme for Geoffrey Crowther. This was a complex and important matter calling for dealings with planning authorities, the Crown Estate, dozens of leaseholders and the Legal and General, who financed the whole project. I had little to do with it and most of the work was being handled by Mike or George Sibbering, but I was able to suggest that they help with rehousing some of my Cleveland House tenants. They were able to fit Wilton's into the former Lyons teashop in Ryder Street behind their own new development, but the rest of the tenants took more than two years to satisfy.

By this time Westland House had been vacated and demolished, and Collins & Collins had moved to No. 6 Bolton Street, also by now the home of Cubitt Nichols and next door to the Sutton Estate. But EIPI was expanding rapidly and clearly, with such large property interests of my own, it was inappropriate for me to stay with the estate agency, so I decided to move.

The timing was just right, for Sackville Street was finished and I moved into the space I had reserved for myself when the development was first let.

With only two exceptions, the staff of W & K had been absorbed by the CU, and at Sackville Street we established the most efficient small office that I have ever known. Norman Kudish came with me from C & C & R. He had first helped us to sell the lease of 59 Brompton Road and, although at the time primarily a specialist in commercial property (and a prickly character), he was a good chartered surveyor with the necessary intelligence to take on the management of our thirteen new properties. The flats were bound to present many novel challenges. Ian Fowler also joined us, a chartered accountant with an economics degree, who has been secretary of the holding company ever since; he came from Peat's, had the tact and intelligence for the job, as well as being an excellent accountant. Ian was helped by Miss Thomas, a splendid girl with a personality that intimidated some of us; and Norman Kudish by Miss Webster, a vivacious, pretty creature, who later married the clerk to a race-course. My secretary Miss Barker completed the team, returning after one of her intermittent absences – it was no good complaining, she was always worth having back.

The two W & K people who stayed were Terry Sessions, a former RSM in the SAS, whose father-in-law, Mr Whiting, was head porter at Campden Hill Court (both held the Military Medal, from successive wars) and who had been clerk-of-works; and Mr Estcourt, a former CPO in the navy, who was staff superintendent and looked after the hundred or so porters and cleaners that we now employed, and continued most ably to do so until his death, by which time we had many more. I thought it a pity that soon afterwards Mike Rawlence decided to leave Collins & Collins and to join Ralli Bros – then a small bank representing Raccanati and Wolfson interests – the agency had a long way to go, and he was very good at his job.

At this point, and apart from financial concepts and controls, which were vital, we had four principal roles: management and improvement of the flats; a few continuing small residential developments; the major planning and development opportunities of our new commercial properties; and our former programme. This last category now included 9-15 Sackville Street, later to be let to the Bank of New South Wales against our purchase from them of their freehold of 47 Berkeley Square, and soon was to take in 16-21 Sackville Street, eventually let to Austin Reed, and 50-52 Curzon Street, quite a large scheme extending along Clarges Street and Half Moon Street; all except Berkeley Square were on the Sutton Estate.

The most time-consuming task was the flats, and it is not surprising that this kind of investment was unpopular: leading developers would have nothing to do with residential property, but I did, because I liked it, and because it was an area which had been overlooked, and where there was worthwhile work to be done. Our flats had for many years been let on a 'fair wear and tear' basis; that is to say, tenants were not even responsible for internal redecorations, and consequently much of the accommodation was in a very neglected condition; but most were well located in areas of high demand. And, as I mentioned earlier, the rental structure was both obsolete and full of anomalies. Our policy was to carry out improvements wherever possible and to achieve open market rents everywhere.

To establish open market rents it was first necessary to take whatever flats were vacant, to modernize them, and to demonstrate their value by letting them. This was clearly going to be the beginning of a large programme, and it seemed best to use outside surveyors for the supervision of the building work. Cubitt Nichols agreed to take on extra staff (including Mr Sessions) on the basis of a fixed annual fee plus 5 per cent of the value of work carried out, and they undertook detailed responsibility for what Norman Kudish and I specified. It soon became clear that the conventional procedure of specification, followed by competitive tenders from small builders, was needlessly slow and troublesome. So we decided to prepare a Schedule of Rates, which three different builders would price on the basis of a random sample of flats, with the winner taking all such work until further notice, moving in on each contract without delay, and being paid by measurement of what he had done against the rates specified in the Schedule. Peter Favell suggested that Bridge Walker should be included on the list of tenderers, and they won: that is how I met Victor Matthews, who had progressed from Trollope & Colls via a directorship of Clark & Fenn to owning his own building company, with the help of the late Victor Hosp, former owner of Clark & Fenn. The work with Victor rose at its highest point to about £250,000 per month, which was a great deal of money in those days, and a large part of his turnover; though the profit margins, which I was to see later, were not excessive.

By buying worthwhile blocks of flats, refurbishing them to a high standard, servicing the blocks properly, and obtaining contemporary rents, we established a good reputation and a high standard of integrity. We sold the lower-quality blocks and created much-enhanced capital values for the rest.

Collins & Collins were intimately involved with it all, and

after Mike's departure, he and the Investment Trust sold the agency in equal shares to Douglas Porcas, George Sibbering and Tony Hinton, who then ran it. I recall that Douglas first established his position as senior partner by being the earliest to arrive on a Monday morning, and moving into Mike's former room; Tony arrived next and took mine; and George, who was late, had no choice but to return to the room he had had before. It was an essential part of every renewal negotiation when a lease expired that Collins & Collins would act as our formal advisers on rental values, and be prepared to prove the point in any dispute.

We had realized even before we took over the W & K properties that the name Eastern International Property Investments conveyed more than one unhelpful connotation for landlord and tenant relationships and for months before the transfer of the properties we discussed, and rejected, numerous alternatives. A new company had been created for each of the thirteen W & K properties and so, of course, we already had a subsidiary called Trafalgar House Limited. Finally I suggested that this was the best name for us, and we chose it in place of EIPI; the Registrar of Companies agreed, and that became our new name. Most companies that change their names seem to have trouble and expense as a result, and some never quite recover their old identity; but in our case the change was made early enough to be carried through without difficulty. It may still have seemed slightly enigmatic at the time of our public issue, but not for long.

Another important change at the time was that Geoffrey Crowther became chairman. The job was not arduous, but the CU wanted someone independent, as they put it; and as they were by now committing over £4 million to Trafalgar, there was no argument about the principle. They put forward various names to me which, for various reasons, I was not happy with – and I said, 'Why not Geoffrey?' The CU were content with the idea, but Geoffrey was not so sure: I recall a day at Bolton Street when he was visiting Oxford for Trust Houses, of which he was chairman, and he telephoned four times to say no, yes, no, and finally yes. I am very glad he agreed. Soon afterwards Francis Sandilands, then chief general manager of the CU, and now knighted and its chairman, became a director and has been so ever since. A special requirement of the CU was for me to sign a twelve-year service agreement as managing director. I did not mind a bit, but I remember Joyce was bitterly against the idea. It did no harm in the end.

I have mentioned already that our plans and those of the CU included the assumption that in due course we would get a Stock Exchange quotation for our shares. By late 1962 we had reached the point at which our assets had risen sufficiently in value (and this was readily calculable) for some form of public issue to be considered for the following year. David was interested in the Investment Trust, because, as had happened before, their investment had again grown to represent an excessively large proportion of the value of their portfolio, and he wanted the issue to take the form of a rights issue of part of Eastern's existing holding to their own individual shareholders. This suited everyone else because it would get us the quotation without the need to dilute our respective interests by the creation of new shares to be issued to the general public. There was an important prerequisite: for Green Park House Investments to become Trafalgar's wholly-owned subsidiary – GPHI was the 55/45 company we had formed with the CU for the W & K properties. This, again, was agreeable to all concerned, but the transaction became quite complicated because some restructuring of GPHI's debt was desirable. At that time the chairman of the CU's finance committee was Sir Mark Turner, a distinguished man with numerous appointments and, in particular, deputy chairman of Kleinwort Benson, the merchant bank. We were going to need a merchant bank for our issue, and Leonard Cooper suggested that we might as well make the appointment straight away so that they could help with the preliminary GPHI work as well. KB seemed a good choice, and Sir Mark recommended his young associate John Gillum to undertake the job.

John and I have been friends ever since, and for the next eight years would be in touch almost every week, and often several times a day. He once told me that it took him twenty years to recover from being a scholar at Winchester, which is a joke, because he is a lean, ascetic-looking Wykehamist, and I cannot imagine that he will ever lose the characteristics or the manner; he had spent a little time in the regular army, a year at Cambridge, and a period at Lloyd's, before joining KB, where he soon became a director. (In 1971 he became deputy chairman of Samuel Montagu.) He is a highly intelligent and numerate man, but does sometimes make things rather complicated: Geoffrey Crowther once said he believed that John drafted all important documents in Greek, before translating them into English for us.

The prospectus for the public issue was published in July 1963 and the event, of the utmost importance to those concerned, created scarcely a ripple of public interest, though the shares were to appear high on the list of leading growth stocks throughout the next ten years. I remember only two items of personal publicity: the *Daily Mirror* featured the story of this being done by someone who was just twenty-eight, with a photograph of Joyce and me toasting one another with champagne (I resolved not to be photographed again with a glass in my hand); and *The Times* ran a small article saying I had made £1·6 million. This also was a salutary lesson, for even they make mistakes, and on this occasion had exaggerated by a factor of five. *The Times* article of 1963 caused Jack de Manio to visit my office with his BBC recording machine, but, when told of the error, he left with a polite apology, exquisitely expressed.

We had by then four million shares in issue, of which 816,000 were offered to shareholders in the Investment Trust at 6s 6d each, and the market closed that day at 8s, capitalizing the company at £1·6 million. At that time the shares were distributed as follows:

Commercial Union	46%
Eastern	12%
Myself	21%
Former shareholders of Eastern	21%

Our friends were given the chance to purchase shares not taken up by the Investment Trust shareholders, and many did so. I gave some to close companions and employees. I spent the day at Westland House feeling both nervous and elated, and my mind was much occupied with the subject of the next chapter.

One incident of the day of the issue is worth recording: I

reached my office at about 9.15 in the morning, and there,
already waiting, was an earnest, pale young man who, he
said, had read an early edition of *The Times* describing my
success, and promptly took a train from the Midlands to visit
me. He had, he claimed, personal control of a concept that
would make millions of pounds in no time at all, and for
which he needed £3,000 at once. The idea concerned the purchase of 'inferior fuels' from the National Coal Board, and
when I heard this I cast about in my mind for the quickest
way to get rid of him, for I was tense, and my concentration
was elsewhere. I asked Miss Barker to telephone Douglas
Porcas to see if he wanted to listen to the tale, which he did,
and I heard nothing more of the matter for several months.
Apparently Douglas had thought the idea worth backing, for
he thought it came from me, and he joined with three friends,
each to give our visitor £750. They never saw him again; apparently 'inferior fuels' were slag heaps.

8

The Three Companies

W & K had offices at Bush Lane House on the south side of Cannon Street. Their landlords were a company called City and West End Properties, who shared the first floor of Bush Lane House with two other property companies under the same management named Consolidated London Properties and Metropolitan Properties Company. When I first saw these three names on the list of tenants in the entrance hall, I made a note and started enquiries. It was hard to believe, but here I had discovered three more firms similar to W & K, larger and with a greater commercial content.

Whilst I was organizing the public issue of Trafalgar, I started delving into the details of these three firms whenever I had a spare moment.

Our stockbrokers at the time of the public issue were Read Hurst Brown & Co. We never had a close relationship with them and, as I shall relate, later we moved on to L. Messel & Co., after David Fremantle decided to retire altogether from the Stock Exchange. Read Hurst Brown were one of the few firms of stockbrokers who specialized in property shares, and when I mentioned the three companies to Alistair Ferguson, the partner in charge, he laughed and told me that he knew of at least fourteen takeover applicants which one or other of these old-established companies had been able to extinguish with ease.

Some companies of the day would regard it as a matter of good public relations to publicize lists of their assets, but these three companies were secretive in the extreme, and the cohesiveness of their unified management was increased by the fact that each company held shares in the other two – and this second point was reinforced by the fact that their preference capitals, of minor nominal value, had high voting rights. It used not to be unusual for preference shares to carry votes, and in the case of companies such as these it was easy to see how they might have entered the 1900s with equal amounts of preference and ordinary shares in issue, carrying equal voting rights, whereas by the 1960s the ordinary capital with unchanged voting rights had become a great deal more valuable (and interesting) than the preference capital.

So the defensive strategy had been simple and effective: potential bidders would be told politely that takeover talks would be fruitless unless there was a firm offer on the table – and the bidder would reply that he could not calculate what a fair offer would amount to until he had details of the properties – which the board would not provide in the absence of a firm bid. This was reinforced in the case of any one of the three companies by the fact that a bidder would know that the votes of the other two would already constitute a decisive opposition. According to our subsequent analysis of the latest available register of shareholders, the detailed position was as follows:

	City and West End Properties, Limited		Consolidated London Properties, Limited		Metropolitan Properties Company, Limited	
	Pref. %	Ordy %	Pref. %	Ordy %	Pref. %	Ordy %
Total given in Board letters of 4 December 1963 as holdings of Directors, members of their families and other two companies	20·7	16·8	24·9	20·1	33·7	28·2
Less: Holdings of other two companies as per latest registers	19·1	11·8	19·4	13·6	29·1	11·1
Presumed personal holdings of Directors and members of their families	1·6%	5·0%	5·5%	6·5%	4·6%	17·1%

What no one seemed to have thought of was that to bid simultaneously for all three would neutralize the effect of the cross holdings.

There was little doubt that the assets and management of these three companies had much in common with W & K: that is to say they owned under-used or under-improved property, some of it with development potential, but they had no development expertise. The problem of absence of information might be overcome by a large programme of investigative analysis; and the problem of the cross holdings would, of course, be eliminated if one bid for all of them. Trafalgar's net worth at the time of the public issue in July 1963 was £1.5 million; and a bid for all three companies, ignoring the cross holdings, was going to cost something over £6 million – so the plan was an audacious one, not just in terms of aggressive growth, but also as regards technical expertise of a high order (to overcome the information problem) and a sophisticated financial approach to deal with these archaic voting structures.

The public encounter lasted from late November 1963 to 30 September 1964, when we were able to write to our shareholders with a summary of what had been done: we had acquired City & West End, the largest and most desirable of the three companies, and we had sold our shares in the other two to William Stern/Freshwater interests, and to Leslie Marler's Capital and Counties Property Company. We were enabled to offer pre-emptive terms for City & West End because of the profit we had made on our shareholdings in the other two companies. With the help of John Gillum and the Commercial Union we were able to rearrange our capital structure in such a way that all our debts were funded for long periods ahead, and most were unsecured, leaving us with a greater reservoir of uncharged property than we had had a year earlier.

In our letter to Trafalgar shareholders we explained that the immediate effect on Trafalgar was that our net asset value per share (ignoring development potential) had increased from 7s 6d to 14s 4d; and our properties, after a few sales that were made in the meantime to protect our financial position, had increased from £4.4 million to £10.9 million. This adventure was totally absorbing to all concerned, and could be described at far greater length than space allows. Having explained what we did, I will now attempt to describe how we did it.

Credit was not easy at the time, and obviously the research would only be worthwhile if we could borrow enough money to carry through the project. Various different financial packages were assembled and then replaced as the story unfolded,

D

and all involved Barclays Bank, Kleinwort Benson and the Commercial Union. All but the first concept involved a loan from Barclays backed by a guarantee from Kleinwort Benson, who relied ultimately on the fact that money would not be lent unless we acquired control; and if, so to speak, the scheme later fell apart, then the Commercial Union would themselves buy sufficient of the properties to put matters right. We, for prudence's sake, conducted our operations through a subsidiary named Maintsmass, and the limit of our liability was never more than £400,000. Barclays and Kleinworts received commitment commissions at various stages, whilst Kleinworts and the Commercial Union had various fee/equity options. Without all this flexible support the transaction would have been impossible. Part of the outcome was that Kleinwort received £150,000 in cash and 150,000 Trafalgar ordinary shares, something well deserved for their part in the venture; and the trust between us was such that they accepted our own valuations and calculations of what would be their proper reward.

But first, of course, came the valuations: there was nothing as easy as telephone directories to help us, as had been the case with W & K, and one of our first techniques was to observe the three companies' offices on pay-days, and to follow the staff who were taking porters' wages to their properties. By this and other means we built up a pattern of ownership and, as the list increased in length, the task became easier. Several of the city properties were bound to have development potential. After we had identified them, Bob Chapman secured aerial photographs from which he could calculate their size; this, with the added assistance of ordnance survey site plans, helped me to be sure that patience and perseverance could make the sites of some of these buildings much more valuable than the buildings themselves. Altogether we identified seventy properties in London, and the next problem was to assess the position regarding tenure and tenants. Our solicitors, Ashurst, Morris, Crisp & Co., D'Arcy Biss' firm, were not available to us for this operation because they had acted for the three companies for many more years than they had acted for Trafalgar. D'Arcy adopted the proper detachment from our affairs, as was appropriate, and we introduced Chris Ruck of Bircham & Co., solicitors to the Commercial Union and North

British, to act for us in the takeovers; for the research, we went to a much smaller firm led by a young lawyer named Michael Rapinet. Michael was friendly with the C & C & R people, and it was with them, of course, that I had developed these investigative techniques.

The work was organized by Douglas Porcas on the residential side and George Sibbering on the commercial side. Security was total, although at stages as many as fifteen or even twenty people must have been involved. Rapinet's work was of particular importance because it was not enough just to identify a property: one had to know if it was freehold or leasehold and, if the latter, one had to know the unexpired term of the lease and the ground rent. What Michael did then cannot be done today, but in those days any solicitor could visit the Land Registry and, once there, provided he knew where to look, could gain access to almost any title documents that he chose to examine: this confirmed our earlier identifications of ownership, as well as giving us the vital details of tenure. Tenants and tenancies were easier, because the pattern was so similar to W & K's; that is to say multiple tenancies of small suites, usually let on a 'fair wear and tear' basis, and generally with half the reversions falling in within a year or two. Nevertheless it was a mammoth task and our credibility with our backers was enhanced as the story unfolded when it transpired that Chamberlain and Willows, who made the valuations for the defence, were less than 5 per cent above us, and this was accounted for by two properties that we had failed to identify – a small factory at Horsham in Sussex, and, surprisingly, a building in the Kingsland Road that was let to the Commercial Union.

By the end of September we had completed the valuation work, begun the financing negotiations and authorized Kleinwort Benson to make the first tentative approach to the three companies. By the end of October, as I see from Trafalgar's Board minutes:

> Mr Broackes reported that Messrs Read and Gillum of Kleinwort Benson Limited had met representatives of the Board of the Three Companies, and had placed the Company's proposals before them.

A director of the Three Companies had subsequently written to Kleinworts saying that they were unable to recommend the proposals to their shareholders, and later attempts to arrange an early meeting for Mr. Broackes to see them had failed.

This completed the sounding-out process and merely confirmed what we had expected. By early November the first financing package was complete: the gross sum required was £7·5 million, and the net sum, excluding cross holdings, £6·5 million. We already had a small shareholding in each company, and before making a formal bid it was necessary to exercise our rights to obtain an up-to-date shareholders' register. This is part of the routine for any takeover, for one needs to know whom to write to. John Gillum despatched the following letter to Mr Andrews, the managing director of the three companies:

R. C. Andrews, Esq.,   7th November 1963
Dear Mr. Andrews,

City & West End Properties Limited
Consolidated London Properties Limited
Metropolitan Properties Company Limited

I am now writing to you as arranged, following the Board Meeting of Trafalgar House Limited last week.

Our clients were disappointed that the respective Boards rejected without comment the proposals which we put forward on their behalf, and also felt unable even to have a meeting to discuss the proposals.

In the present circumstances, our clients have inevitably to make decisions without the benefit of discussions with you and, whilst they remain ready to meet your Boards at any time, they have now instructed us to apply to you, in accordance with Section 113(2) of the Companies Act, 1948, for up-to-date copies of the Registers of Members of the above three Companies and we should be grateful to receive these copy registers within the statutory period.

Yours sincerely,

J. R. GILLUM

John Gillum and I went personally to visit Mr Andrews with our written offer on the afternoon of Thursday, 21 November 1963. We were still prepared to talk on a friendly basis, but as this was not possible, our formal printed offers were sent to shareholders on 27 November. The three companies retained Michael Andrews of Phillip Hill, Higginson, Erlangers, to advise them, and they wrote to their shareholders on 4 December to say they had ordered an independent professional valuation of all their properties; ordinary stockholders should await this valuation, and preference stockholders should certainly reject our offers because the three companies themselves were going to repay their preference stocks 'on terms no less favourable than those now offered by Trafalgar House'. We answered on 12 December, pointing out that our offers were well above recent market prices (and apparent net asset values), and that, as the three companies had given no indication of when the proposed revaluations would be completed, it might be that they would not publish them until after our offers had lapsed. We also pointed out that, although the directors had boasted of the strength of their cross holdings, it was only their personal holdings that would be material to a bid for all six classes of securities; furthermore, the preference repayment would require approval of the Court and approval of shareholders by separate class meetings – and it should not be assumed that the ordinary shareholders would support the premium payment to the preference holders which we had provoked – for it was the former whose funds would be used to pay for the latter. They responded with concrete proposals to pay for the preference at higher prices than we had offered (we had expected this), so instantly we replied with another 6d of our own.

All that had taken place up to now in the public engagement can be regarded as fairly typical of the time, apart from the fact that we were bidding for six separate securities in three interconnected companies: no one else had attempted to take on more than one at a time. It was clear that a considerable number of ordinary shareholders would feel (rightly) that they had nothing to lose by waiting for the revaluation announcement which, predictably, was not announced until after our offers had lapsed. The preference response was diluted to the extent that quite a number of preference holders also held ordinary shares, and therefore decided to do nothing with either for the time being.

The affair assumed a very different complexion when we decided that we would declare all six offers unconditional at acceptance levels that most bidders would regard as inadequate. Thus over the Christmas period we reorganized our financing arrangements (which related to control) to accommodate the necessary level of borrowing that would give us a significant first stake in each of the companies. On 1 January 1964 we announced that the bids were all unconditional and open for acceptance until 10 January. The percentages of the preference and ordinary stock of the three companies, and of the votes, owned by Trafalgar were by then as follows:

	Preference Stock %	Ordinary Stock %	Votes %
City and West End Properties Limited	23·1	12·0	15·9
Consolidated London Properties Limited	30·7	19·4	23·9
Metropolitan Properties Company Limited	24·4	19·2	21·8

What we had done would not be allowed today (as I explain later in the case of Trollope & Colls). It astonished the opposition but ensured our long-term success. Now there was a new twist: to repay the preference shares required in each case a 75 per cent majority vote by holders of the preference stock, and we announced on 6 January (that is to say before the final closing date) that we would oppose repayment with holdings that were already 24 per cent, 32 per cent and 24 per cent respectively. This was a neat tactical move at that particular point, but of no long-term effect because the articles of association of each of the three companies denied voting rights to shareholders until they had been registered holders for two months. Therefore, towards the end of January, we withdrew our opposition and were quite glad to see our investment reduced by the repayments that we ourselves received. The three companies had themselves removed one of their protections.

At this point Joyce and I left for a short skiing holiday in

Arosa. The bids had not generated any great deal of public interest or enthusiasm; it was a momentous experience for me, but few others knew of, or bothered to understand, the importance of what was taking place. Those who had followed events closely may generally have assumed that the enterprise had failed and that we might find it difficult to get our money back if and when we withdrew altogether from the engagement. But I was reasonably confident that within an unspecified period of time we would win an outright victory. We continued to buy shares in all three companies on the Stock Exchange and had invested nearly £1·4 million in them, after deducting the £280,000 which was returned to us with the repayment of the preference stocks.

Towards the end of February 1964 Kleinwort Benson were approached by Leslie Marler, chairman of Capital and Counties, who disclosed that his company held 10·9 per cent of City & West End's capital, and 2·6 per cent of the capital of Consolidated London Properties. I met Marler at his Broadway, Victoria office on the morning of 26 February. He claimed a good relationship with the three companies' directors and offered a vague partnership which might result in our both achieving our separate objectives. In particular we agreed not to compete with one another in buying stock in City & West End, but to buy it jointly, half to be for the separate account of each of us, and he was to abstain from buying any stock in CLP or MPC. John Read and John Gillum shared Marler's optimism that this procedure would ease the way to a solution where we would all be successful and divide the assets between us. No particular time scale was envisaged at this point. In May, however, we heard from Marler that he wanted to end the share purchase understanding. We agreed to this, and John Gillum reported that on 26 May he had told Michael Andrews that Trafalgar intended to make fresh bids and would prefer the board's co-operation. Michael replied to reiterate that they would not talk to us, and disclosed that by this time the three companies were collaborating with Capital and Counties to form a joint company for redevelopment of City & West End's interests in Leadenhall Street in the City of London. John Gillum promptly made the point that any transaction of this magnitude should have the prior approval of stockholders in C & WE.

We then settled upon a contingent strategy of the kind that rarely proves effective – but in this case it did. We made a bid for CLP in the knowledge that, if Marler were to confirm his role as friend and protector of the three companies, he would have to make a better one; and if he did, we would accept it, and use the profit to make a pre-emptive offer for C & WE, the company we most wanted.

The Leadenhall Street proposal turned out to concern Billiter Buildings. We continued to press that any agreement of this kind should be the subject of stockholders' approval, and C & WE reluctantly agreed to convene an extraordinary general meeting for this purpose.

But by this time Capital and Counties had announced their higher bid for CLP, and I felt a moment's intense elation. We promptly delivered our pre-emptive bid for C & WE conditional on acceptance by CLP and MPC, and also conditional on Capital and Counties declaring their bid for CLP unconditional. The board then repudiated their plans for Billiter. None of these shares were major securities in market terms, but for a few hours the Stock Exchange suspended dealings in the securities of all five participants to give people a chance to digest the latest developments. The result followed our best expectations: we got the best company, City & West End; Marler got CLP, giving us the profit we used for the premium on our successful bid; Michael Andrews gave us every chance to offer a little more for MPC but, by this time, we did not really want it. We sold our interest to William Stern and his father-in-law Osias Freshwater who, between them, completed their bid for MPC – which became the holding company for disasters of great magnitude in 1974.

Some of the staff came to me and some went to Collins & Collins, and this was a good thing for all concerned. Apart from the main board, all of whose members departed, only a few opted for cash compensation for loss of office, and those who stayed on with us have enhanced their careers and have helped us. At the time of the takeover the chairman was seventy-nine and his deputy was eighty-one. They led what can only be called a rather old-fashioned concern, but their subordinates were able, well-disciplined people of a calibre one would find hard to recruit today, and they responded excellently to new direction. Time and again this has been our experience with takeovers.

By now I was thirty years old and had graduated in several respects. The rest of this book describes what we made of the springboard that was constructed through the events of earlier chapters.

9

Preparing for More

By late 1963 it seemed reasonably certain that Labour would win the next election. The Profumo scandal was a symptom that the Macmillan Government was gradually losing its grip, and the failure of Reggie Maudling's 'dash for growth' confirmed that the Conservatives no longer had a coherent or relevant theme. Not that Labour had either, but they had announced plenty of new ideas, and it was wise to prepare for the ones that would affect us. In the case of the proposal to re-introduce taxation of unrealized planning and development gains through some form of betterment levy, all one could do was to press on as quickly as possible to get planning consents for whatever might be worthwhile in the foreseeable future, and to start work as soon as possible, wherever possible, because either of these events was likely to be a 'chargeable act' under any new legislation. In the case of the proposal to introduce a Corporation Tax, it seemed best to visit other countries which already had one, and to find out how our kind of business coped with it. So I used some of the January-June interval in the Three Companies' affair to visit New York and Australia.

The Australian visit was also prompted by an invitation from Boodle Hatfield, the solicitors, to examine various properties there which a client of theirs had purchased to avoid death duties during the time that real estate held overseas by a UK resident was exempt from UK death duty, and were no longer worthwhile since the law had been changed to bring such properties into charge. As so often happens when assets are acquired for a purpose unrelated to them, these particular properties in Brisbane, Sydney, Melbourne and Adelaide had no intrinsic interest or appeal; but during my visit I was able to confirm what I had found in New York: they had no equivalents to the conventional English property company, because under Corporation Tax this was just about the least attractive way in which to own a continuing interest in property. This conclusion is self-evident, but was not generally understood for some time, and in our case led to the determination to amend our structure so as to operate in the best possible way under the new tax system, and to identify other companies which, if they failed to do so, would become vulnerable to take-overs and would in turn be profitable in our hands: in other words we sought to derive positive benefit from what to others might be a burden. This did not involve leaving the property business – far from it, and there was much useful work to be done; but we would do it in a different way and use our property base to support a far wider enterprise. The ideas were all completed in 1964, but I made no comprehensive public statement on the subject until January 1967, when I spoke to a meeting of the Chartered Auctioneers' and Estate Agents' Institute and set out the thesis in some detail. A copy of this speech is in the Appendix on pages 259–69.

The difference between Corporation Tax and the former Profits Tax was only one of degree, but it was large enough to convince me that the conventional property company, which was not much different to Trafalgar at the time, had to use its resources to greater effect if it was not to become irrelevant. The new tax was a positive incentive to generate profits for retention rather than for distribution, and the ability of a property company to create wealth in the form of capital values seemed to me the ideal basis for growth into other industries and activities, which could create income but not necessarily capital values.

The point was that conventional property companies had been formed as an investment medium for shareholders who required a secure income, and such companies were expected to distribute virtually all of each year's revenue by way of dividends. This new and greater degree of double taxation bore most heavily on such companies and their shareholders, and my thesis was simply that under the new regime they had an opportunity to use their resources (as distinct from their revenues to greater effect – as we did. Readers will see that I assumed an annual inflation rate of $3\frac{1}{2}$ per cent to illustrate part of my theme – this was reinforced by what happened later! Probably none of the points I made seem surprising or unexpected today, and what *is* surprising is that few people understood them at the time. These thoughts were to determine Trafalgar's subsequent growth and gave us a definite policy, whilst others merely felt sorry for themselves.

The first practical expression of this policy had been the acquisition in 1964 of a 49 per cent interest in Bridge Walker, the builders, with options over the remainder of the capital. I have explained how, after the W & K transaction, we undertook a large and steady volume of building and conversion work at our blocks of flats, and how most of this came to be placed with Victor Matthews. City and West End owned several office blocks in the City which were not unlike the flats in the sense that they had been built around 1900 to be let in small, self-contained suites which, by the time we arrived, were mostly obsolete and decayed. There were hundreds of them and, although all these buildings were to be rebuilt in due course, the potential yield on modernization in the meantime was so high that we embarked on a renovation programme similar in scale to the flats-improvement project, with the result that the volume of work with Victor at one time reached the level of £3 million a year, three-fifths of his business, and employed several hundred of his men plus many sub-contractors. This was at a time when the economy of the country was grossly overstretched by the 'dash for growth' superimposed on a pre-election boom, and there was an acute shortage of craftsmen in the building industry. Bridge Walker's net worth was not much over £100,000, so Victor's finances were finely balanced, and one of the reasons he liked Trafalgar was that we paid promptly, and the same-day settlement of weekly certificates was related directly to his weekly wage bill. Thus there was a substantial measure of interdependence between us.

In June 1964 Jimmy (now Lord) Remnant telephoned to introduce a client of his, David Parkes. Jimmy was then a partner in Touche Ross, our auditors, and David ran a greyhound race-track and a housebuilding business called Wandsworth Stadiums. As I wanted Trafalgar to increase its small housing programme, which had continued without interruption since Worcester Road, and as David was thinking of taking in a partner, it seemed worth having a meeting. He came to

see me at Westland House one afternoon. We had a friendly
talk and agreed to spend two or three days together visiting
our respective interests, and in the course of one of these
journeys I introduced him to Victor at his offices in Effra Road,
Brixton, where we discussed construction questions. A few
days later David told me that there was no point in pursuing
the housing concept any further because there was not room
for both of us to have a dominant role, and there the matter
rested for some weeks.

Then Victor telephoned me to announce that he had agreed
to sell Bridge Walker to Wandsworth Stadiums; and soon
after David phoned to apologize for not telling me earlier of
his plans, and to seek my reassurance that this change of ownership would not affect Trafalgar's relationship with Bridge
Walker. I had to tell him that I feared it would; and before
long Victor made contact again to complain that Parkes had
withdrawn and I had sabotaged his transaction. I offered to
consider the proposition for Trafalgar, because in the immediate future we needed to be sure of some such reservoir of
craftsmen and, in the longer term, we would need skilled
management with greater experience and ability than mine to
lead and control a large labour force. Victor seemed to fit
the bill in all respects, and the negotiations did not take long,
because he gave me a copy of the report which Touche Ross
had prepared on their investigation of his business for David
Parkes, which we were quite happy to rely on. We agreed a
valuation of £130,000 for the share capital, bought 49 per cent
for cash, and, as I said earlier, took options over the remainder;
we both then made additional loans to the business and we
started a new housebuilding company named Bridge Walker
Homes in which Trafalgar held 51 per cent. Both investments
were held through a new subsidiary of Trafalgar which, at
Geoffrey Crowther's suggestion, we called Footbridge Holdings.

The winter of 1962–3 had been quite exceptionally severe,
and a worry to Victor. Trafalgar at the time was developing
sixteen new houses on an attractive site at Magnolia Wharf,
Strand-on-the Green, by the Thames, and something like ten
weeks' production had been lost because of the snow and the
ground freezing to a considerable depth. Victor, who must

have been forty-three by the time we made our first investment, wanted to have more stability and substance to his life,
and, ironically enough, he sought this security through an
income from rents, whilst I was looking for higher, but less
certain, returns from trading activities, which I hoped he
would run. Victor had made a very bold move in acquiring
Bridge Walker in the first place, for his resources were small,
and when he first came to see me at Sackville Street in 1961,
and we went on afterwards to lunch at Brown's Hotel, he explained to me that the reason he ran a cream and black Rolls-
Royce was primarily to make it clear to creditors and suppliers
that he was doing very well – which, indeed, he was. He looked
then just as he does today, seventeen years later: tough and
purposeful, of middle height, with a pronounced nose, brown
eyes and a full head of black hair. He had married (his wife is
also called Joyce) during the war, but their only child, Ian,
was not born until 1961. They lived the life of thousands of
other successful Londoners who owned medium-sized businesses; even today it is much the same, except that he now
owns more land, and they spend as much on race-horses as
we spend on domestic staff, holidays and entertaining.

We had become friends at our first meeting, probably because it was immediately clear to each of us that the other was
totally absorbed in his business, and our mutual respect was
assisted by the fact that in every other way we were quite
different: that is to say in terms of age, education, social background, business experience and recreations.

My theories on the effects of Corporation Tax led me to
compose in 1964 with John Gray, David Fremantle's assistant,
a list of ten public companies most likely to fail to cope with
the new situation, and to become attractive for us to take
over. As one of the companies on the list was Trollope & Colls,
where Victor had worked for some years after the war, the
bond became even closer, and after our first purchase of the
initial stake in Bridge Walker I would see him three or four
times a month; I would visit him at Brixton once a month for
board meetings and we collaborated closely on our first housebuilding scheme: seven houses on a good site at Petersham,
where we produced a design for a 4/5 bedroom, 2 bathroom,
3 reception room, double garage property which still sells as

well as ever. He contributed the Ionic portico and dentil-cornice, and I suggested the louvered shutters to the first-floor windows: the design has lasted well, and since that time we have built 'Petershams', as we call them, on sites all over the country.

In the meantime, of course, we had been moving offices from time to time as the staff increased with the size of the business. after Sackville Street we took on lease the new building on the site of Collins & Collins' former offices in Curzon Street, which the new owners had so far failed to let. We sub-let the space we did not need for ourselves, and it was there that the Three Companies' bids were put into effect, and the City & West End offer was completed.

Westland House then proved to be too small for us so we took the eighth floor at the Economist Building, where Geoffrey Crowther had his private suite on the fourteenth floor, and Collins & Collins were letting the surplus space. The Bridge Walker transaction was completed there, and much productive work was carried out during this period by our growing staff and by myself. My office was on the north-east corner, and visitors would remark that it must be hard to work with such a marvellous view: but the truth was that one soon became unaware of it, and my only lasting recollections are the fact that I got from the GPO the number TRAfalgar 1805 for my private telephone; that once my wastepaper basket caught fire whilst I was on the phone to John Gillum; and that, for Victor, the Bridge Walker completion was facilitated by our offices being arranged round a continuous corridor enclosing the central core of the building. This was important because he had certain backers and shareholders to satisfy whilst he concluded his transaction with us, and it was possible to place and rotate them in sequence in a clockwise direction so that none met the others, and each ended up on his own at the lift lobby after fulfilling whatever was expected of him. By now the 50–52 Curzon Street development was nearing completion; part of the office space was let to RCA, and the flats went well, but about 9,000 square feet of offices remained unlet and I persuaded Victor to bring his head office there, as well as moving there myself from the Economist Building. It was from these offices that we planned and carried out the acquisitions of Ideal Building Corporation and Trollope & Colls.

It will be clear from what I have said that by 1965–6 Trafalgar had become quite a large, though unconventional, company. There was nothing else quite like us, and we were becoming equipped and ready for very considerable and deliberate expansion beyond the boundaries of conventional property companies. Routine activities of the time were much the same as they had been four years earlier, but the scale was larger. Labour had won the 1964 election and were re-elected in 1966, two events which filled Victor with gloom. I remember having a drink with him in my office at the Economist Building on the evening of the announcement of the first result and stating with complete confidence that, however much one might be apprehensive in the national interest, I had no doubts at all that Trafalgar could live with Labour, and that we were poised to prosper to a greater extent than could have been anticipated under a continuation of the previous regime. Victor's main preoccupation at the time was with the accounts of Bridge Walker: he had had a series of inadequate chief accountants and was nearing the point of resignedly accepting that nothing better could be expected. I nagged steadily, and Victor exerted himself once more to find the man he needed. The result was to exceed all our expectations, and the successful applicant for this much-advertised job was a thirty-year-old chartered accountant from Taylor Woodrow named Eric Parker; he quickly got everything straightened out and began to introduce the systems that have been indispensable to all our subsequent growth and organization. Eric started as Bridge Walker's chief accountant and is now managing director of the entire Trafalgar Group, apart from the newspapers and magazines. I mention him at this point to illustrate another indispensable facet of the way in which we were getting ourselves prepared for a significant move into business on a large scale.

Labour introduced the Land Commission and appointed my friend Sir Henry Wells (with whom I had been associated for some years in my charitable housing work) as its chairman. It was not particularly relevant to our operations, but could have been helpful to bona-fide developers in the assembly of sites. As it was, it created employment for several thousand civil servants and produced derisory revenues. The Conservatives abolished it, and Sir Henry died later in Australia; I remember being a lone voice on the council of what is now the British Property Federation, where I said we should lobby for the Land Commission to be made useful rather than scrapped, because otherwise, in due course, we would get something even worse, as indeed was to happen. It was clear to me that both the main parties would eventually agree that some form of betterment levy was essential.

George Brown, a great man in many ways, announced his office building ban on 4 November 1964, and this contributed to the gradual doubling, or even trebling, of office rents that was to follow; and it created a scarcity which was the salvation of several developers who had over-committed themselves to poorly located office schemes. I got the news whilst George Brown was still speaking in the House of Commons, where he announced that the ban would take effect that midnight. We quickly reviewed our plans and within three or four hours executed a number of important contracts, particularly the one for Cleveland House. All were witnessed by a solicitor in case, subsequently, there was any question that they might have been signed later and pre-dated.

Although at this stage Cleveland House was beyond the normal scope of Bridge Walker, we gave all the building contracts to Victor, because I could not be sure that other builders would not take advantage of the situation. This was doubly unfortunate for Trollope & Colls, as we were soon to find out, because they needed more work of the kind we had given to Victor and, failing to get ours, took other contracts that day on terms that were too favourable to their clients, as well as being unsuitable for Trollope & Colls. Bridge Walker's gain was reinforced when Victor took on personnel experienced in large contracts, particularly Harry Reeves, who became a director of the company and is now managing director of Trollope & Colls. Harry had been a foreman bricklayer with Victor only fifteen years earlier.

Another Labour move was the reintroduction of rent control over a wide range of residential properties; this led us to abandon gradually the concept of renting flats, and instead we decided to sell them. We continued our policy of modernization and improvement whenever a flat fell vacant, but now it would be sold; and in the case of newly controlled, existing tenants we offered concessionary terms to purchase, or alternatively a premium for possession.

I regret that this absurd legislation drained the reservoir of London's market of residential accommodation available to rent, but it is only fair to point out that the same folly had been committed in many other countries. In our case, no one suffered: those who bought acquired an appreciating asset at a discounted price; those who left took a worthwhile capital sum with them, which would not otherwise have been available, and those who preferred to stay and rent were obviously quite free to do so. This programme released large amounts of money to Trafalgar, which was soon to be redeployed. We were different in all this from the 'break-up' specialists who later entered the market, because we provided an established and continuing management service. Other traditional residential landlords for the most part sold their mansion blocks to speculators, and we bought several, because, as I have implied, we knew quite a lot about the business by now, it was profitable, and we were able to give a good service to tenants.

I mentioned earlier that Mike Rawlence left Collins & Collins in 1962 and that the business was then sold to Douglas Porcas, George Sibbering and Tony Hinton. Early in 1963, in the course of a single day, each of these three came separately to see me at Sackville Street – and each, unknown to the others, had the same message: life as equal partners had become intolerable, so would we be prepared to 'return' as the leading shareholder? We did, taking 40 per cent initially, with the others having 20 per cent each. Subsequently Tony moved elsewhere and George joined Trafalgar for a while; and today we have 50 per cent, Douglas owns 25 per cent, and other partners share the remaining 25 per cent.

Soon after I persuaded Douglas that they should buy Hampton's, a much larger business, but unprofitable at the time, and we helped with the finance. The Collins & Collins personnel moved into Hampton's premises in Arlington Street, Douglas became senior partner, and the former name ceased to be used. This has been an excellent investment for all concerned, and in a poor month Hampton's net profit is more than a year's turnover of the firm I joined twenty years ago. Douglas proved to be even better at running an estate agency than he was as an estate agent, and Hamilton Verschoyle has led his department to become the most successful residential agency in London. Other departments have flourished, and Trafalgar is one of their largest clients: we represent about 8 per cent of their annual fee income, and the only other agent to earn more from us is Healey & Baker, who are stronger on the commercial side. Though not significant in overall terms, Hampton's remains our close associate.

We were at the same time developing our strategies for Trafalgar in the longer term, and these took preliminary form with a number of investments, accumulated gradually and unobtrusively through nominees, in the shares of companies which later were to be taken over – Trollope & Colls, for example. In the early months of 1966 we acquired the Woodgate Investment Trust, and also formed a new company called Trafalgar House Investments Limited to take over Trafalgar – this was an expression of the tax-saving techniques described in the Appendix at the end of my paper for the Chartered Auctioneers. This had the further advantage that shareholders, after receiving their allocation of new shares and loan stock in the new company, could sell the latter without reducing their equity in the business; the Capital Gains tax basis happened to be quite favourable, and in my case the sale of the loan stock produced more money than had been the value of my entire holding at the time of our floatation less than three years earlier. Woodgate was a small, quoted investment trust with a property owning subsidiary called Corbett and Newson; the terms were fair at the time, and the motive for sale must have been family reasons amongst the controlling shareholders, who were quite happy to sell. We were to make a considerable amount of money from rebuilding their offices in Great St Helens, in the City, and from what became our share in the site of the Bishopsgate Tower, which Trollope & Colls were to build for a number of partners, who included Felix Fenston. We sold our share in the latter site to Hambro interests for several times what we had paid for the whole of Woodgate.

This chapter has described some of the many thoughts and events of our first four years of life as a public company. I will now go back to 1960, and the next chapter deals with my private life and some of the non-Trafalgar activities that were to occupy me during the period.

10

In the Meantime

I have explained how Joyce and I moved in 1959 to a rented flat at Hornton Court above Chesterton's, the estate agents, in Kensington High Street. In 1961 we bought our first house, a 96-year lease in Abbotsbury Road on the west side of Holland Park, where Simo Properties and Wimpeys had carried out one of the more attractive and successful post-war housing developments in London. There must have been a hundred new houses in the scheme, arranged in short terraces along the main road, punctuated by closes, each of ten or twelve houses, set behind. Ours was 6 Abbotsbury Close, and it had four bedrooms, two bathrooms, a drawing room on the first floor overlooking the park; and a dining room, kitchen and garage on the ground floor, with a small, agreeable garden facing west at the back. This is a fairly standard design for a London terrace and, apart from the garage, not much different in layout to what Nicholas Barbon was building three hundred years earlier: but post-war architecture generally followed what I regarded as the 'utility era' and was more influenced by contemporary styles introduced for the Festival of Britain than by what had gone before. In this case the architects, Stone Toms & Partners, had followed Georgian elevations which, with good bricks and careful landscaping, produced a most pleasing result which looks even better today than it did then, for by now all the new trees and shrubs are firmly established. The house had cost £9,750 when new, and we bought it from the first owner, a director of Mowlems, the builders, for less than £11,000 – today, in similar condition, it would be worth £100,000. I make this point to remind people that the best investment for almost anyone since the war has been his house: house prices have out-performed inflation, whilst equities generally, and throughout the free world, have failed to do so.

We were not there for very long, and the most notable event of our time at Number 6 was the birth of Victoria at the end of 1961. We moved, as we became more prosperous, to a pair of similar houses on the main road, with the result that by the beginning of 1963 we were living in greater comfort at 17/19 Abbotsbury Road, where we stayed until we moved into Wargrave Manor four years later. At 17/19 the previous owner had removed one of the staircases, with the result that this double house had larger reception rooms than Number 6, as well as more bedrooms, an extra garage, a study and a large nursery. Justin by now was at the Scarsdale School, to which he and I would walk each morning, holding hands and talking incessantly. His next school was St David's in Elvaston Place, which was then a pre-prep school for those who were going later to a boarding school, and for others provided a full education up to the age of thirteen or so. It belonged to the headmaster, a large, elderly man named D. Dudley Durnford, who was an old-fashioned disciplinarian with a gift for making the boys work. I sometimes think Justin's later academic successes all date from this period.

At weekends I would always go to my office on Saturday mornings, because I found I could do my best work there when I was alone – alone, that is, apart from Justin, who generally would accompany me. In the autumn of 1963 I spent ten hours a day alone at the office during a three-day bank holiday to collate and interpret all that we had discovered about the Three Companies. Otherwise Sundays were days off and would usually start with the 10 a.m. Children's Service at St Barnabas Church in Addison Road. Then we would go for a Wimpy at Lyons by the Cumberland Hotel before taking a walk in Regent's Park or on Hampstead Heath. By this time Victoria was old enough to join in, and almost every week we would follow this Sunday morning programme with Basil Kelly, who lived nearby, and his three children, Rosamund, Natasha and Ralph. It was a very ordered and orderly existence, and we all enjoyed it. On Saturday and Sunday afternoons Joyce would come too, and the four of us would all go to Richmond Park or to Kew Gardens. It was a clear and distinct part of my life, and our subsequent moves related as much to the children's education as to anything else;

I was glad to move on to each section of my life and, although the previous one had been happy and complete, I felt no nostalgia or regret, because requirements changed with circumstances, and circumstances were changing all the time. I must admit, however, that we were more nomadic than most people, in terms of houses as well as offices.

By now, as well as a nanny, we had a daily cook, and I had my first chauffeur, George Foster. George, after spending the war in the army, had been a bus driver and an ambulance driver before becoming chauffeur to the editor of *The Economist*. He then gave up this work for a period and took industrial employment to be near his married daughter at Hemel Hempstead; but this didn't suit the Fosters, and when Geoffrey Crowther heard that George was thinking of returning to chauffeuring he told me at once, and gave a strong recommendation. George is a kind and rugged man who knows London better than any taxi driver and is very fast. He has been with us ever since and he has 'seen it all', as they say, in terms of the children growing up and also in terms of the growth of the business. At first we did a lot of driving, and he would even take the weekly pay packets to the porters at all our properties. Today, of course, there is less driving because my life centres round the office in Berkeley Street, and even for lunch I rarely go further afield than the Ritz. Ten years ago it was very different. George would drive through the night to meet Victor and me at Glasgow or Edinburgh airport and take us to visit various building contracts, housing sites, quarries and factories all the way from Scotland down to the Midlands.

Joyce and I continued to take more than one holiday a year, and until 1964 we went abroad without children. Nannies changed fairly frequently, but my mother was always there to provide authority and moral support.

My mother had always been an excellent draughtswoman and designer, and a good painter of portraits and landscapes. Her first important prize was presented to her at Leeds by Dame Barbara Hepworth, one of whose last major works, 'The Family of Man', consisting of nine, large, abstract, bronze figures, we bought a few years ago and have lent to the Government for indefinite display in Hyde Park. My mother's work had been intermittent during my childhood, but after the war she resumed a semi-professional career. In the early years of my marriage she had travelled extensively in the Middle East, but now she was back in London and living in the smallest of our new houses at Strand-on-the-Green, where she remained until she emigrated to Switzerland in 1969.

In the early 1960s she would supervise our children if we were away, sometimes staying at our house and sometimes in her own. I felt that two or three holidays a year were necessary to refresh Joyce and me, to keep us in trim through what was a busy time in terms of physical activity, and a more demanding one in terms of stress and inventiveness. It was not until 1964, after the City and West End acquisition, that I felt the time had come for a longer holiday, including children and nanny for the first time.

We had by now a new, dark-green Rolls-Royce with the number 888 HUV, a number we kept for successive cars until 1973, when I felt it had become rather conspicuous. Joyce and I drove to Dover, where we took the car ferry to Calais, and travelled through north-eastern France to some of the more attractive parts of Switzerland, staying the night wherever the scenery appealed to us. We continued southwards over the St Gotthard pass to Lugano and then, after a day or two, drove down to Italy towards Venice, where the children were to arrive by air a week after we had left London. We took rooms in what must have been the second-best hotel on the Lido, the Grand Hôtel des Bains; and the book, the film, and Benjamin Britten's opera, *Death in Venice*, all remind me powerfully of the atmosphere. We had a tent on the beach and almost every day would take a *vaporette* to Venice itself to walk and explore a little more of this unique city. After a fortnight the children returned to London with their nanny, and Joyce and I proceeded westwards towards the South of France. We spent a night at Vicenza and two days admiring the surrounding Roman and Palladian architecture which marked the end of the beginning, and the beginning of the end, of two high points in European culture, separated by a thousand years: I have no scholarly knowledge of these things and my sense of history is much assisted by seeing physical objects.

We travelled through Genoa to Beaulieu where we spent
three days at La Réserve, which must be one of the best small
hotels in France, and certainly has one of the best restaurants,
and then we drove for two or three hours to Le Club at
Cavalière, where at the time was one of the best chefs in
France, Monsieur Vergé. Le Club then belonged to an elderly
French senator and comprised twenty or thirty rooms, with
an excellent beach of silver-coloured sand surrounded by
characteristic trees and countryside of quite a different kind to
the area between Cannes and Cap Ferrat that we knew better.
Monsieur Vergé then had the concession for the restaurant
and bar, and we see him today with several of the same staff
at the Moulin de Mougins, where he has a small hotel and a
restaurant that must be quite the best in the South of France:
Simon and I have had our birthday lunches there every year
since July 1970.

Simon, our third child, was born on 31 July 1966, and by
this time we had bought Wargrave Manor, a fine house where
we spent nine happy and successful years before moving to
something smaller a few miles away. At the beginning of that
year Joyce began to yearn for a cottage in the country, and the
first three months of the year, apart from a short holiday in
Morocco, had been spent in a fruitless search for something
small and attractive in the Thames Valley, the most convenient
place for us in view of the easy access by the new motorway,
the M4. I had become exasperated with the project, and with
the endless series of hopeless houses which we were sent to
see by local agents; so I spoke to Aubrey Orchard-Lisle, who
was then the senior partner of the estate agents, Healey and
Baker, and who had a weekend house at Marlow.

We had met Aubrey during the previous winter at Round
Hill in Jamaica. He said the only man he knew who might be
able to help was Roderick Sergentson, the owner of a small
agency called Hibbert & Co. in Henley. Roderick suggested a
house at Hambleden which was being sold by Pat Matthews,
then running the First National Finance Corporation, later to
be one of the major collapses of the seventies. We arranged to
meet on the following Sunday, and for some reason the rendezvous was arranged for the car park of the George and Dragon
at Wargrave. We arrived there a little early on a cold, foggy,

March morning and, as I strolled along the road leading to Henley, I paused: and as I did so the mists cleared to reveal a large, white, colonnaded house set beyond parkland above the road. I returned to Joyce and asked her to come and have a look: I told her that I had never had much interest in the idea of a weekend cottage, and what enthusiasm I had had was fast evaporating – but if she would consider a proper house such as the one we were looking at, we might make the major move to the country, and live there most of the time, which would make sense in a number of other respects, particularly for the children. Roderick arrived and took us to Hambleden where we met Pat Matthews and agreed that his house came nearer to our original specification than anything else we had seen; but in the previous hour the specification had changed.

Roderick took the point, but said that in the case of Wargrave Manor there really was not the remotest chance: the Cain family, whose money came from Walker Cain, the brewers, had lived there since before the First World War, and there was no more reason for them to sell it now than there had been at any other time. We returned to our Sunday lunch at Abbotsbury Road with very little to say to one another, for clearly the earlier plan was eclipsed by the new one, and there was no practical object in view for the new one, though it changed everything. Justin by now had gone to Brambletye, my former prep school; Victoria would soon be five and was looking forward to country life with ponies, and our next child would have no particular schooling requirements for some years. I wanted a more spacious and reflective existence, and by now Trafalgar had management which did not need detailed supervision – but did require direction in terms of the overall concept. And we both wanted something on a larger scale where we could live calmly with good staff and the minimum of aggravation.

The following Wednesday Roderick telephoned to say that Wargrave Manor was indeed going to be sold, and Knight Frank & Rutley were about to prepare particulars. I cancelled my luncheon appointment, phoned Joyce, and we drove down eating sandwiches in the back of the car. We spent nearly two hours there, and agreed to buy it; which must have surprised

Lady Cain and Sir Ernest, who only that morning had agreed to this sudden appointment.

The house had about twenty acres of garden, much of it lawn, three or four acres of woodland, and a small farm of just over fifty acres; once there had been another six hundred acres of land, but unfortunately this had been sold some years earlier.

The central part of this white stucco house was built in about 1775 for a lawyer from London named Hussey, and the large hall and dining room were added in 1810. On the ground floor were five good reception rooms, two of them panelled in oak; the first floor contained eight bedrooms with four bathrooms; and on the top floor we installed three bedrooms and two bathrooms, with much additional space to spare in the attics, and a separate housekeeper's flat above my study. There were two lodges and a good detached house for the head gardener; the farm buildings for the most part were thatched; and in the centre of this small estate was a Georgian stables block with two cottages and a massive, red-brick water-tower built about 1860.

Evidently there had been two distinct periods of work to the property since the additions of 1810 – that is to say the construction of lodges and so forth in 1861, and the addition of bathrooms and extra servants' quarters about 1910. At its Edwardian peak, we were told, there had been fifteen staff in the house and sixteen gardeners, but the Cains seemed by now to be living quite comfortably with a resident maid, a male secretary for Sir Ernest, and four gardeners, only one of whom then earned more than £10 a week, and most of whom spent nearly half the year mowing the lawns – there were no motor mowers until we arrived. The additions of 1910 had made the house unnecessarily dark. The whole of the central area of the ground floor had been filled in with a mass of windowless little rooms, and extra bathrooms on the first floor had been placed against the corridor windows and were carried on steel joists over the central yard. After all this was stripped away the house became bright and easily manageable.

When we moved there in January 1967 our domestic staff was at its highest level, consisting of housekeeper, butler and cook, nanny and nurserymaid, and four charladies. Within two or three years this contracted without problems to butler and cook, nanny and two charladies, and we have kept to this level, apart from the nanny, ever since, with the butler now driving the same charladies to and from Wargrave to nearby Sonning, where today we live for weekends. One of the four gardeners had retired before we moved in to Wargrave Manor; Owen, the head gardener, died suddenly a few years later; Champion had a stroke and had to retire; and May, a timid man who spent his entire working life in the greenhouses, had to be left there when we sold the house in 1975. The other vacancies were quickly filled as they arose by Don Ewers and Doug Knapp, who later moved with us to Sonning. People sometimes wonder why we are not plagued with staff troubles, and I really do not know the answer. We do not over-pay, though we value these people highly; I am very determined to have harmony and continuity at home, and the credit must go to Joyce. Our two Sonning gardeners also look after the garden of our house in London. It goes without saying that this standard of living, commonplace not long before, could not be supported out of taxed income: we live partly off capital and, unlike most other people, we have created capital.

The day after we moved into Wargrave Manor in January 1967 I took Victoria to her new school, Rupert House at Henley, and this served her well until a little London education became desirable in 1971; Simon started at Rupert House in 1970. We would spend six nights a week at Wargrave and had a flat, and later a house, in London for the seventh night, generally a Tuesday or a Wednesday. On Fridays I would usually spend all day in the country, with Miss Barker and a telex machine, and this became the most productive day of the week. Travelling to and from London on the other days was not burdensome; the journey to the West End then took only about fifty minutes.

The only thing that did not please me was the farm. It was too small to be effective, and this, in turn, made it difficult to get good managers. We went in for milk production with between thirty and seventy Friesians, and never found the right formula. If I had this part of my life to live again, the only thing I would change is the farm; I would use almost the whole area to grow specimen trees, some in tubs and some in the ground, with tarmac paths to keep one's feet dry in the winter. Clearly I am not suited temperamentally to being a farmer or to real countryside – I regarded Wargrave more as a remote suburb of London. The only benefit from the farm was the paddock for Victoria's pony and Mrs Judge, the farm manager's wife, who taught her to ride.

One of the reasons we all enjoyed the place so much was the scale of the house and the garden; another was that our move coincided with those of many other families of similar age, and now our children had many more friends and parties than in London. It is well known that for most middle-class people, this mid/late sixties period marked a peak of individual prosperity, from which standards have declined ever since. Certainly our own morale was influenced by this, and much of the conceptual work for Trafalgar's expansion was done at Wargrave, including Ideal Building Corporation, Trollope & Colls, Cementation and Cunard, as well as some of the failures; and with IBC and T & C our shares doubled and doubled again in price within a year.

It suited me well to detach myself a little from the day-to-day management of Trafalgar, and this was beneficial to the company. I had proved, at least to my own satisfaction, that I could be unusually successful in combining property skills with financial ones, and I had no desire to continue with repetitive work. I knew that Trafalgar's scope in the next few years would be considerable, and I wanted its breadth of management capability to grow, something that can be hindered by the continuous presence of the man who started the business. A relationship of total confidence was developing with Victor Matthews, and with Eric Parker, and without being clear about the route, I was sure of the destination: the structure we have today. Also, after ten years of very hard work, I wanted to become more reclusive and contemplative. I was thinking all the time about the future, and in terms of the consequences of completing transactions that we had not yet commenced. Within my restricted commercial circle I had become something of a minor cult figure, but I think I was alone in realizing how much further the business had to go: the only thing to surprise me subsequently was the speed at which it all happened.

My property skills were at their peak in the mid/late sixties, and it is ironic to reflect that my judgement is more frequently called for today than it was then. My interest is undiminished, but I suppose part of the truth of the matter is that, when I have satisfied myself that I can do something well, I want to do something else; not instead, but in addition. This must have contributed to the diversity of Trafalgar, as has the fact that I have no business interests outside Trafalgar. I keep a strong interest in what we do and in what we have done; I do not get bored with what is complete, but I like to withdraw a little and to contemplate it.

I suppose another factor which influenced our wish to settle for a few years with a large house in the country, but not too far from London, was the thought of catching up, so to speak, with a more sociable existence. We were never unfriendly, but the pace of work from the late fifties had made it hard to see as much of our friends as, by now, I wanted to do.

Quite apart from the social lives of the children, there was at that time in and around Wargrave an extraordinary amount of adult social activity, with two or three parties a week from early June to late September, many including dinner and dancing, and some lasting till dawn. This small society consisted largely of people of our own age who had left London for reasons similar to ours, and most departed eight or ten years later, just as we did. For many of them this life would no longer be financially possible; for some the reason was divorce; but for nearly all it related to children going to other schools, combined with the desire to reduce the time it took to travel to work.

From 1963 to 1970 I was involved with charitable housing trusts. With Diana Paul, then chairman of the Kensington Council Planning Committee, Henry Wells, who became chairman of the Kensington Housing Trust, and Brenda Breakwell, a most remarkable woman who was manager of the Trust and later became Mayor of Dartmouth, we developed and put into effect some novel concepts which much enlarged the ability of the Trust to extend its good work in North Kensington. KHT had been founded in 1928 by a group of local philanthropists led by Lord Balfour of Burleigh, who provided the initial finance to build flats in some of the more dilapidated parts of the Borough. This produced employment as well as accommodation, and the flats would be let at modest rents, just sufficient to service the cost of construction, which in those days was low. Many tenants had social as well as financial problems, and when I became treasurer of the Trust in 1963 its work was as much concerned with matters of welfare as with being a landlord.

We had at that time about six hundred and fifty dwellings, and were encouraged by the local council to buy three- and four-floored houses in the neighbourhood, which then could be bought for £4,000 or so, and converted into self-contained flats to let at what was, in effect, a cost rent. New building, by this time, was uneconomical for us, but one last new block of flats was built at Wornington Road and named Peplar House after the previous chairman, Lady Peplar. But gradually even our conversion schemes became uneconomic, for construction costs began to rise even faster than house prices. Our assets were worth far more than they had cost, but we had no liquid resources left to cover the revenue deficits that were beginning to emerge. The Council was most helpful (and rightly so, since we were doing work that lightened a load they knew they would find more costly to carry) and the Campden Charity gave us money each year; but nevertheless we reached a point at which, unless rents were raised to a more realistic level, the Trust would have to cease to add every year to the stock of decent housing in North Kensington. The rental picture was as confused as W & K's had been, though for more virtuous reasons and, although there were plenty of needy and deprived tenants, there were also plenty of more prosperous ones. Labour had by now introduced its new Rent Act, with the concept of fair rents, though charitable housing was not subject to the new legislation. We decided to opt firmly for the elementary concept of subsidizing individual tenants rather than indiscriminately subsidizing accommodation, and we set about establishing the equivalent of a fair rent for every dwelling. This was a large valuation programme which called for expert professional help. I suggested the name of Geoffrey Carter, who then owned the estate agency Marsh & Parsons in Kensington Church Street, and was our agent for the

Kensington Vicarage development at the time (Geoff, incidentally, joined Trafalgar later, and now runs our Property Division – he is also chairman of KHT, which these days operates more as a direct extension of the Council, and has grown substantially).

He agreed to undertake all these valuations, and the result confirmed that the rents we were charging were about £130,000 per annum below what would have been the level of fair rents, had they applied. About £80,000 per annum of this subsidy was found to be justified by the circumstances of individual tenants – and some actually found they were paying less than before – but the net gain of £50,000 per annum became available to the Trust to subsidize its continuing programme and to create more accommodation. This was not accomplished without protests, and the overall concept was not a new one – but the remarkable thing is that we did it, and it worked. One must be firm about protests of this kind, for usually they come from those who could pay more, but find it worthwhile in their lives to adopt a theatrical or political posture, which often works to help them financially – without helping those who really need assistance and are less vocal.

It was through this work that I met Sir Keith Joseph and became deputy chairman of a similar Trust that he started in Paddington, the Mulberry Housing Trust. I also joined the board of the London Housing Trust which became very large after uniting with Quadrant to co-ordinate similar enterprises all over London. Today, of course, all these organizations operate within strict government control, rents are no longer collected personally, and the social involvement of the landlord has largely been lost. Much good has been done by the movement, but a few more KHTs would have made it even better.

I retired from these various appointments when I felt that I had done all I could to help. I was saddened as the preliminary effects of current inflation rates came to bear on our work. There were three characteristics: the earlier doctrine of self-help, which in these charities meant giving time and thought to what would benefit the recipients as well as the tax-payer, no longer applied; government-encouraged, inflationary expectations put our costs beyond the ability of our tenants to

My mother and father

When I was eighteen

One of my mother's commercial designs

ABOVE LEFT Soon after our
marriage

ABOVE An early development;
I drew the picture myself

LEFT Ravenswood, 1958 – we
might have lived there

BELOW LEFT 22–25A Sackville
Street, the first major development on the Sutton Estate,
1958/59

Green Park House, the first scheme in
the West End, 1956

Magnolia Wharf, Strand-on-the-
Green, one of many small
residential developments

Bush Lane House, Cannon Street, 1963.
The home of Three Companies

Bush Lane House, 1976, as
reconstruction was being completed

Topping out at Cleveland House, 1966. From left to right: Sir Geoffrey (later Lord) Crowther, Bertie Waddell, myself and Victor Matthews

Cleveland House, soon after completion

Mortimer House

Wargrave Manor

The hall at Wargrave

The drawing room at Mortimer House

Cunard's fleet of passenger liners, 1961. From left to right, front row:
Caronia, Mauretania, Britannic, Queen Elizabeth, Queen Mary; middle
row: Saxonia, Ivernia, Sylvania, Carinthia; back row: Media, Parthia, Scythia

The *QE2*, Sydney, Australia, February 1978

The Barbara Hepworth figures in Hyde Park

ABOVE TOP The Trafalgar House
Board of Directors at the Annual
General Meeting, January 1979

ABOVE MIDDLE Some of my
silverwork

LEFT Ro Fisher's bronze of me
writing the book

The family at Sonning, March 1977

Young Businessman of the Year, 1978

pay without subsidy; and the personal touch, particularly represented by personal rent collection, began to decline because of economic and staffing pressures.

Keith Joseph and I became friends, and I accepted his invitation to join the board of Bovis's new property subsidiary. Keith's family, with the Salmons and Glucksteins, had established Bovis the builders not long after starting the J. Lyons business; Keith was deputy chairman of Bovis, and the chairman, Harry Vincent, had been born a Gluckstein. I remember in 1966 that within a week Harry asked me if I would follow him as chairman of Bovis, and Keith, on a separate occasion, asked if I would like to become their chief executive. I told them both that Trafalgar was already larger than they realized, and neither of their objectives could be achieved except through a takeover by Trafalgar. Subsequently, through Harry's brother Neville, they made their deal with Frank Sanderson, which did not work out well. I remember, before they were taken over by P & O, but soon after they had competed with us for Cementation, that Keith brought Frank Sanderson to see Victor and me to discuss whether merger proposals could be explored between us: when I pointed out that this could only succeed with a single chief executive (quite apart from many other problems), Frank said that he would be quite happy to leave, if the terms were right for the shareholders – and Victor, laughing, said so would he.

The only other non-executive directorship of a business concern that I took during this period – or subsequently – was of Trust Houses. During my 1964 visit to Australia I found time to meet, at Geoffrey Crowther's suggestion, Alan Greenaway, then chairman of TraveLodge, the motel chain, and I explored the possibilities for some link with Trust Houses. It was clear that TraveLodge would welcome something of the kind, because they were short of money – but so, as it happened, were Trust Houses; we were tempted to do it through Trafalgar, but rejected the idea, for I had already decided in the case of routine property development that it could only be controlled and understood if Joyce and I first went to live in Australia for a year, and the figures were not large enough to justify this. It is an attractive continent with a marvellous climate, but I had the firm conviction that (for me, at least) there was

E

more to do in London; that is to say, from my London office, and often within walking distance from it: that is one of the reasons I find the metropolis so fascinating.

Geoffrey's problems with Trust Houses were unnecessary, and at one point I told him so, after he had tentatively explored the possibility of a merger with Trafalgar. In 1966 he told me that he had despaired of the existing management and would like me to join the board with a view to succeeding him as chairman in due course. I agreed to the former and said that we must wait and see what was appropriate in terms of subsequent developments. I have little experience of boards apart from my own, where it might now be said that the executive committee (Victor, Eric and I) has a degree of authority that makes the other directors' attendance at our formal meetings relatively and generally a matter of routine exchanges of information. Trust Houses was the reverse: the non-executive directors who dominated board meetings were for the most part distinguished people with strong personalities, full of good intentions, but lacking commercial involvement with the business or the industry. There was little I could do. I must not be unhelpfully critical of this situation, but in Trafalgar's case, when we acquire a company, we move in with unquestioned authority as the new owners, and even companies which for generations have been unused to the idea of 'owners' will accept without argument that this is now the case. It is more difficult to reform from within, spontaneously, particularly when the nominal leader has no significant financial involvement. Trust Houses had recruited and promoted worthy executives, but there was no one there of the vision, experience and stature that their large business called for.

In the summer of 1968 Joyce and I rented the Château de Clavary, below Grasse, from Peter Wilson, the chairman of Sotheby's. We spent two or three weeks there with our family and, at a party, I mentioned to Count Kapnist, who ran an estate agency on Cap d'Antibes, that we had much enjoyed our visits to La Violetta in the late 1950s, when David Fremantle used to borrow the house from his friend Pat Egan. Vadim Kapnist told us that this villa was again up for sale, and in due course we bought it. When we had last seen the house it had been a small, old-fashioned property with an orchard, sixty yards from the sea; Pat Egan had later sold it to an Englishman named John Gibson, whose family business was the Harrison Gibson furniture store, and John Gibson had carried out some extraordinary improvements, including an annexe for guests and a large, very deep, swimming pool of unusual shape.

It was there, in the summer of 1969, as I prowled morbidly round and round the pool one evening, that Joyce said, 'Don't worry so much, perhaps you've already done all that you're going to do.' By this time I was chairman of Trafalgar and I was thinking of Costain, Cementation and Cunard; I was not exactly worried, but I must admit that I was in a troubled state of mind, for I knew that by now there was scarcely anything that Trafalgar could not do given patience and planning, but I was fearful of binding myself more inextricably to what I had done much to create. It has been inaccurately described as the Alexander Syndrome, an exaggeration in any case, but Joyce's point was relevant, though not precisely on the target. I did not want to stop what I was doing, but I did not want to become committed to a treadmill which required me to do it for ever. I had found out that responsibility for events, good or bad, brought out my best qualities: but, as I see now, I was entering the period of doubt and analysis that we all go through on the way to middle age, rather early in my case; I had done a great deal and I had a very wide spectrum from which to choose what I wanted for the future. Trafalgar remains my largest investment, and I do not know of a better one, but it suited me by now to be chairman on a basis that was mainly non-executive but virtually full-time, and therefore incompatible with much else.

In 1966 Trafalgar tendered successfully for a building lease of 50/52 Hyde Park Gate, where we built an excellent block of flats, overlooking Kensington Gardens, called Broadwalk House. This, incidentally, was the last property development that I handled personally – others have done this work since then. It was characteristic of the effect of the planning regulations, combined with marketing considerations, that the maxi-

mum number of 'habitable rooms', as calculated under the
assumed occupancies of the 'persons per acre' zoning, should
be concentrated in the main block facing the park, subject
only to height controls: at the rear was a mews house, which
we renovated, and a large garden where all that could be built
was a single house for sale – in fact we bought this house ourselves; but this was a pale shadow of the house that could
have been constructed on this site combined with the site of
the mews. We had considered Bob Chapman's remarkable
designs for what might have been built there, but rejected
the idea on grounds of cost and lack of public appeal. It
would have been one of the most exceptional houses in London, and I much regret that we did not build it – and buy it.

Another error of judgement concerned our farthest field at
Wargrave, eight acres with unrepeatable views. We knew
quite well that in due course our needs would become inconsistent with Wargrave Manor itself, and, despite all the planning restrictions, we might have got consent to build a very
special house on this remote site. It would have been a delight
to do it next door, so to speak, and to have two or three years
in which to create and establish a garden and all its architecture before moving into the house. It would have been of
classical appearance, completing a quadrangle with steps leading up to the front door, and a very large stone-floored hall
with a staircase leading down again to ground level where,
in particular, I would have had my study overlooking an enclosed Dutch water-garden. I made sketch designs and then
abandoned the project, because the cost then would have
been £400,000, perhaps the equivalent of £2 million today; but
we had the means and the ability to do it, and nothing of the
kind has happened since. I suppose in both these concepts I
was influenced by recollections of Stowe, and both houses
would have had halls which rose to the eaves, with glass domes
above.

I find I feel grateful towards everything I did during this
period, and all I regret are a few things I could also have done,
but did not do. My hesitancy was not laziness or timidity; it
was a sense of financial caution which, on the whole, has stood
me in good stead. What surprises me now is the purposeful-

ness with which I planned for other things which duly followed. My confidence might have been confused with arrogance and, looking back, as I said earlier, what most surprises me is the speed of what followed.

11

A Larger Scale

As I explained earlier, we outgrew our floor at the Economist Building and, as the association with Victor Matthews developed, Trafalgar moved to unlet office space in our development at 50/52 Curzon Street where we each took a floor and he brought with him some of his key staff from Brixton. We were about to embark on a series of takeovers following which he would do the executive work and assume responsibility for larger numbers of people; and this called for our physical proximity for discussions, often three hours a day, four days a week; it was also essential for our financial interests to coincide. So, as part of the events of 1967/8, which I am about to describe, we exercised our options over his remaining shares in Bridge Walker, and his business became a wholly owned subsidiary of Trafalgar. He joined the board, and for nearly two years we were joint managing directors; but, although our financial objectives by now were identical, he was sometimes a troublesome companion because his nature is to concentrate on one thing at a time to the exclusion of all other considerations and if, for example, there were a dispute between Trafalgar House Management and Bridge Walker over some builder's final account, or a question of work that had to be re-done, he would instinctively revert to his former role.

The only serious argument we had was about Eric Parker, when Victor wanted Eric to be concerned only with his, Victor's, side of the business, whereas I wanted all financial and administrative matters for the enlarged group to become integrated under Eric's control. In all other areas, that is to say issues involving third parties and outside opportunities, we would invariably reach agreement, as we do today – though we still often reach identical conclusions for quite different reasons, but without either of us troubling to demolish the reasoning of the other, provided the conclusion is agreeable to us both. We issued new shares in Trafalgar for the acquisition of the remainder of Victor's interest in his former business, and before long they had risen in value sufficiently to make him a millionaire.

Only five years earlier he had felt content to contemplate the fulfilment of his ambitions with the ownership of Bridge Walker in Brixton. Now the horizons were expanding rapidly, and Victor hardly faltered; Douglas Porcas, by now head of Hampton's, was for a while on the board of our housebuilding company, and so far as I know it was only to Douglas that Victor confided that I was taking 'a hell of a risk' in assuming that he could mould, and create, the organization to manage all the things I wanted Trafalgar to do. I was confident, and I think Victor would acknowledge that neither of us could have done it on his own. I remember an occasion a year or two later when Stanley Morton (soon to be Sir Stanley, chairman of the Abbey National Building Society) came to lunch with us at Cleveland House and said, pointing at me, 'You're Svengali and Victor's Trilby!' It was an offensive remark, meant kindly.

These steps towards integration were being taken at the same time as our first proposed acquisitions of public companies engaged in contracting and housebuilding were approaching the point of decision and action. In particular what we wanted was Trollope & Colls. Of all the major builders in London, Trollope & Colls were the best; others may have excelled in one particular area or another, but none had this pre-eminence of skills, crafts and capabilities for work of the highest quality in Central London. The takeover was also to assume great importance for us in another way, since opposition of high quality developed from another quarter. We were building up a 9·9 per cent shareholding, the most that could be held without disclosure, and planned the acquisition for early 1968, after the publication of Trollope & Colls' figures, which we anticipated would be bad. We also planned to follow this acquisition with another of lower quality: a housebuilding concern where large, but less sustainable, profits could be generated quite quickly. I suppose it could have been said that our plan was to secure a high-quality rating for profits which were not in fact entirely of the highest quality. But, if that was a consideration, it was not the main one: we preferred our chosen sequence because we feared that, if we were already characterized as a large housebuilding business, we would be even less acceptable to the board of Trollope & Colls, who, in turn, would find it easier to defend themselves by pointing to the flawed calibre of their aspirant.

By early 1967 we were as well prepared as we could be for both, but in each case the timing was beyond our control, and the opportunities came up in the wrong order.

Ideal Building Corporation had developed from the New Ideal Homes business started by Leo Mayer in the early 1930s, and the investment trusts of Harley Drayton held about 30 per cent of IBC's capital. By 1967 Mayer had died, Drayton had died, and so had Sir Herbert Butcher, the most recent chairman of IBC, and the job was being done on a temporary basis by Martin Rich of Drayton's. I knew all this and made a tentative, preliminary approach via Dick Lomer and Angus Ogilvie. Dick was a solicitor whom I had met through the Mulberry Housing Trust and who had created two large housebuilding finance companies (Glamford and Builders Amalgamated) which Drayton bought, and Angus Ogilvie ran. We bought them later, after Hambros became involved, but in the meantime they had encountered severe difficulties, and these problems coincided with others at IBC where Eric Wollard, Mayer's former right-hand man, proved to be less effective on his own as managing director. So when I went to Martin Rich's office one afternoon in April, intending to prepare the ground for a deal in about a year's time, I was taken aback to be told that my visit was welcome and timely, because Drayton's were fed up with the whole situation and would make a swift deal with us; and, if not with us, with someone else. This led to much soul-searching on our part, for we would have preferred to take over Trollope & Colls first; but the conclusion was inescapable: we could not reject what was available just to preserve our posture for something which might in any case prove impossible.

We were able to negotiate arrangements for IBC which were unusual in the case of a public company takeover, but were not inappropriate in these particular circumstances: we contracted with Drayton's to make an offer to all shareholders, which their trusts would accept, at a stated price (in cash), but subject to our first having access to all their sites and records to confirm that the net assets of IBC were indeed as stated in their published accounts. These terms were announced publicly, and may have done something to prevent the exodus from our shares that we had feared. The investigation lasted about six weeks, and we conducted it ourselves, with outside professional help as required.

IBC in those days built altogether about two thousand houses a year in the South-East, the Midlands, the North of England and Scotland, and were responsible for about 1¼ per cent of this country's production of houses for sale. The Epsom head office contained about 120 people, and there were two regional offices. As well as the housebuilding companies, which developed estates of private houses for sale, there was also a construction company named Carlton which built for local authorities. It soon became clear that IBC's records were good, but parts of the business were not; they had just undergone a study by management consultants, which gave them sound systems but no commercial assistance.

This is a good point at which to explain our attitude to management consultants; often we would arrive on the scene soon after they had left, and in Cunard's case there were no fewer than three. If a company has deteriorated beyond the control of its board and senior executives, then the consultant can give limited help, but no more, and only in a number of technical respects. Trust Houses called in consultants in one of Geoffrey Crowther's periods of disenchantment, and on that occasion the report had the value of expressing as an independent opinion what was already clear to most of the board, but was unacceptable to them until they got it in black and white from McKinsey's. At one point in the 1960s consultancy became very fashionable, an indispensable cure-all; but when things got tougher it became clear that these people were more of a luxury than a necessity: when a company found itself in a mess it would have to find its own commercial solutions or submit to a takeover, and allow someone else to settle its problems. We are not hostile to management consultants, but we do not use them. Most people see business in terms of management and labour; but we think very much in terms of a third component, direction, and this is where the commercial thrust originates.

Direction, of course, is dependent on information, and many of the systems we use today in Trafalgar were developed under Eric Parker's direction after we bought IBC. Two concepts dating from that time, for which I was mainly responsible, are 'the blueprint', and the practice of charging notional interest for the cost of Trafalgar's investment in every operation. The 'blueprint', as introduced whilst we were investigating IBC, is a formal appraisal of an operation's resources and market, expressed in terms of what profits a detached observer could reasonably expect it to make in the current and future years. All our businesses prepare blueprints once a year; these are synthesized into figures for each division and for Trafalgar itself, and compared each month with results achieved to date and with updated forecasts reflecting current experience; much work goes into all this, but it is the best system I know to make top management aware of change. The notional interest calculation is used for internal accounting and reporting, so as to make it clear to those concerned that if, for example, we have paid £4·6 million for a company, as was the case with IBC, we do not regard it as having made a profit until it has earned what would have been the cost of borrowing the money to buy it. These are matters of financial imagination and internal accounting. Just as important, if not more so, is to identify and liberate the individual talents which invariably are to be found in the new acquisition of an old company. These people, as a rule, are somewhere below the level of the main board and respond well to the operating strategy and tactics which we have already rehearsed before embarking on the takeover. With us they broaden their horizons, and they comprise a caucus of talent that it would be hard to recruit *de novo*.

Two bonuses that came with IBC were people who joined the central management of Trafalgar: Miss Colebrook, who had been Eric Wollard's secretary, clearly capable of greater things, and has been with Victor ever since; and 'Jimmy' Jimson, a retiring personality with great technical ability, who became our group chief accountant and spent some time later as finance director of Fleet Publishing International, the division which contains the newspaper and publishing interests.

The relative importance of IBC within Trafalgar as a whole was to recede as we grew bigger, so I will deal now with its subsequent developments: for six years it did well, and then it became a source of aggravation for two quite separate reasons. Financial returns were spectacular initially, and for two consecutive years the company earned more than it had cost; but after the UK market collapsed in 1974 we had to make provisions totalling £4 million in our accounts to cover the fall in the value of our stock of land. Today it is profitable again, but has a capital employed of over £30 million, which is both too much and too little, because the returns are inadequate, but the price of the new land required to maintain production has risen excessively, partly as a result of the government's Development Land Tax; and we must either put in more money, or be content with a diminishing business: the decision has not yet been taken.

The main aggravation came from Carlton, the local authority housing specialist. Victor had up to then avoided local-authority contracts for houses and flats, because the margins were too small; but in this case the company seemed to have special skills, and he allowed it to continue. After two or three years of moderate profits from efficient operations in the South of England, we ran into losses in the North; our investigation disclosed that several employees in the Leeds office had been cheating the company; Victor phoned me in disgust when he learned of these malpractices, and I agreed that we must prosecute. The police made a thorough investigation, which confirmed our suspicions, and those concerned were arrested, tried, convicted and sent to prison. As a result, however, of certain remarks passed at the trial, further investigations followed, and led to Carlton's managing director being convicted for making a corrupt payment to a councillor in the North. The police sought to establish whether anyone more senior had authorized the payment: they had not, but the whole episode proved an unwelcome distraction and for more than a year much senior management time was directed to it.

When the acquisition of IBC was completed in June 1967 we all went down to IBC's Epsom offices one afternoon where Victor addressed the staff through a loudspeaker system which

had been installed for the purpose. He was to become chairman, and would run the company from these offices for the
first few months so as to get to understand everything that
went on there and to get a better idea of the company's capabilities. This is a procedure we have followed ever since:
Victor would become chairman of the newly acquired company,
Eric would join the board, and I would attend most of the
meetings. Today, of course, things are slightly different because
acquisitions of this size go straight into one of our divisions,
but the principles are the same. Apart from our executive committee of three, we now have seven divisional managing directors; either Victor or Eric is chairman of each division, and its
managing director is chairman of its operating subsidiaries.
Currently we have seven divisions, about one hundred and
eighty subsidiaries, over three hundred subsidiary directors
and our total labour force is now about 37,000. I have mentioned these various matters of organization at this stage
because, although IBC was relatively small, it illustrates how
we handle most of our acquisitions, and will save repetitive
explanations later in the book. Now let me return to Trollope
& Colls, our most important objective.

The Trollopes are of the same family as the Victorian
novelist. In the 1920s the company and the controlling families
ran into a number of problems, and the company's bankers,
the Royal Bank of Scotland, lent money to a young engineer
named McNamara who bought shares in T & C, put the company back on its feet and became its chairman – a post which
he retained until his retirement in 1963. Most of his colleagues
on the board were close to McNamara's age and succession
problems were inevitable. By the mid 1960s it could have been
said that although T & C was still the best builder's in London,
it had failed fully to exploit its unique connections in the City
in terms of development opportunities for its own account. It
owned about £13 million's worth of properties, but one need
only look at Wimpey to see how much more could have been
done.

Lord Mais succeeded McNamara as chairman in 1963.
Raymond Mais had had a distinguished war record with the
Royal Engineers, and afterwards formed his own firm of
quantity surveyors. It was in that capacity that he came into

contact with Trollope & Colls, where earlier attempts to find management succession had failed; McNamara asked Lord Mais to join the board, and he became managing director in 1957.

By 1967 Mais was both chairman and managing director; he was also much involved with City Corporation affairs and soon to become Lord Mayor; and for this reason the unresolved management problem remained potentially as serious as it had been before. Younger men were introduced from outside the business, but none quite made the grade – in this connection it is ironic that Victor, once a successful contracts manager, had left them ten years earlier because he was dissatisfied with his prospects for promotion.

By the autumn of 1967 we were completing the surreptitious assembly of our 9·9 per cent shareholding in nominee names; our research had established the value and extent of the T & C properties, and Victor had assessed the general condition of the company which we would have been ready to take over at some time in 1968. But at this point, as so often happens, something unexpected occurred: Lord Mais asked his secretary to approach Geoffrey Crowther's with the request for a private meeting on a confidential subject. The two men did not know one another and, as Geoffrey said to me at the time, 'This might be for his favourite charity, but I doubt it: you'd better be there'. The meeting took place on a November afternoon at Geoffrey's Trust Houses office in Holborn. Raymond Mais came quickly to the point and said there had been steady buying of his company's shares at a price unsupported by their recent trading performance, and he wondered if by any chance Trafalgar was assembling a stake with a view to making a bid: and if this were the case, he would prefer a private negotiation to a public battle. We acknowledged our interest, whereupon Raymond conceded that from his point of view the idea was not to be ruled out; because he had several unresolved problems and considerable respect for what he knew of Victor Matthew's abilities. We parted on the basis that our respective proposals would be set out in writing, and I visited Geoffrey at his house in Putney the following Sunday evening to discuss the drafts he had himself prepared that day. Correspondence continued for a few more days and at one point it seemed quite possible that we would win the bid without opposition; what we did not know was that Raymond had taken these negotiations to this advanced stage without consulting his board.

A few days later the shares of Trollope & Colls rose on the Stock Exchange and it seemed clear that there had been a leak. This made it imperative for us to announce our intentions without delay, which we did on the afternoon of 13 December 1967. In fact the announcement was made simultaneously to the Stock Exchange and to the annual luncheon that IBC were giving for their suppliers at the RAC country club at Epsom. I was sitting next to Owen Aisher who, as chairman of Marley, was our most important supplier and guest, and before he rose to make his speech I stood up and told the assembled company of the news that was just then being released. Owen Aisher made a witty speech, but some of our guests were preoccupied, if not stunned, by the news. They could understand a success-ful property company like Trafalgar being able to buy IBC, but Trollope & Colls was something altogether different in calibre and importance.

It soon became clear that the directors of Trollope & Colls did not necessarily agree with their chairman; but of far greater importance to us was the competition. From the start we had regarded Trollope & Colls as a highly important prize to be fought for, but the quality of the competition which sud-denly emerged made our ultimate victory even more significant. Our competitors turned out to be the Church Commissioners for England in association with the builders Higgs & Hill, and their joint plan was to separate the properties from the con-tracting business, with the Church taking the property. John Gillum of Kleinwort Benson was, as usual, acting for us; John Baring of Baring Bros acted for the Church; and Daniel Meinertzhagen of Lazard Brothers acted for Trollope & Colls – Daniel was a director of Trollope & Colls and McNamara's son-in-law.

There were several factors that helped us to win against this high-quality opposition, and I will now describe four of them: the board of Trollope & Colls was split, and the extent of their disagreement with Raymond Mais was illustrated by their decision that if all bids failed and the company remained independent, Mais would leave them and receive £75,000 compensation for loss of office; and there was a misunderstanding by Lord Silsoe, First Church Estates Commissioner, who gave an interview to the *Financial Times* which reported his declaration that the Church Commissioners would not have pursued the matter without the unanimous support of the Trollope & Colls board – which Trollope & Colls promptly stated did not exist. Two other reasons were the equity option devised by John Gillum, and the very high quality of support and advice given by Jock Hunter, then senior partner of L. Messel & Co., our new stockbrokers.

The essence of the equity option was this: the bid was expressed primarily in a partly convertible unsecured loan stock, but those who accepted by the first closing date could receive the consideration entirely in shares if they so wished, whereas those who accepted later would have no such choice. There was much public doubt and scepticism about our chances of success, but little doubt that if by any chance we were going to succeed, the equity option would be a powerful stimulus to early acceptance by those who might otherwise have hesitated. This device would not be allowed today by the Takeover Panel, who require all holders to be treated alike; and we certainly would not have been allowed to declare the offer unconditional at less than 50 per cent acceptance – the reason being that we might have ended up with something less than control, having issued Trafalgar shares to acquire a minority holding from shareholders who would only have wanted our paper in the event of us gaining control. But in those days, as with the Three Companies, there was more scope for flexibility, and we decided that there would be a good chance of turning a trickle of acceptances into a flood if we let it be known in the City that we would declare the offer unconditional at the first closing date provided we had acceptances of anything over 30 per cent. John Gillum and Jock Hunter advised that the odds would then be in our favour, but we all knew that if we failed subsequently to get control we would encounter serious criticism from the financial community at large, and might find ourselves in a nasty mess.

The bid by now was worth about £14 million, and we could

only contemplate the proposal to 'go unconditional' at 30 per cent with the unanimous agreement of our board.

The decision had to be taken in January 1968, and by this time Geoffrey Crowther was in Barbados at Trust Houses' Sandy Lane Hotel. Joyce and I went to see him there, and Geoffrey and I talked for several hours a day, for several days. He was well aware of the risks involved in the course we wanted to follow, and it must be admitted that he had more to lose and less to gain than the rest of us – his share interest was not large, whereas his public reputation was considerable. After four days he agreed, reluctantly, but with a good grace. He said at the time that he only agreed because he did not think we would get even 30 per cent. The word went back to London, and tipped the scales.

This was not much of a holiday for us because I was on the telephone to London for much of the time, and I remember one evening during dinner when I was called to the hotel manager's office and spent nearly an hour with two telephone lines open to London where John Gillum and Michael Gampell were sitting in their respective offices and transmitting sections of the critical circular by telex to Sandy Lane for my comments prior to publication the next day.

The next evening I flew back to London, arriving at Wargrave in time for a late breakfast on a mild Sunday morning. I spent an hour or two on the telephone to Victor, John Gillum, Jock Hunter, David Fremantle and others. Victor said at the time that I could quite easily have completed the holiday in Barbados, because by then he was completely confident of the outcome, but I am glad I returned, if only to witness a demonstration of Geoffrey's virtuosity at Finsbury Square the following afternoon. Victor was confident, but personally I never count on these things until they have actually happened. The first closing date was 3 p.m. on the Monday afternoon, and we made provisional arrangements to visit T & C to address the staff at 5 p.m. that day, provided that we had by then received sufficient acceptances to declare that we had control.

We had, by this time, completed the Cleveland House development, where we had moved our offices into the first floor and kept three other floors unlet in case we would need them in connection with Trollope & Colls. Geoffrey had returned from Barbados that morning. He had arranged that if all went well he would come from the Economist Building to Cleveland House at 4.30 p.m. to give Victor and myself a lift to Trollope & Colls' City headquarters.

Geoffrey arrived in his Rover, and it was clear that he had given no thought to what he would say at the meeting. Victor, on the other hand, was particularly concerned to be word-perfect, and had spent much time preparing what by then was the typed text in his pocket. Victor's concern, of course, arose from the fact that he had spent many years working with or for the people at Trollope & Colls who had so bitterly resented our bid, and he was particularly anxious to strike the right note when he spoke to the staff. I suggested that, as Victor would be the third of us to speak, and as I had nothing very complicated to say, Geoffrey should quickly read through Victor's script to get the feeling of the occasion and to avoid duplications; this he did, and returned the document to Victor.

When we arrived Raymond Mais was courteous and relaxed, but we encountered a sea of stony and bewildered faces as we entered the basement canteen: these people simply could not believe what had happened to what they regarded as their company. Raymond rose and made the formal announcement that more than 50 per cent of their shareholders had already accepted our bid and consequently Trollope & Colls was now Trafalgar's subsidiary; then Geoffrey stood up and, without notes or hesitation, delivered from memory much of what Victor had proposed to say, having edited out in his mind the personal bits, which were all that Victor was left with. Afterwards we were too surprised to protest and Geoffrey, evidently feeling rather pleased with himself, said, 'That will teach you to show people your speeches!'

This experience stood me in good stead when, ten years later, I found myself seated next to the Prime Minister at the Mansion House. He was speaking before me and on three occasions asked me what I was going to say, to which I replied with platitudes concerning tributes to colleagues and so forth. This was fortunate, because Mr Callaghan effortlessly introduced into his speech two other things that I had told him during lunch, and if he had known what I was going to say (which was critical of the Government in two particular pects) he could certainly have demolished my modest work before I opened my mouth.

On the Wednesday following my quick trip from Barbados, I returned there because I had to collect Joyce and take her to a party that was being given for us by Peter and Allison Sharp at the Carlyle Hotel in New York. This was a tiring sequence of travel, and by the time I got back to London Victor was firmly established in Finsbury Square, where he ran the business for the next few weeks whilst accommodation at Cleveland House was being prepared to bring together the top two hundred and fifty or so employees of Trollope & Colls and the rest of the group. This was to be our headquarters until 1973, but as different sections of the business became better organized they moved out to less costly accommodation. Victor's first task with Trollope & Colls was, with Eric's help, to break it down into separate, separately accountable, profit centres. This was soon accomplished and the staff, once they knew which sectors were profitable and which were not, quickly saw the point of what Trafalgar had done, and all pulled together to put the company on the right course. Trollope & Colls' sense of individuality has, if anything, improved over the last ten years. As with other companies which we acquired, they benefited from the direction, resources and central services of a larger group, but were encouraged to retain their separate identity in terms of personnel and relationships with clients.

Victor's anxieties about Trollope & Colls had included the apprehension that some of its clientele might depart in view of the new ownership. Indeed there were some worrying incidents, but the only permanent losses concerned a small amount of work for other developers who were reluctant to place contracts with a building company that belonged to one of their competitors. Today this is no longer the case, and in the intervening years it turned out rather well for us because, in the depression of the 1970s, we were not dependent on developers' work, having cherished all Trollope & Colls' connections with the banks, insurance companies and so on, whose plans were less interrupted than those of developers. The price we had paid made allowance for losses on recently acquired contracts and the profit performance ever since has reflected the restoration and improvement of the company's standing.

David Fremantle had not been happy to find himself nominally in charge of Trafalgar whilst Geoffrey and I were abroad settling the crucial decision for the T & C bid. He had been deputy chairman since Geoffrey Crowther became chairman in 1962 and was, of course, the indispensable source of so much that had happened since 1956. David had already retired from stockbroking, and after the T & C takeover he told me he would like to retire from Trafalgar; I assured him that he would be welcome to stay in virtually whatever role he chose for himself, but his mind was made up, and it was arranged for us to take over Eastern International Investment Trust, our original parent, from which also he would then retire. I am inclined to think this withdrawal was a mistake. He must have been in his early sixties at the time, and we would have been glad to have him as a companion for many more years. He sold his London house and moved to Gloucestershire where, unfortunately, first his marriage broke up, and then he became ill. Joyce and I see him once or twice a year, and he comes to Trafalgar's annual luncheon for retired directors, from his new house at Chiswick.

I mentioned earlier that David had left Montagu Loebl Stanley after becoming chairman of Eastern International Trust. He moved to Arthur B. Winch and then to Read Hurst Brown & Co., who were our stockbrokers at the time of the public issue in 1963. Throughout the period his assistant was John Gray, and when David retired from the Stock Exchange he arranged for John to take their clients with him to L. Messel & Co., who became Trafalgar's official brokers in 1965.

John Gray, when I first met him, was a young chartered accountant with a considerable interest in music and an ability to undertake prodigious tasks of financial analysis with bursts of great energy; Messel's were glad to have him because of the quality of his work on the investment trust market. He had been a supporter of Trafalgar from the beginning, and his faith was probably greater than David's. He must have made almost £200,000 by the early 1970s, when he decided to leave Messel's, and by this time he was becoming distinctly eccentric. He had married Messel's cook, his third wife, and soon it became clear that he planned to leave this wife (and this country) when he bought a large sailing boat and announced his intention to proceed gradually to the West Indies where he would charter the yacht to foreign visitors and live happily in the sun.

We were always on good terms, and when he came to say goodbye, Victor and I invited him to stay for lunch at Cleveland House. He brought a tattered black suitcase into the dining room and, when we asked him how he was going to finance this new life (he had been generous to his previous wives), he crossed the room and returned with the suitcase: without a word he snapped back the locks and opened the lid to reveal an interior crammed with bank notes.

Only a few days later Joyce drew my attention to an astonishing paragraph in the *Daily Express*: a customs launch had arrested John and his boat a few miles outside Portsmouth, and had seized a suitcase containing £60,000 in cash. John lost the money as well as the boat because, of course, it was illegal to export money without official consent. It is hard to imagine who gave the tip-off to the authorities, but there must have been one; in any event, John returned to London for a while, but not for long.

A few years ago he wrote from Grenada in the Caribbean seeking support for an insurance company he wanted to establish on the island. He said that he now had another yacht, this time much older, and mortgaged to various of his former wives. The last time I saw him was one winter evening in Bond Street: he looked small and shabby in a black overcoat and bowler hat. His companion, presumably his fourth wife, was almost a foot taller than he, and black. He died of a heart attack a few months later in Grenada: I did not moralize about waste or lost opportunities – John was just being himself.

It was through John Gray that we met Jock Hunter, then Messel's senior partner. Jock first became closely involved with Trafalgar at the time of the T & C bid, and he was an indispensable supporter. He is a quiet, kind man who represents the best qualities to be found in the City: authority, integrity and modesty, with a wide circle of friends who understand these qualities and respect his judgement. We were sorry

when in 1972 he insisted on retiring from Messel's at the age of
64: we get on splendidly with Giles Coode Adams, who has
done most of our work at Messel's for the last ten years, but
Giles would be the first to agree that Jock had some irreplace-
able qualities which we all miss.

One of Jock's numerous activities was to be chairman of the
Square Mile Club, an informal group of thirty or so youngish
men from the City and from industry who meet five or six
times a year to entertain a distinguished guest. I remember
once at Brooks's Club where we were listening to Len Murray.
I was seated between John Baring and Jacob Rothschild feeling more and more depressed as this well-dressed, fluent, but
above all, grey, man told us of his earlier membership of the
Communist Party and his views about the future – in which
evidently there was little place for us. There was a sudden
crash of breaking glass, a moment's silence, and then a loud
explosion in the room underneath the first-floor library in
which we were having dinner. Red wine spilled across the
white tablecloth, books tumbled from the shelves and the room
gradually filled with smoke from the landing outside. Two
waiters were injured, one seriously. The bombers had cast first
a brick and then the bomb through the window of the room
in which we normally used to meet: it was only because this
room was being redecorated that we were using the library
above.

Another figure much involved with our affairs until the early
1970s was Michael Gampell, D'Arcy's former assistant at
Ashurst, Morris, Crisp & Co., who had helped me at the time
of the Tratt débâcle in 1958. Michael is an ingenious, energetic
and inventive solicitor, and we were sorry when he left
Ashursts. He had, at one time, been a director of our property
management subsidiary and was involved with much of our
routine legal work as well as, more critically, with the takeovers. Most of our legal work now remains with Ashursts, but
we use other firms who have had long-standing connections
with companies we acquired, or who have particular specialist
skills – two examples of this being Berwin Leighton and
Kingsley Napley. Michael Gampell did much of Geoffrey
Crowther's more important legal work, and I remember
Geoffrey once affectionately said of him: 'If he would comb

his hair once a day and clean his shoes once a week, he might do even better.' We paid Michael a retainer for a few years after his departure to help him get established in his new firm, but he changed his life again.

Throughout the late 1960s and early 1970s, when our take-over activities were at their peak, Victor and I would constantly be in touch with all the people I have described. Life today is rather different because company acquisitions are less frequent and we are more preoccupied with running the empire.

By March 1968 our gross assets had reached the £50 million mark and the first part of our plan from the mid-sixties was complete. As well as being established as a significant force in the property business, we were now engaged on a national scale with construction and housebuilding. Our shares had performed well on the Stock Exchange and our reputation was high. I was thirty-three, I had progressed in twelve years from a very small business to quite a large one, and had accumulated an unusual amount of experience in the process. Those were the days when people like Jim Slater were first becoming well known, and public opinion was favourable towards the restructuring of industry and commerce through mergers and takeovers. Jim typified the adventure-motivated financier and Arnold (now Sir Arnold) Weinstock the creative industrialist; Slater Walker had been established four years earlier, and Jim was then thirty-nine. Arnold would have been forty-four at the time and had just completed the crucial acquisition of AEI for his General Electric Company. These men illustrate two different extremes of the new generation that came to dominate their respective markets. I like to think that Trafalgar was as competent and adroit as anyone in terms of financial and technical expertise, and we used our skills to create a large continuing business in conformity with a preconceived strategy. Arnold prospered, of course, and on a larger scale than Trafalgar; Jim failed.

As the second half of this book develops, readers will get the impression that my time and energies were mainly concerned with takeovers. To an extent that is true, but, as I shall explain, we were just as much concerned with direct investment and the development of our existing business. Our technique of integration was not developed as an alternative to the 'liberation of assets' (asset stripping) procedures of others, it was an earlier concept which we continued to follow. I planned to withdraw from day-to-day management, but to be involved closely in whatever was happening within the divisions of our business. The takeovers captured public interest, but in our own domestic terms the continuing business was the most captivating interest of all. This coincided happily with the broadening of my private life which I have described in the last chapter. The routine of running the business was the main concern of all of us, but has not the characteristics to be described in a book; and there were many smaller takeovers which were important, but not of general interest now, nor at the time they took place. I write about landmarks rather than milestones so as to give a panoramic view of what we do.

12

What Next?

For some time one of our long-term objectives had been to acquire the City of London Real Property Company, but we were not in a great hurry and we knew that our chances would be slender until our market capitalization was over £100 million (today it is more than twice that figure, but in 1968 it was only about £35 million). In the meantime we were not much concerned about competition: Jack Cotton, who had made an unsuccessful attempt on CLRP in 1961, had died, and his City Centre Property Group was virtually immobilized through having too many financial heavy-weights as non-executive directors on the board; Harold Samuel could certainly have done it for Land Securities, but he seemed in a withdrawn condition following the tragic loss of one of his children; and Metropolitan Estates and Property Corporation might have gained the necessary financial muscle under the recent chairmanship of Sir Charles Hardie, but they lacked the required development skills. For all these reasons we took a relaxed and patient view and had not even begun to assemble a strategic share stake, though we had been through the routine of identifying and valuing their assets.

CLRP, as its name implies, had large holdings in the City of London; they were well respected for routine management skills but their attitude to new building was more a question of replacement than redevelopment, though they had gone in for rebuilding. Indeed, it could be demonstrated that their shareholders would have faired better if they had leased their bombed sites to others, and concentrated on running their numerous Victorian and Edwardian office blocks, which were so much like the Billiter Buildings, Africa House, West India House, Leadenhall House, Broad Street House and Bush Lane House that we had assembled through the Three Companies takeover, and were planning soon to redevelop to great advantage. That programme, incidentally, is now nearly complete, and will have taken almost fifteen years from conception to completion of the final sales; it will have produced receipts of £80 million for an outlay of less than £40 million. The same thing could have been done with CLRP on several times the scale but it needed the full-time dedication and supervision of an expert. The nearest CLRP got to this solution on their own was to appoint Gerald (now Sir Gerald) Glover, an associate of McAlpine, as non-executive chairman.

One sunny morning in the autumn of 1968, Victor and I were walking from Cleveland House to have lunch with Geoffrey at the Economist Building, when we saw an *Evening Standard* placard, 'Giant Property Bid'. Land Securities had agreed to take over City Centre Properties, and I realized instantly that if Harold Samuel was prepared to undertake that relatively unrewarding task, it could only be a matter of time before he went for CLRP. Our chance of success would be slight, but the only chance we would get would be to act at once whilst Harold was occupied with the early months of sorting out CCP. Geoffrey was sceptical about this reasoning, and I remember a few minutes later in his dining room that he said, 'Harold must be sixty-five and too old to want any more of that kind of thing.' My researches had been good, so when I said that Harold Samuel was only fifty-seven, I was glad to accept Geoffrey's bet of ten shillings, which he paid a few moments later after consulting *Who's Who*.

We went through the familiar process of soul-searching and expressions of regret that the timing was not of our choice; but we resolved to proceed. The bid got quite a fair reception from the public, although it was really rather cheeky and audacious at the time; CLRP's share price quickly outstripped the value of our £95 million offer and MEPC decided to enter the fray, but that did little to alter our earlier assessment of the situation. Our formal offer was published on 5 December 1968 and it is worth examining two extracts from the document. Geoffrey's letter is interesting because he wrote it entirely himself, and it demonstrates his style as well as his attitude. He was a man of extraordinary talent, and on this occasion, after we had spent an hour or two on tedious drafting, he said he must leave, but would write this circular for us himself that evening; he typed it himself, without corrections, and delivered it the following morning in the form it was published. The graphs spare my own modesty by showing that our performance in the first five and a half years of life as a public company had been exceptional, as had been the record during the preceding seven years before we got our quotation on the Stock Exchange in 1963.

5th December, 1968.

To the Members of the City of London Real Property Company Limited.

Dear Sir or Madam,

The later pages of this document contain the formal offers made on behalf of Trafalgar House Investments Limited ('Trafalgar') to acquire the issued capital of the The City of London Real Property Company Limited ('CLRP'). In order to comply with the provisions of the law, of the City Code, and of established practice, these documents must be formal, precise and voluminous. My purpose in this introductory letter is to try to explain in less formal language why Trafalgar is making these offers and why we believe it will be to your advantage to accept them.

What is Trafalgar?

By comparison with CLRP, Trafalgar is a new company and a small one – but not so new that it does not have a record of very rapid growth in earning power, and not so small (the gross assets are in excess of £50 million) that it cannot claim a plentiful and varied experience in the management of real property.

In its origins, Trafalgar was, like CLRP, a pure property-holding company, a vehicle by which a number of shareholders could come together to own and develop real property. Like CLRP, our properties are heavily concentrated in London, and especially in the City of London. Much of the success that we have enjoyed in recent years, however, has been due to a decision to extend the traditional activities of the property company into other, but closely related, fields. We arrived at this decision because we believed it to be industrially logical and because we possessed the management talent; furthermore, because we were among the first to realise that the new system of taxation embodied in the Finance Act of 1965 – and especially the introduction of Corporation Tax and Capital Gains Tax – would undermine the basis of the traditional property-holding company. We saw that it would be necessary, if we were to escape the penalties of the Act, to adopt new policies, both in respect of the management of our properties (with heavier emphasis on development and on improvements) and also in the financial structure of the company, by taking the fullest advantage of 'gearing' to reduce the impact of heavier taxation. That Trafalgar is one of the few property companies to have shown steady improvement in earnings per share of its capital throughout this troubled period has not been due to good luck or to improvisation, however brilliant, but to very careful analysis and intensive thought leading to deliberate policy decisions.

As part of this policy, Trafalgar has set out to acquire businesses ancillary to its main purpose of owning property. This had led us into the building of houses both for sale and under contract to local authorities, into general building and contracting, and into the manufacture of building components. This also has been deliberate and, we think, logical, for although these companies are closely concerned with our chosen field of property, they are in financial structure opposite and complementary to the ownership of property itself – they produce profits without requiring a heavy permanent investment of capital. But they remain ancillary to our main purpose, which is that of a property company. To manage this expanding group, we have built up a management structure that possesses strength in depth – there are more than 60 full time Directors of the subsidiary companies. What is more important, this very competent team of professionals is given firm and consistent direction from the top.

That the price of Trafalgar Ordinary shares on the Stock Exchange values the company on a much higher ratio to earnings than is true of the generality of property companies is, we think, a recognition by the market of the validity of our policies.

We present ourselves to you, therefore, as a young, efficiently managed company, in the same field as your own, with a demonstrated ability to adjust to changing times and to pursue

active policies with success and with benefit to the shareholders.

Why do we want CLRP?

Not for its size. Our reason is that, after careful research extending over many months, we came to the conclusion that the
properties owned by CLRP offer by far the most fruitful field
for the further development of the management techniques we
have built up. Your company owns the same sort of assets, in
the same place, as we do ourselves. (We believe we are the next
largest property company owner, after CLRP, of commercial
rented property in the City of London.) These assets present
precisely the same opportunities for enhancement of values and
income as those we have already demonstrated our ability to
turn to advantage.

Nor are our terms offered as a blind guess. We have been engaged for months past on a careful analysis of CLRP's assets,
their present value and prospective earnings. Naturally our
information cannot be as accurate or as complete as that of
your Board. But we believe that it is not far off the mark. Our
object in devising the terms was to effect an amalgamation of
the two companies on a basis that would be fair to both bodies
of shareholders. After all, if we are successful, the two bodies
of shareholders will become one, of which the ex-CLRP shareholders will (after the exercise of all conversion and subscription rights) represent 61 per cent. of the total. The future responsibility of the management will be to both bodies of shareholders alike.

What are the advantages of acceptance?

The immediate advantages are set out in the offer document.
The capital value of the securities offered in exchange for the
Ordinary Stock is considerably in excess of the price at which
that stock was quoted in the market until very recently. The
immediate increase in gross income is 54 per cent. for the
Ordinary and 16 per cent. for the Preference.

What you are offered is not cash, but (for the Ordinary)
three different classes of security in Trafalgar, one of them pure
equity, the second fully convertible into equity, and the third
having, through the subscription rights, an equity element.
The future value of the securities offered to you will therefore

depend on the prosperity of the combined company. This has a number of implications that I would like to draw to your attention.

As I have said, our offer is based on a close estimate of what we believe the assets of CLRP are worth. In immediate value it is, we recognise, below our estimate of the calculated net asset value per share of the company. So it must be if it is not to injure the growth prospects for those who are already shareholders in Trafalgar – and it will not escape you that 'break-up value' is a theoretical concept that could not be realised in practice save at the cost of substantial assessments to Capital Gains Tax both on CLRP and on individual shareholders. In any event, our proposals are the complete opposite of 'break-up', since we are offering you what we believe to be the maximum continuing interest in the equity of the combined company, that is consistent with the interests of our existing shareholders.

The offer document places a value of par on the Convertible Unsecured Loan Stock and on the Unsecured Loan Stock with subscription rights of Trafalgar, while the Ordinary shares of Trafalgar are taken at their recent market value. But we are confident that, if the offers are accepted, the strength of the combined company, under active management, will be such as to put higher values than these, within a short time, on the company's equity securities.

This is not an idle boast. Five times within the last three years Trafalgar has acquired, by public offer, the capitals of other public companies, giving its own equity or equity-linked securities in exchange. In each case, doubts might have been (and sometimes were) expressed about the ability of these securities to maintain their values. In each case, the securities given in exchange have risen rapidly and considerably above their values at the time of the offer, so that accepting shareholders have gained considerably more than was held out to them.

It is our belief that this will happen again if the present offers are accepted. We cannot, of course, foresee the general course of the markets, but if there is no general fall in values, we look forward to being able to demonstrate once again that a logical amalgamation of two complementary businesses, combined with skilful management, can produce a total value greater than the sum of its two parts.

Your Choice

You now have to choose between two courses. One is to accept a participation in the capital (and very largely the equity capital) of a combined company with the management and policies that I have attempted to describe. The other is to reject the offers and thereby forfeit the opportunity of benefiting from the future growth that we see for the combined company; at the same time you would risk seeing your holdings revert to the investment rating at which they were assessed by the market until recently.

This letter, which I sign as Chairman of Trafalgar, is of necessity an immodest document. Let me therefore conclude by saying that it is the policy of the Board to entrust the management of the company to the Managing Directors, Mr Nigel Broackes and Mr Victor Matthews, and that neither I nor my other non-executive colleagues would wish to take away from them and the team that they lead any of the credit for what the company has hitherto achieved.

Yours faithfully,

CROWTHER

Chairman.

MARKET VALUES

This chart illustrates the market values of comparative investments in Trafalgar and CLRP over the last five years together with the movement of the Financial Times Actuaries Index of Property Shares over the same period. 23rd July, 1963, was the first day of dealings in the shares of Trafalgar House Limited, the predecessor company of Trafalgar.

NOTE: The chart assumes that all capitalisation issues of Trafalgar (and Trafalgar House Limited) have been retained, together with the holding of Unsecured Debenture Stock received by Ordinary Shareholders as part of the reconstruction in 1966.

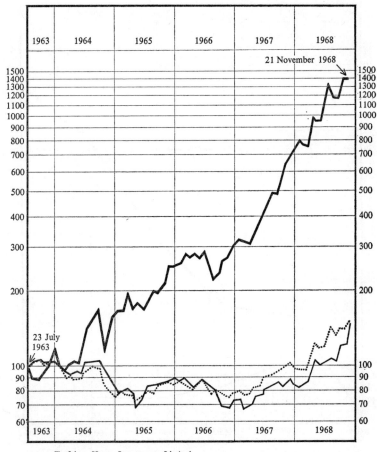

——— Trafalgar House Investments Limited

••••••••• Financial Times Actuaries Property Index

——— The City of London Real Property Company Limited

EARNINGS

This chart illustrates the relative earnings performance of Trafalgar and CLRP during the five years 1963/64 to 1967/68 inclusive together with Trafalgar's estimated earnings for 1968/69. The earnings have been computed by reference to an investment of £100 in both companies made on 23rd July, 1963 and are shown on a 'gross' basis (after corporate taxes but before withholding taxes such as Schedule F) which is arrived at by 'times covered' on actual dividend costs over the period. In the case of Trafalgar, interest on the Unsecured Debenture Stock received by a Shareholder under the reconstruction in 1966 has been added, less Corporation Tax at appropriate rates.

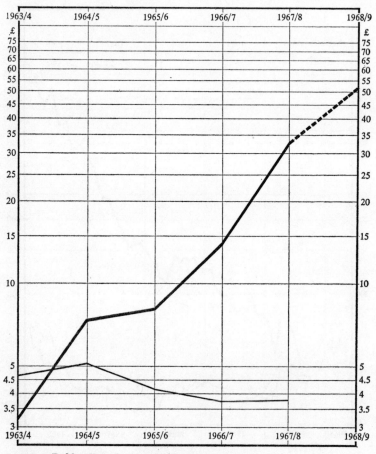

Trafalgar House Investments Limited

Trafalgar Estimate for 1968/9

The City of London Real Property Company Limited

The decisive event occurred in January 1969 when Land Securities announced their intention to bid for CLRP. For them success was inevitable. We came to no harm through the experience, indeed it may even have added a little to Trafalgar's reputation for being willing to attempt what was, for us, a difficult task which, none the less, was clearly worthwhile. Harold Samuel asked me to lunch at the Ritz soon afterwards and said, 'I want to thank you for making your bid for CLRP because if you hadn't started it, I wouldn't have got it.' He also confirmed that he had been quite sufficiently preoccupied with CCP to have been hesitant about attempting CLRP at the same time. Until the last moment he was uncertain, but his reasoning had been similar to ours: there would never be another opportunity like this one, and this was his last chance as well.

We entered 1969 full of confidence and plans for the future. Victor, who had joined the board in 1967, became joint managing director in October 1968. At the same time I became deputy chairman (as well as being the other joint managing director), and Eric Parker joined the board as group finance director. We were already putting together a first-class, central, management team. Our policy was, and continued to be, to choose the best technical people from companies we had acquired and to give them broader responsibilities covering the whole group. There was little outside recruitment and few if any redundancies: the pattern, nearly always, was to retire or release main board directors after acquiring a company, to assess its senior management, and to make promotions. Often we would find much previously-overlooked talent at lower levels, and the effect on morale was beneficial. Our administration was in good order, our reporting systems were working well, and market conditions looked favourable for further strategic acquisitions during the next few years.

The stock market had receded from earlier heights, Roy Jenkins was a sound and conservative Chancellor of the Exchequer, and Trafalgar itself had a stable balance sheet with the prospect of substantial inflows of cash over the years ahead. Despite the recent devaluation of sterling, we still had doubts about the domestic situation and, as well as having specific

F

industrial targets, we had the more nebulous desire to move rapidly into foreign currencies. This was reinforced when, early in the Health administration, we became more worried about things at home.

At this point I should explain that we had taken care with our acquisitions to issue unsecured loan stocks wherever possible. These were either irredeemable or redeemable at the end of the century and, as a result, although our gearing might have looked high, most of our assets were uncharged and we were in a position of great flexibility. We had resolved to sell some of the Trollope & Colls properties: the properties themselves were excellent, but they were nearly all leasehold and most had been let on long leases with rent reviews at twenty-one-year intervals. It is as well that we made these sales when we did, because today's investment market dislikes properties with infrequent reviews and consequently we got better prices in the period 1969/70 than could have been obtained at any time subsequently. Also Trollope & Colls had interests in various joint companies that had been formed with partners to carry out particular projects and which, by then, had no function other than to collect rents. Our policy was clear, and has not changed since: we are happy to take part in a joint venture to accomplish some particular task, but afterwards we like to withdraw; generally speaking we have no interest in retaining minority interests in inactive unquoted companies. By the early 1970s most of these joint ventures were unwound to the general satisfaction of all concerned.

I mentioned earlier in this book how I would prowl round the swimming pool at La Violetta. Joyce wondered if I had done all that I was going to do, but the truth of the matter was that there was a great deal more to be done, and already our planning had identified specific companies for the acquisitions that were to follow. At the same time we were proposing other ventures which would be developed from scratch, so to speak. Indeed, we would always consider direct investment in people, plant and machinery as an alternative to a company acquisition – and both courses have proceeded in parallel ever since. The company acquisitions captured the headlines, but we only make them when they represent the best means to satisfy some particular objective. The last few years our direct investment of cash in plant, machinery, ships and aircraft, has fluctuated between £25 and £40 million per annum, and we wish it could be higher. We reflect the national malaise that not enough new investment is worthwhile in current circumstances. Our technique is (as it should be) opportunistic, but we have never been in what came to be called the 'break-up business' and have only bought companies that we wanted to keep. A detached observer might even claim that we have shown too little willingness to consider sales where prospects have deteriorated. We only do this where we see no prospect whatsoever for a recovery in the foreseeable future: the Trocoll Industries' concrete pipe business came into that category, as did Cunard's recent sale of our fleet of bulkers and our earlier sale of Sun Air/Lunn Poly.

We now chose hotels for direct investment. I must make it clear that this was not as an alternative to our other work, but as an addition to what was to follow. We had plenty of scope financially and wanted to progress on any front that was worthwhile. We were doing as much as we wanted to do in the conventional property business and had no difficulty in defining broader boundaries for ourselves. Central London hotels were an obvious area to enter, but my relationship with Trust Houses meant that we would rather do it with them. The point was that other property companies in this country eschewed management, whereas Victor was keen to introduce it. The underlying reasoning followed what we termed the 'accommodation concept', namely that we had progressed from owning and renting real property to the point where we were building, and developing for sale to others, and a logical extension would seem to be the ownership and operation of hotels. This was to lead us further toward leisure concepts with travel and cruising in mind. I make the point at this juncture to illustrate what I have said in the previous paragraph. In one form or another we were going into the hotel business, and, as an extension of this thought, we had examined the alternatives of building or buying passenger ships before it became clear that the best course would be to buy Cunard.

So we had the ideas, the personnel and the financial resources to do considerably more at a time when it seemed that economic conditions nationally and internationally would continue to be favourable for some years to come. If we had acquired CLRP our share price would probably have risen by a pound or two before long, but I had little doubt that this would happen in any case. In fact CLRP would have been a reverse takeover, and to have increased our equity by one and a half times for that purpose would obviously have diluted the benefits of the many other things that we were going to do. Furthermore, although the acquisition, if successful, would have been hailed as the coup of the decade, it would irrevocably have categorized me as a property developer, and there was so much more I wanted to do with my life. In fact I had found myself in an uncertain state of mind during the CLRP affair. I was happy with everything that I was doing, and content to continue with it indefinitely; but I did not want to be irrevocably committed for ever to one product, so to speak. The proposition is hypothetical, but I felt at one time during the bid that if it was successful I would quite shortly afterwards withdraw wholly or partially from Trafalgar, rather than return to full-time, property work which, however worthwhile, would have set me in too rigid a mould.

The answers to questions of this kind cannot be simulated, and one practical test which I encountered was in 1973 when I was offered £11 million in cash for my holding in Trafalgar, on the condition that I would retire from the business and an offer for the remainder of the capital might, or might not, follow some time later (it was not available at the time). I had little difficulty in resolving my sentiments when faced with this concrete proposal, and I was surprised to find how much my pride in Trafalgar affected my judgement. I held more shares then than I do today, and the price was considerably above anything we have seen since; but I had no regrets or second thoughts about my rejection of the offer. On an earlier occasion I encountered the problem in terms of conflicts of interest, as opposed to money: in 1970 Peter Walker asked me to become chairman of the New Towns Commission. I could have done the job quite well, and would have enjoyed it; but I could not take a step which would inevitably reduce my role in Trafalgar, and also curtail the large amount of construction work we were doing for the New Towns.

13

Lord Crowther

This short chapter deals with a bizarre period of a few months during which the relationship with Geoffrey Crowther passed from admiration to enmity. What happened was inevitable, but it was a waste.

In February 1969, after the CLRP affair, Joyce and I again went to Barbados, hoping to combine a fortnight's holiday with a little work with Geoffrey on our respective plans for the future. These included earlier ideas for resort developments in collaboration with Trust Houses on the basis that large sites at attractive locations in the Caribbean would be developed between us: Trust Houses would operate an hotel and Trafalgar would develop houses or sell building plots on the surrounding land to people who would be attracted by the proximity of the hotel. Sandy Lane itself was an example of such a development, and the process made sense at the time, although subsequent political developments would rule it out today. In 1967 we had formed a joint company with Alan Godsal to carry out Trafalgar's role in the proposed partnership. Alan has good connections in the West Indies, and his family had owned sugar plantations in Barbados since Cromwell's time. We first purchased sixty acres or so of beach-land on the island of Tobago, a few miles from Trinidad. It had proved extraordinarily difficult to agree designs or commercial terms with Trust Houses and eventually we had sold the land for a good profit to an American group. We offered none of the profit to Trust Houses because, in our view, they had done more to frustrate the transaction than to promote it; but this incident may have been a factor that influenced individual attitudes in what was to follow.

At that time Alan Godsal had a house by the beach at Sandy Lane, and an important meeting took place there one evening with Geoffrey: the three of us agreed that the overall plan was still worth following, but our previous technique of segregating our roles had proved to be inoperable. I suggested, and Geoffrey agreed, that henceforth we should be equal partners in every facet of the operation; that is to say we would buy the land jointly, share the costs and revenues from the hotel, and divide between us the profits from the sales of the surrounding land. On this basis Geoffrey agreed straightaway for our two companies to purchase nearly 100 acres of land by the sea in St Lucia. I reported all this to the Trafalgar board when I returned, and Geoffrey, who was in the chair, had nothing to add to what I had said. Trust Houses paid their half of the cost of the St Lucia site and we waited for them to confirm formally the agreement we had reached with Geoffrey in Barbados. By one means or another Trafalgar wanted to get into the hotel business. It seemed preferable to do so with Trust Houses, if they wanted the benefit of our property expertise; but otherwise we would do it on our own. At Trust Houses board meetings I had done my best to explain that they were placing too much emphasis on the provinces, and too little on Central London; and we had offered them participation in two excellent London schemes.

At this point let me try to explain Geoffrey's role in both companies: with us he was a non-executive chairman; with Trust Houses he was a cross between being a busy, part-time chairman and an inexperienced part-time chief executive, relying on a number of managing directors who had been promoted to, or beyond, the limits of their abilities. I have mentioned some of his periods of exasperation with Trust Houses, but there were also periods of elation, and clearly, having been principally a journalist until his mid-fifties, he relished the idea of becoming a tycoon, and this job fascinated him. He was also ambitious to make money, but Trust Houses did not feature in that aspect of his plans. He had come to accept that a full-time group managing director would have to be found from elsewhere, and he told me that in due course he, Geoffrey, would retire from Trust Houses and look upon Trafalgar as 'a job for my old age'.

The managing director he chose for Trust Houses was a chartered accountant called Michael Pickard, who arrived fresh from recent problems at the British Printing Corporation where his old mentor, Sir Charles Hardie, was now chairman.

I hoped that now Michael was safely installed, communications between Trafalgar and Trust Houses would improve.

The Tobago incident may have soured relationships between us at the operating level, but Geoffrey and I were on the boards of both companies and I was optimistic that our agreement over St Lucia would put things right. Alas, I was wrong, and matters built up fairly swiftly to a climax which resulted in Geoffrey's resignation. It is hard to explain the step-by-step sequence of events which made this inevitable, and I will start by reproducing the schedule of irritants which I sent him early in May 1969 with my formal letter stating the more fundamental reasons why I would resign from Trust Houses and he must leave Trafalgar. Ten years later some of these incidents seem individually trivial, but I am surprised to be reminded how numerous they were. The people referred to by Christian names are Michael Pickard, Diana Self (Planning), and Sir Oliver Chesterton, a non-executive director with great property knowledge. Mr Brady supervised their construction programme. Below is the schedule sent with my letter.

TRUST HOUSES

1. *London Properties*

(a) A year ago, Trafalgar tendered for the Hovis site under the impression that Trust Houses were in it with us, we missed it by a very narrow margin, which perhaps was a good thing because a few days after the tender, Trust Houses wrote to say they must reduce the rent they had indicated they would pay. I wrote to Michael and went to see him in the most genuine endeavour to indicate how these things would have to be handled if you wanted to get into Central London development of hotels with any normal commercial developer.

(b) Then came the Berkeley where you dropped out in good time but we were successful. We got 50% more rooms and an offer of 40% more rent per room than the plan we had based our tender on. I spoke to Michael to say that proper, detailed pre-tender negotiation and co-operation could have got this for you on 'ground floor' terms. He told me the point was now understood, but that at the time Trust Houses had not got a full appreciation of current Central London potential – he said that the new appreciation was clearly evidenced by the degree of co-operation with Trafalgar when you looked at the Berkeley for the second time and Diana and Brady conducted the most detailed analysis and examination of alternative plans with Geoff Carter. I accepted this at the time but learned later that there had been absolutely no communication of any sort between the time Michael saw the drawings and a month later when you told me you still weren't interested. Michael wrote a few days ago to say he had only just learned that the analysis and replanning had been carried out within your office and without discussing it with us at all.

2. *Caribbean*

(a) You have already stated that you felt ill-used over Tobago where we made a profit and all you got was a bill for a site survey. If this has coloured Trust Houses' attitude to us, I feel I should record that it was in July 1967 that you expressed interest in principle and though in the meantime you drafted figures and heads of agreement, you said you could not possibly make a firm commitment until you saw the property in January 1968. By that time, as we know, Hilton, etc, had intervened and got the local government to specify a minimum size of development which exceeded your maximum. The point is that during this time the vendor had refused to wait any longer unless we bought something. Trafalgar bought its site, with your knowledge, and later, at your request, declined to sell out to Hilton at a very large profit (more, in dollars, than we eventually made but fortuitously less in pounds due to devaluation), although you had made it clear that you weren't committed in any way to underwrite our position. In my view, we took the risk and earned the profit. The extent of the risk is illustrated by current rumours that Hilton are not going to develop at all.

(b) This winter I'm sure we shared the desire to set up the complete joint arrangement that I had proposed in Barbados and when I got back I carried the impression that you wanted to as much as I did. But this was turned down by Trust Houses and we were only offered a minor role.

3. *Construction*

No one would disagree that the Sandy Lane extension is an unsatisfactory illustration of how to handle building work in the Caribbean. Bray asked Victor for help and T & C sent two senior and experienced men out there to meet him. We confirmed that we could sort the matter out in the way that Brady had proposed and we had the clear impression that you wanted us to. Then Victor was astonished to receive a letter saying that our help was not, after all, necessary and assumed that you must have chosen another contractor, for it was quite clear that the present one could not do the job. It was even more mystifying to be told recently that in fact Trust Houses had not accepted other help and the job was in more trouble than ever.

4. *TraveLodge*
You'll appreciate that I feel a personal interest in this because I introduced it, Trafalgar nearly took a major interest in it at one time, and Alan Greenaway is a friend. When the question of his appointment to the Trust Houses Board came up, I asked if he was to be told that Trust Houses had decided to start buying shares in his company; when I learned that he'd discovered draft plans for a bid for his company, I was absolutely amazed. I can't say more because I don't know the facts – and was not told. I'm bound to assume that this must have an undesirable effect on relationships.

5. *Shorts Gardens*
We met in February and it was agreed to see what could be done to maximise Trust Houses' site value before considering sale. Brady stated that he was capable of doing the work and even resisted the idea of getting an architect, which Oliver and I pressed. Having heard nothing more, I was baffled to learn in April that the property was being offered to Trafalgar. Obviously, having advised you not to sell, we couldn't bid for it. I wrote last week to Michael asking what was going on.

N.B. / 13.5.69

What had happened beforehand was this: the regular monthly meeting of the Trafalgar board took place on 16 April. I remarked to Geoffrey that we were puzzled still to have heard nothing from Trust Houses about the Caribbean joint venture, and he said that really he could not become further involved in what might become a disagreement between the senior executives of two companies of which he was chairman. He suggested that Victor and I should lose no time in obtaining clarification from Michael Pickard, who was then in Majorca, and we arranged to meet in Palma on the afternoon of the following day. In the meantime I saw Francis Sandilands who, as chief general manager of the Commercial Union, represented our biggest shareholder and had appointed Geoffrey as our chairman in the first place: it seemed possible that hotel development co-operation with Trust Houses was not going to work, and we might have to consider a change of chairmanship unless Trafalgar was prepared to abandon its hotel ambitions.

Victor, Michael and I met for dinner at the Hotel Villamil in Majorca. We exerted ourselves to break down Michael's evident resistance to the St Lucia deal, and we told him of the choices that would face us if Trust Houses would not confirm the agreement reached with Geoffrey two months earlier. For the first time, Michael was explicit that he did not want joint ventures with us in the West Indies or anywhere else; and the following day, with some regret, I began to draft the letter I would have to write to Geoffrey. Later we bought Trust Houses' share in the St Lucia site and carried out the development ourselves.

After talks with D'Arcy Biss and Francis Sandilands it was agreed that we would not abandon our hotel ambitions and that Geoffrey would have to go; and, of course, I would resign from Trust Houses. Francis felt that he should be the one to tell Geoffrey of the decision, and it may have contributed to Geoffrey's violent reaction that this was done on the telephone – the reaction was extreme, although not long before he had said he would be quite willing to stand down.

Once it was clear that Trust Houses and I would have to part company, Geoffrey asked me to speak to Michael Pickard again. Michael came to see me at Cleveland House and told me that he accepted that this severance was inevitable; but he said he would prefer the announcement of my resignation to be delayed for a month or two, because they proposed before long to have a public issue of convertible loan stock, and he felt that any main board resignation from Trust Houses in the meantime would make it more difficult. I made a mistake in agreeing to this deferment of the announcement.

In the meantime Geoffrey was not idle, and he asked Victor to see him at his penthouse at Broadwalk House, which Trafalgar had built. Victor told me of the invitation, saying he could not think what it was about: I guessed, but did not tell him, that Geoffrey wanted to present an alternative. Geoffrey in turn did not quite come to the point, but it was perfectly clear that he had taken our decision very badly. One of his subsequent exertions was an unsuccessful attempt to prevent Francis Sandilands becoming chairman of the Commercial Union.

The deferment to which I had agreed at Michael Pickard's request proved to be unfortunate for a reason which none of us could have anticipated. I had ceased to attend Trust Houses' board meetings, I was not sent the board papers, and I knew nothing of their plans to buy an apartment hotel in London called Kensington Close.

The first I heard of the property was when George Sibbering of Hampton's came to see me on a Monday morning in mid-June to tell me that the owners wanted to sell the property and had asked him to find out if we wanted to buy it. Victor and I went to see it, we liked it, and our board (Geoffrey had absented himself just as I had from Trust Houses) agreed that we should make an offer, which we did. That evening Trust Houses' company secretary rang me up to say that Mr Pickard had asked him to speak to all directors to get their approval to the bid which Trust Houses proposed to make for Kensington Close. I asked to speak to Pickard, I explained our interest and we agreed that this charade would end forthwith. Geoffrey's resignation was announced on the evening of 18 June and I became chairman of Trafalgar, with Victor as deputy chairman and sole group managing director. Geoffrey promptly sold all his shares – but, characteristically, re-invested the proceeds in Trafalgar warrants. (A warrant is a quoted security giving, for small cost, the right at some future date to subscribe for shares at a stated price.) After his death I was told that the value of the warrants equalled the value of his net estate.

The aggravation over Kensington Close was to intensify. Our offers had been similar, but Michael Andrews, then of Samuel Montagu, who were acting for the vendors, advised that Trust Houses' paper was better than Trafalgar's. Schroders were acting for Trust Houses and I learned later that they were responsible for a vindictive article in the *Financial Times* which could have been read to imply that Trafalgar had made a competitive bid for Kensington Close at a time when I knew of Trust Houses' desire to buy it. For the first time I realized that Geoffrey and Michael Pickard had not told their colleagues that to all intents and purposes I had left them two months earlier and remained, in name only, at their request. This angered me extremely, and when Geoffrey heard that I was taking legal advice on their omission he wrote a conciliatory letter offering to explain the whole history of the matter to all concerned.

Subsequent events at Trust Houses are fairly well known: they merged with Forte; he (Sir Charles Forte) moved for Michael Pickard's dismissal; Geoffrey, still chairman, supported Michael, and lost. On more than one previous occasion Geoffrey had rejected the idea of a merger with Charles Forte, and later I was told that what made him change his mind was pressure from Michael and from Charles Hardie. For Trust Houses the merger was probably the best thing that could have happened, but Geoffrey's own position, predictably, became untenable.

He embarked on a journey round the world to bid farewell to all the executives who ran the foreign interests that had been acquired during his regime. This almost amounted to an act of self-destruction, because the timetable was arduous, despite Geoffrey's having been urged to take more care of himself following an earlier heart attack. As it was, he died at London Airport on the morning of his return, and I delivered a letter of condolence to his widow, Peggy, that afternoon. I was pleased to hear later from one of his sons that, before departing on this fateful journey, he had taken a walk with Peggy in Kensington Gardens and said, 'It really is time that we remade friends with Nigel and Joyce.'

Geoffrey had become an extremely distinguished man and, if the University Parliamentary Seats had not been abolished at the end of the war, he would probably have become MP for Oxford or Cambridge. As it was, he had gone to the House of Lords too late to take a very active role. At the time of his death he was hard at work as chairman of the Commission on the Constitution, and had recently completed his report on Consumer Credit, which was not unrelated to some of the banking excesses that occurred a few years later. He was Chancellor of the Open University and had many other prestigious appointments which reflected his qualities; but he was not a businessman, and I think those who are old enough will remember him best for his war-time work as a member of the Brains Trust. Joyce and I went to his memorial service at Westminster Abbey where a string quartet played Schubert's 'Death and the Maiden', and we were reminded how much we missed him. Oddly enough, he did not seem musical at all, although he listed music as one of his recreations in *Who's Who*.

14

Plans Mature

The graph on page 149 shows how in five years' life as a public company, starting in 1963, our shares had appreciated by fifteen times or so; in the seven years before the public issue the factor had been more than thirty and, with growth from the original investment by a multiple of nearly five hundred, our record was a remarkable one. We had achieved this substance and status from an original subscribed capital of £36,000 at the time I bought my shares, and now we had the resources to press forward with growth of a more varied kind. I mentioned earlier that Victor Matthews had become joint managing director in 1968, and was now sole managing director; and now I was chairman on what I have described as largely a non-executive basis, but a fairly full-time one. I will try to explain the reason for this: in my view the chairman of a large and diverse public company should not handle individual, routine, trading transactions, and should not identify himself too closely with any one particular division. He should be impartially concerned with all of them, and it is they (the divisions) who must deal with the outside world. At this point my association with property was still so strong that it was particularly important to step back if Trafalgar was to be, and appear to be, a cohesive unit as opposed to a conglomeration of loosely associated businesses identified only by a common shareholder. I give more details of how we have worked ever since on page 205.

In my published statement with our 1976 accounts I summarized what had been our objectives since 1970, and what had been the outcome, with these words:

'To develop our UK business within the limits imposed by a prudent assessment of a poor political and economic outlook.

'To take on much more business overseas.

'To develop strong positive cash flows with particular emphasis on foreign currencies.

'To add further strength to the balance sheet, the quality and quantity of earnings per share, and the asset backing.

'To support the foregoing with complete integration of direction and policy, and with management backed by group technical services of the highest calibre.

'The only significant diversification during the period was our entry into the shipping business, and Cunard can be seen to fit the criteria listed above. We were never involved in so-called 'break-up' situations or purely financial opportunism.

'Several objectives were supported by company acquisitions, but we never bought anything that we did not intend to integrate, manage and hold indefinitely. The degree to which we have succeeded in achieving our objectives can be illustrated by the following statistics:

Turnover increased from £57 million in 1970 to £448 million in the year just ended.

Sales in foreign currencies increased from less than £1 million to £200 million.

Earnings per share rose from 3·4p to 14·4p.

Pre-tax profits grew from £3·4 million to £33·6 million and gross assets from £83 million to £436 million.

'I have chosen this particular period for this brief and, I hope, detached summary for three reasons: it starts after our decision to begin our gradual and deliberate disengagement from primary dependence on the property business; it covers a sufficient number of years to give some sense of perspective; and it extends up to the present day – when shorter-term judgements are unavoidable, but often of dubious quality. The achievements of the 1970s were, of course, planned in the 1960s, and it is only fair to add that in today's conditions it would be foolhardy to try to plan in such detail for the 1980s.'

That was written nearly three years ago, and now our turnover approaches the £1,000 million mark, with profits in the region of £60 million for 1978, admittedly including £20 million of non-recurrent items.

Obviously the earlier rate of increase in the value of our

shares had to slow down as we became bigger, but the performance continued to be good, except during the period 1974-5, when there was universal depression. The graph which follows shows how our shares performed from 1969 onwards and how the Financial Times Index compared with us. Readers can relate this graph to the events I record in the last third of this book.

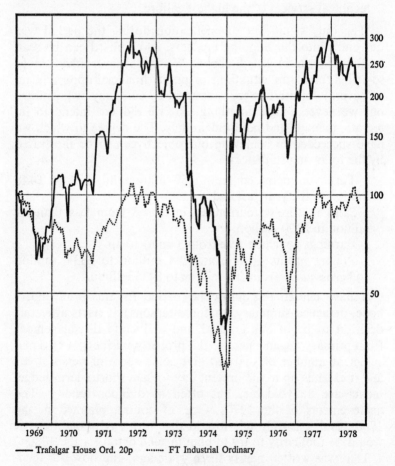

—— Trafalgar House Ord. 20p ······· FT Industrial Ordinary

By 1969 we had a good rating on the Stock Exchange, and also a good banking rating to borrow money and to generate cash and, just as indispensable, we had good personnel. I remember giving an interview some years earlier to Bill Davis (then City editor of the *Evening Standard*, who recently joined us from *Punch* as editorial director of our publishing interests), in which I said I was not good at picking staff. This may have been offensive to some of our employees, and I realized that what I meant was that we had very good staff, and that I was fortunate that they had chosen to join me.

After I became chairman, we settled our general plans for the next few years. The business, as already constituted, was well organized and performing satisfactorily: construction, housebuilding and property development were all progressing well. In the case of hotels we examined various takeover possibilities, but rejected them all apart from beginning to buy a significant stake in the Savoy Hotel Company, which I will mention again later. We planned no more takeovers in housebuilding and decided to grow in that business by direct investment; in the case of construction we wanted higher technology, a broader spread of activities and access to overseas markets. This goal was to be achieved by takeovers. Cunard had been identified as the best route to passenger shipping, an extension of the accommodation concept. There were also to be two unexpected (and unsuccessful) takeover situations, Metropolitan Estate and Property, and Bowater. Our provisional targets for takeover were Costain, Cementation and Cunard, but finally we rejected the first of these.

We built up a stake of just under 10 per cent in Costain, but it seemed an uncertain prospect, so we sold our shares to Slater Walker, who subsequently put his stake together with their own and mounted an unsuccessful bid by Hanson Trust. The shares in question have for the most part ended up in Arab hands. Cementation seemed a more promising and attractive purchase for us, and our acquisition was completed in June 1970.

The Cementation Company had been founded in 1919 by a Belgian engineer named François. They specialized in mining, grouting (a patented cement and chemical process) and, by 1970, had added civil engineering, tunnels, reservoirs, piling, bridge-building, motorways and general construction to their activities. They possess many unique skills, and one of their attractions to us was an excellent international reputation and a UK-based staff who were accustomed to travel all over the world to undertake specific contracts. It may be wondered why, with all these qualities, they became available for take-over. Their administration was good but their profit record was poor, and for this there were two principal reasons: their resources were insufficient to cover such a wide range of activities, and their management had got into the habit of relying on one or two very large overseas jobs, to the detriment of the more routine side of their business. Their work on the Kariba Dam and the giant steelworks at Dugrapur in India are two examples of the larger contract that sometimes obsessed them.

Denis Oppé, a director of Kleinwort Benson, was on the Cementation board, and he arranged for me to meet Henry Longden, the chairman of Cementation, at Kleinwort's Fenchurch Street offices (which T & C had built) one afternoon in January 1970. We quickly established a rapport, and it became clear that, if Cementation would benefit from membership of a larger group, Trafalgar would be the most attractive one to join. The bid was published on 3 February, but the ultimate acquisition was not completed until June because counter bids were made by Bovis and by Tarmac. The eventual cost was nearly £17 million, perhaps rather a high figure, and certainly unnecessarily so. At one stage Bovis's bid was similar to ours; we still had the recommendation at the Cementation board, but Bovis bought a large amount of Cementation shares on the stock market. The outcome was assured when we bought these shares from Bovis, but the incident was marred by a disagreement with the Takeover Panel: when Bovis were buying their shares we complained to the Panel that they should be obliged to underwrite their offer, so that all shareholders would have the option to receive cash, just as a few had done. The Panel rejected our request at the time and it was inconvenient later, after we bought Bovis' shares, to be told by the Panel that the whole of our offer would now have to be underwritten – these were the same shares that Bovis had bought piecemeal. We felt ill-used, but Kleinwort's promptly agreed to undertake the entire commitment without charge; otherwise we might well have withdrawn the offer, because we felt this requirement was unfair. Kleinwort's had done us a good turn, but they were also motivated by the desire to support whatever the Panel wanted. This incident did not turn out to be as cost-free as we had expected, because Kleinwort's were left with more than two million Trafalgar shares which they sold slowly, and in small quantities, for nearly a year, restraining the price of our shares.

The integration of our respective trading activities proceeded apace, but on this occasion Victor did not move into the Cementation head office for any length of time. Several of the company's technical and specialist functions remained in much the same form as had been the case before the acquisition, but their general construction and civil engineering activities were harmonized with our own ; and our modest overseas construction interests were merged with theirs under the name Cementation International.

Since that time we have built a second office block at the site of their Mitcham headquarters where we now accommodate about 1,600 people in what has become the base for most of the central services of the whole Trafalgar group. Indeed, it was the Cementation acquisition that completed the foundations of our central service departments, which have been largely unchanged since 1971. Several of these thirteen principal departments are headed by people who came from Cementation. Ian Fowler, who joined Trafalgar in 1962, has been secretary for the Holding Company ever since, and Alan Ford, a most talented administrator from Cementation, did much of the work to bring the subsequent structure into being.

I have mentioned Jimmy Jimson, who came from IBC. Trevor Winter, who runs our internal audit department, came from T & C; John Ewing, our head of legal services, followed Joe Crean, who came from IBC, but died suddenly; and Henry Berens, who runs our investment department, was recruited from Whitehall Securities because no equivalent person existed in any of the companies we acquired. All the others came from Cementation, namely: John Blagden (data processing and computers), Peter Coles (personnel), Frank Bateman (premises), Gerry Lyons (purchasing), Ron Heather (taxation), and John Lawford (group treasurer). I have listed these individuals by name to pay tribute to them and to illustrate how the range of our central services is supported by people whose careers expanded appreciably as a result of our takeovers. We rarely lose these people, and attach great value to continuity. This structure, which was established under the direction of Eric

Parker, is virtually unchanged today and serves us well, though it could be said that it would demonstrate its usefulness even more clearly if further acquisitions could now be made, although official policy on mergers and monopolies has, of course, become more repressive in recent years. It may have been unfortunate that Victor's personal commitment to the integration of Cementation's trading interests was interrupted by the Metropolitan Estate and Property transaction, which came suddenly to a head in July 1970, only a few weeks after the Cementation acquisition was completed.

The MEPC story was a strange one, and in a sense it originated from a chance winter meeting with Charles Hardie and his wife Angela in Barbados. Charles had been chairman of MEPC for four or five years and had done a great deal to strengthen the company's finances and reputation, and perhaps these two characteristics had overtaken the company's property and development expertise. In any event, Charles' eyes were fixed on more distant horizons, and one evening after dinner at Sandy Lane he described a most ambitious plan. He was soon, he told me, to become a director of Hill Samuel, the merchant bank, and his intention was to merge it with MEPC, then to acquire Trafalgar, with himself becoming chairman of the much enlarged unit, and me as chief executive. I said, 'But what about Kenneth Keith?' (now Sir Kenneth). He replied that he felt sure Keith would be amenable, and was in any case much interested in farming. Privately I was most sceptical about this, but I mentioned the matter to colleagues when I got back to England in terms that made it clear how surprised I would be if we heard any more of the matter.

In the late spring of 1970 there was a joint announcement by Hill Samuel and MEPC of their intention to merge. I had had no further talks with Charles in the meantime and took a detached interest in what was going on. The announcement had been made late in the afternoon, which generally improves the chances of an uncritical press the next day; the initial reaction was not unfavourable, but gradually institutional hostility to the proposal began to crystallize, and in due course Victor and I were asked by Sir Mark Turner, then deputy chairman of Kleinwort's and a director of the Commercial Union, to attend a private meeting on the subject. The meeting took place on the afternoon of 7 July at the flat which Klein-wort's maintain for such purposes in Arlington House. Mark Turner, who was accompanied by John Gillum, told us that the Commercial Union proposed to make a bid for MEPC, conditional on the Hill Samuel proposal being scrapped. The Commercial Union wanted Trafalgar to join them as junior partners who, if the offer succeeded, would take on all MEPC's residential properties. These included many thousands of flats from MEPC's recent acquisition of London Country Freehold and Leasehold (Key Flats), and this was at a time just before Central London residential values began to accelerate.

Clearly we would be interested, but I would have liked to know if Charles had given any further thought to the completion of the plan he had described to me that evening in Barbados. It would have been wrong to tell Mark what Charles had proposed, so I asked, 'Will the CU go ahead with this bid even if Trafalgar does not take part?' Mark confirmed that they would, and consequently I knew that, whatever the outcome of the CU's offer, the Hill Samuel/MEPC proposal would fail. The Hill Samuel plan, by now, had become distinctly unpopular with institutional shareholders and would not be supported in preference to a premium offer for MEPC by the CU (though that, too, eventually was to fail). As soon as this was clear, Victor and I confirmed our interest; our colleagues subsequently agreed, and CU's offer was announced at a press conference ten days later.

The initial public reaction was one of relief that the Hill Samuel proposals were bound to collapse, but a current of hostility from other institutions began to develop towards our own plans. It may well have been that those who supported our proposals in the first place included a number of people who were primarily concerned to see Hill Samuel fail and, once that was achieved, were relatively indifferent to the outcome of the CU offer. MEPC's defence was led by Philip Shelbourne, today the chairman of Samuel Montagu, but then with Rothschilds. Philip is a lawyer who had been our tax adviser ten years earlier when he was at the Bar. His campaign was vigorous and effective ; it centred on a revaluation of assets in which proposed developments were valued as if they had been completed and let, though some had not even been started, and the only deduction that was made was for the cost of construction. This was an unreal concept, but by this time things were not going our way and people were not particularly interested in our protests. Francis agreed that I should take charge of our press relations, and this part of the campaign recovered; but I have never deluded myself that a good press will secure victory – the point is that a bad press generally will ensure failure.

Philip Shelbourne's task for MEPC was made easier by the fact that we, that is CU and Trafalgar, were proposing to proceed by way of a Scheme of Arrangement: this requires Court sanction and is difficult enough between consenting parties and had never been used before for an opposed bid. The technique had been chosen to simplify the division of properties between CU and Trafalgar, and it would have saved Stamp Duty; but it meant that our timetable was protracted and inflexible, and when the level of acceptances proved to be inadequate it was too late to raise the price by a shilling or two, because the whole process would have had to start again and would have dragged on into the following spring. So the bid lapsed, rather than failed, through inadequate acceptances. We would have made a lot of money from the flats, but then we would have been associated with the odium which developed through the fringe banks' operations in that field a few years later. Sometimes I think that Trafalgar's good fortune relates as much to what we did not do as to what we did, and this was almost as much a matter of luck as of good judgement.

As with CLRP, we came to no particular harm as a result of our involvement and for the CU the outcome was of no great significance. They had wanted to increase their property holdings and the transaction would have had some of the characteristics of a rights issue at the same time, but neither of these considerations was particularly important. The only losers were the shareholders of MEPC, because the company resolved to brighten up its image by embarking on an even more ambitious development programme and as a result the shares performed poorly in the forthcoming crisis.

Hill Samuel would have done very well out of the deal as originally conceived, because their capital and reserves would have increased very considerably, with a commensurate addi-

tion to their banking scope; they tried later to do something
of the kind with Slater Walker, and must now be relieved that
the plan also came to nothing. The directors of MEPC had
flattered themselves with the thought that they were buying a
bank ; but, of course, the truth of the matter was the reverse,
and their future role would have been minor: it was the bank
which would have benefited.

Merchant banking then was a more glamorous occupation than
it is today, but thoughtful observers realized that inflation, in
particular, had already eroded the real resources of such organizations, and their financial significance was starting to diminish
at a time when the joint stock banks, and overseas banks, were
rapidly improving the services and facilities which they offered
in London and elsewhere. Most of our merchant banks possess
particular specialist skills, and generally they have nowadays
to live more on their wits than on their resources. Their heyday
lasted from the late fifties to the early seventies when, with a
mixture of panache and self-assurance, they became the indispensable counsel to many large public companies. But, as
things got tougher, it emerged that in some cases they were
more of a luxury than a necessity ; without questioning merchant bankers' abilities, companies found they had to improve
their internal capabilities. I have made the same point concerning management consultants. One might say that Jim Slater
got in on the act just as the play was about to finish.

After Geoffrey's departure we clarified our hotel objectives
which, as a first stage, contemplated the investment of £15
million in Central London and £10 million in the Caribbean,
equivalent to about 2,000 bedrooms. The Caribbean concept
already anticipated the ownership of passenger ships, although
another year would pass before we acquired Cunard. We had
for some time been friendly with John Young of Court Line;
and although we were sceptical about his business, we liked
him and some of his ideas ; indeed, the concept of hotels leading to cruise ships originated with Court Line's subsidiary
shipbuilder, Appledore, who proposed a giant catamaran which
would support a floating hotel. Conventional ships are contained within an envelope of gradual curves, and the idea of
putting a rectangular accommodation structure on to two

ship-shaped hulls would certainly have saved a lot of money.

We had in mind two clear ideas: (a) that Central London hotels were a neglected and promising area, which is what I had been trying to convey to Trust Houses in 1967, and (b) that Caribbean hotels, as well as complementing adjacent construction and sales, should be used for what we call fly/ stay/cruise programmes which involved ships.

At this point I must ask readers to cast their minds back to the pre-Arab/Israeli war period, when such visions were fashionable and realistic. As things have turned out, of course, the West Indies have proved troublesome for indigenous reasons and the price of oil has changed travel patterns and their volume.

In the meantime, London hotels have passed through an awkward period before fulfilling our earlier predictions. The interruptions and reverses to this market have been so great that today I often wonder if we might not have done best of all to release Geoffrey, as we did, but to have restricted our hotel interests to the centre of Central London, proceeding with Cunard, but with less emphasis on integrated holiday plans.

In the winter of 1969/70 we bought the Montego Beach Hotel in Jamaica, Paradise Beach in Barbados, and Trust Houses' interest in St Lucia where we built the Hotel La Toc. In London we built the Hotel Bristol on the site of the old Berkeley, we bought the London International Hotel in Cromwell Road, when it was half-built, and we built the Cunard International at Hammersmith. Everything looked fine until the oil crisis, and one must remember that, although this led to what is probably the worst world-wide depression since the 1930s (and the worst of the century in the case of shipping), we in this country were in any case heading for our own financial crisis as a result of the Health/Barber policies and the banking excesses they facilitated.

The case of the Hammersmith hotel is an interesting reminder of how unrecognizably different so many things were a few years ago. In 1969 there was the imminent prospect of this part of Hammersmith being transformed, and there was an acute shortage of accommodation for package tour visitors, a business growing particularly fast in the case of Americans. The geographical considerations were these: the underground railway link to Heathrow Airport would pass through Hammersmith, and the local council were going to build a full, first-floor, walk-way system linking us and many other proposed new buildings with each other and with the underground station; it would be an important terminus on the route from the channel tunnel to the White City; J. Lyons & Co. were going to develop about twelve acres of the Cadby Hall site on the north side of Hammersmith Road with flats, offices, and several thousand hotel bedrooms; and St Martin's Property Co. were going to develop many acres to the north-west of Hammersmith Circus. All this would have moved London's centre of gravity to the west. Now, nine years later, all that we have got is the under-ground link with Heathrow, part of the St Martin's scheme, an office block for Bechtel International and our hotel; and St Martin's now belongs to the Kuwait Investment Office.

We have just started to build a 130,000-square-foot office block for our own occupation on a site next to the Cunard Hotel, which was part of the original deal, but was held up by the delayed removal of the London Transport bus depot from the land ; and some of the other schemes are beginning to show renewed signs of life – but in the meantime we are placed between a motorway and several acres of cleared land within a giant traffic system, and it is no secret that we have lost millions of pounds ; last July was the first profitable month since 1973. It was bad luck that this should be the first major new development for which Victor was responsible; we had bought the Cromwell Road hotel from two American gentle-men, the Danziger brothers and, as part of the settlement of a dispute concerning construction costs, we accepted a majority interest in the Hammersmith site. Like so many things, it seemed a good idea at the time.

Two of our hotels were sold later, and this produced an overall profit; the others trade profitably and perhaps we were lucky not to have proceeded with a chain of provincial hotels related to housing developments and local shopping centres: that was the plan, but it got no further than Bar Hill near Cambridge, where we have built nearly a thou-sand houses, many acres of warehousing and factories, shops, offices and our Cambridgeshire Hotel – all on a site of several hundred acres which we bought from Holland, Hannen and Cubitts in those halcyon days of 1969.

This reminds me again of John Young, whose Court Line used the word 'Halcyon' for hotels, holidays and even ships. John led the development of a huge, package tour business with vision and drive, but, at best, the economics of £40 for a fortnight in Spain were fragile, and this was a sector which we examined, and rejected. Readers will recall that when Court Line began to falter in the summer of 1974 there was widespread public concern, because of the enormous number of people whose holidays plans were in jeopardy. In August of that year the Official Receiver was appointed, and in April 1976 the statement of affairs was published: it disclosed a deficiency of nearly £73 million.

The crisis of 1974 would have happened even without the action of the Arabs, which increased our fuel bill for the *QE2* alone by £3 million per annum. The Arab/Israeli war turned what would have been a domestic recession into a world-wide depression.

Of course we make mistakes, and so does everyone else; but we showed rising profits throughout the period and avoided excessive involvement with property and hotels, which it would have been so easy to undertake in the early Heath boom period. Credit was plentiful and we could have taken on hundreds of millions of pounds' worth of property development work in the early 1970s. But our response to the accelerating boom was restrained and before long we were more concerned with property sales than we were with purchases.

We were busy enough putting together an international construction group and planning for Cunard, though there is no doubt that the investing public were puzzled that what had been regarded as primarily a property group (conventionally this means the ownership and development of offices, shops, factories and warehouses) should bother with all these distractions and ignore what seemed to be the biggest boom in property since the war. We even had to resist pressure from certain wise and well-known figures in the City who reproached us for not being more active and aggressive in the worlds of Jim, Ronnie Lyon and William Stern. One of our inbuilt protections was Victor's temperament: he has a keen sense of humour, he responds well to flattery, and to others must seem a cheerful, contented man; but in private he is often morose and pessimistic, doubtful and suspicious of the future. This is nothing new: he was just the same fifteen years ago, and in the meantime he repeatedly has considered (and rejected) ideas for retirement, or emigration, or both. I am generally more optimistic than Victor, but on this occasion, as the boom was building up, I shared his conviction that things were bound to 'go off pop', as he put it.

I confirmed this conclusion after a dinner at Chequers in January 1972, which I will describe now – although it took place after some of the events of the next chapter – because it gives a fair account of what had begun to go wrong with Britain two years earlier. The Conservatives' victory in the general election of June 1970 had been somewhat unexpected, and Ted Heath's personal prestige was all the higher for that reason. He was hailed as the Prime Minister most likely to succeed of any since the war, and offered the promise of firm, no-nonsense government, rather than flabby Socialism or pink-tinted Conservatism. But, as I shall relate when we come to the collapse of 1974, the economy was not responding to him as he required it to, and the endeavour to stimulate it with money was to lead to an extremely dangerous situation.

Mr Heath's companions at the Chequers dinner included Anthony (now Lord) Barber, Robert (now Lord) Carr, John Davies, Lord Rothschild and Sir William (now Lord) Armstrong, then head of the Civil Service. The other guests were Jim Slater, Malcolm Horsman, Neill Wates and Jacob Rothschild; I suppose we had been chosen for this meeting to see if any of us would make satisfactory younger alternatives for business communications to Lords Stokes and Kearton, who had been prominent in the role before. This was the time when the 'lame-duck' thesis was still current, and I politely contrasted Rolls-Royce with Cammell Laird in terms of cost effectiveness, and made passing reference to the former Land Commission and the IRC.

Chequers is large and comfortable, but not particularly gracious. I was interested to see how a bachelor kept such an establishment together, and quickly identified the youngish lady housekeeper who unobtrusively saw to it that administration and comforts were immaculate. There was a fine open fire in the hall where we assembled for drinks just before

6 p.m. Then the Prime Minister appeared and led us to a long, narrow sitting room on the first floor where we settled for the first session. The Government's two main concerns were lack of investment by industrialists and the prospect of rising unemployment and we, the guests, expressing our particular sectional worries, had little general comfort to offer. The inconsistencies in Government thinking were fairly obvious: all the non-interventionist, free enterprise, 'Selsdon Man' and 'lame-duck' policies had sounded fine a year or two earlier, and they were still accepted doctrine to the Cabinet. But they could not understand why employment was rising and they appeared not to see that an endeavour to start an industrial recovery by monetary means was inconsistent with their other doctrines.

It was particularly disappointing that the Tories had made little impact on the level of public spending and apparently none on the level of bureaucracy in this country. To print money would lead to inflation; financial stringency would raise interest rates. The honeymoon was almost over, and there had been no sign from the Government of significant reductions in personal taxation; so success was still penalized, though failures were no longer given convalescent help.

Refreshments were offered throughout this period, and after nearly two hours we were taken downstairs to an ante-room where a distinguished butler offered good champagne. At dinner, where WAAF sergeants served pheasant and a very good claret, talk was general and the Chancellor, sitting next to me, leant close and asked in a confidential tone, 'Would you mind telling me how much money you've actually made?' I laughed, and whispered the answer; we were on easy terms because his brother Noel is a friend. Tony is now chairman of the Standard and Chartered Bank where I had lunch a few weeks ago, and I wondered if he would ask the same question (he did not) – but of those five visitors to Chequers that evening, only Jacob and I are still in what might be termed remotely equivalent positions.

After dinner we returned to the upstairs sitting room where I made what to me, at least, was my only memorable remark: Mr Heath opened with the statement, 'You have told me that none of you want to invest north of a line from Bristol to the Wash' (which seemed a funny way of putting it) and I replied,

'So far as I'm concerned, Prime Minister, Trafalgar would not invest north of Oxford Street, the way things look.' The conversation returned again and again to the inconsistencies between the 'lame-duck' policy, concern about unemployment, and the problems of worn-out or obsolete industry in the North and in Scotland. More than once I pressed my point that at least there should be contingency plans in case the 'lame-duck' policy failed, and finally Mr Heath stated sharply that contingency plans were subversive and sapped people's determination, at which Sir William nodded sagely. Mr Heath then continued to say that throughout history civilizations had developed where they were useful, and declined when they were not; if Clydeside came into the latter category, it was just too bad. I am paraphrasing, of course – his language was more direct and specific. The Prime Minister seemed to treat his colleagues somewhat brusquely; he was polite to his guests, but the message was unmistakable: he, by his Herculean endeavours, was giving Britain a dose of medicine that was long overdue; and we, the businessmen who ought to support him, were letting him down by our failure to invest. Harold Wilson, of course, had said something similar before, and Julian Amery did much the same thing later, when house prices were rising rapidly, and builders were accused of hoarding land. I am, I hope, a calm and realistic man, and I could only repeat that our problems lay in the fields of excessive public spending, bureaucracy, taxation, and lack of respect for our currency. Any leader who supports realism in these matters has my loyalty, and I am well aware that the problems he (or she) faces include not only the electorate but also the Civil Service.

Drinks were offered throughout the evening, but only Mr Heath, Lord Rothschild and I consumed what I would regard as a normal amount; we broke up at midnight and I felt faintly deflated, but in another sense exhilarated: I had confirmed at first hand that the Prime Minister was just as determined as ever to pursue a stubborn policy which was not working. A change of course was inevitable, and no thought had been given to its form. Contingency planning was not only absent, evidently it was forbidden.

Not long afterwards came the April Budget, the U-turn, the further expansion of credit, the fringe bank phenomenon, and finally, less than two years later, the indexation of wage in-creases (and Civil Service pensions), control of office rents and a fresh set of property taxes. The money that had been created went to the wrong places and soon after, when Harold Wilson was back in office, inflation was approaching 30 per cent per annum, people were saying that Britain was ungovernable and two men (General Walker and Colonel Stirling) achieved tem-porary public credibility with their plans to start private armies. It really was a dreadful mess, and my reason for covering what took four years to unfold in a single paragraph is to set the background of what, for us, was a period of cautious anxiety, whilst others were euphoric: we feared that in Britain things would 'go off pop', as Victor used to say, and we planned more and more foreign involvement; but the oil crisis came as a complete surprise, and we had not expected the rest of the free world to 'let us down', as an agile-minded politician might have put it.

What I have said about Chequers explains why I shared Victor's pessimism about the UK at that time – generally I take a more expansionist view. We increased our efforts to add to our overseas work and revenues. UK hotels, of course, were not inconsistent with this because a weak currency in an attractive country leads to a tourist boom.

In 1969 we had started to buy shares in the Savoy, knowing that less than 2 per cent of the shares (known as 'B' shares) controlled nearly 50 per cent of the votes, and we gradually put together a holding of more than a quarter of the equity, and about 16 per cent of the votes. The company, of course, also owned the Berkeley, Claridge's and the Connaught; the shares were cheap and the cost of the investment was not large. After we had disclosed what we were doing the Savoy chairman, Hugh (later Sir Hugh and Lord Mayor of London) Wontner asked me to lunch at his corner table overlooking the Embank-ment and the Thames ; with great clarity and courtesy he explained how all our leading hoteliers (Charles Forte and Max Joseph in particular) had agreed to respect the Savoy Group's independence, because they set the standards and trained the staff for the whole of our metropolis. I did not disagree with what he said, but we continued to buy the shares. Then Sir Hugh asked Victor and myself to a suite at Claridge's where we had a good lunch and met someone who helps with their administration and used to know my mother. The message was the same, and we continued to buy the shares. We had no concrete basis to expect ever to be able to acquire the company, but the law might change as regards distorted voting structures, and we were always attracted by great names – the Savoy and the Ritz still displayed details of Cunard sailings.

It is sometimes thought that we made a takeover attempt, but that is not so: what happened was that in 1970 the Savoy decided to acquire the Hotel Lancaster in Paris, and convened an extraordinary general meeting to allow them to do so, predominantly with new 'B' shares, the ones which had the extra votes. We made a public protest, because this would distort the voting structure still further but, predictably, our protests were in vain, because the board already owned or influenced enough stock to vote the proposal through; but the point was worth making. The vendor of the Lancaster was a man named Wolf, who had settled in Switzerland. It was an extraordinary coincidence to discover that he lived in a flat overlooking Lake Geneva on the Quai des Fleurs at Montreux – almost next door to my mother. They met, and he would joke that all these 'B' shares were for his children, and afterwards for his grandchildren.

Then Mr Wolf became ill, and as his wife in the meantime had had an argument with Sir Hugh about discounts and the ownership of a clock at the Hotel Lancaster, she approached my mother to see if we (Trafalgar) would like to buy their 'B' shares.

She took her husband to convalesce at Monte Carlo in the autumn of 1975, and we sent Henry Berens, the manager of our investment department, to see them there. I was interested beyond the degree of the importance of the transaction, and took Joyce to our house at Cap d'Antibes for a few days to get a first-hand account of the transaction, without meeting the vendors. Strangely enough, we discovered, they had very few 'B' shares: at the completion meeting five years earlier nearly £750,000 worth of shares had been issued to Mr Wolf, but most were promptly exchanged for a banker's draft drawn on a Swiss bank for an unknown purchaser; and all the Wolfs had left was £24,000 worth, which we bought. We kept these shares until 1978 when we sold them to Maxwell Joseph for £75,000. So the journey was not wasted – but the mystery remains: where are the other 'B' shares?

Only a fortnight ago Victor and I were having lunch with Maxwell Joseph at the Casino his company has created in space they have rented from us at the Ritz in Piccadilly: our conversation ranged from charges for croupiers' accommodation on the *QE2* via a reconstruction contract for Berners Hotel in Bloomsbury to the question of freight arrangements for shipments of J & B Scotch Whisky to North America, but casually he revived an earlier possibility – that we would sell him our Savoy holding. We gave him an option for twenty-four hours; he phoned by tea-time to ask for a meeting that evening, and came at 6 p.m. to see me at our house in Chelsea Square. The answer was yes, and we agreed it without even shaking hands; Victor was at Fleet Street and I phoned him on his private line to give him the news. The sale produced £5·1 million cash compared with a written-down, book cost of just over £1 million – but the true profit was negligible because the shares had yielded around 2 per cent per annum for the last eight years.

Perhaps by the time this book is published Max will have made more progress with the investment than we did. It has been an interesting situation for twenty-five years now, and sooner or later something is bound to happen. The Savoy are exceptionally self-protective, or at least, they used to be: Jimmy Goldsmith's father was a director when, in the mid-1950s, he discussed takeover possibilities with Charles Clore at a Paris race-course. Charles made a proposal, Harold Samuel made a controversial bid, and the Savoy responded with a plan to transfer their properties to their staff pension fund – whose current trustees would appoint their successors. The Berkeley Hotel, which we eventually rebuilt, was the main objective, and it was at that time that Clore made his investment in the Ritz. This was all in the late 1950s. It was from a file which Harold Samuel lent me that I realized that by the time he withdrew, he in fact had control of the Savoy. He was disgusted by the anti-semitic nature of the defence, and lost his voice for several weeks – although he continued regularly to go to the Savoy to have his hair cut. Wontner and his supporters bought Harold's shares, and later they proposed the division of the company's capital into 'A' shares and 'B' shares. This was approved by a majority of shareholders. They kept their portion of the 'B' shares, which carried privileged voting rights, and sold many of the 'A's.

Earlier unsuccessful takeover attempts for other companies, such as MEPC, did not matter very much; those that had succeeded like Cementation were fully and beneficially integrated with what was a growing and cohesive business, we were expanding by direct investment, we had reduced our emphasis on UK property development, and we sought more foreign currency earnings. The Cunard plan looked better than ever, and their spring announcement of poor results set the scene for early action.

Cunard is one of the most famous names in the world. Samuel Cunard, a Canadian, started the business in 1840 and their dominant presence in the North Atlantic was reinforced when in 1934 they acquired the White Star Line. Apart from the *Queens*, they had owned such well-known ships as the four-funnelled *Mauretania* and *Aquitania*, also the *Titanic* and the *Lusitania*, and even as recently as 1960 they had no less than eleven ocean-going passenger liners. Jet travel, of course, had a devastating effect on the whole industry throughout the world, and the 1960s for Cunard were years of great trauma: the passenger side was inexorably dismantled and reduced; their cargo interests were extended, and many of their traditional cargo-liner trades were developed with others into the container consortia, which subsequently built and now operate the modern container ships. This long-established traditional business of not only Cunard but also of its principal subsidiaries, Brocklebank and Port Line, had to transform itself in a very short time, and at a time when there was no logical succession on the main board. Sir Basil Smallpiece came in firstly as a non-executive director from BOAC in 1964, and was then appointed chairman after Sir John Brocklebank; within a year or two almost the entire board had changed. It was a bold decision to build the *QE2*, and the management pressures must have been considerable: the directors were

G

unused to the business, and the management, whilst experienced, had mainly been concerned with routine matters and were unprepared for violent change. It is surprising that they did as well as they did, because the company's resources were scarcely adequate for the task they had no choice but to undertake.

We were interested in Cunard as a link between our hotels and our leisure interests. It would be cheaper to buy the company rather than to build our own ships. Only three of their seventy ships were passenger vessels but, as sometimes happens, the closer I came to the proposition, the better it looked – and what was wrong with cargo ships, anyway? But it had been hard enough, only four years earlier, to convince the investing public that a conventional property company could effectively acquire contractors and housebuilders. Today, eight years after the event, and after P & O have taken over Bovis, the builders, the idea may not seem so startling, but I can assure readers that at the time it was little short of revolutionary, indeed I am grateful that my colleagues came to share my confidence in the idea as rapidly as they did.

It is not generally known that in the early 1960s Cotton and Clore wanted to bid for Cunard, but were prevented from doing so by the representatives of two of their major shareholders on the board of City Centre Properties. Public opinion in these matters is crucial, and in our case the results of many years' concentration on building a reputation were to prove indispensable. It had not mattered to lose other takeovers in allied fields, but this was to be our most dramatic diversification and, as well as attracting the Cunard shareholders, we had to keep our own happy. Most companies and entrepreneurs, when they need support from the press, get their PR people to fix up a lunch or a conference, and that is the last time they will see the press until they need them again. I knew all the significant City editors and journalists personally, and would see them regularly whether we were active or not at the time; and although we use Derek Dale, an independent consultant, to organize our formal financial PR, I still maintain my contacts, and many are personal friends. Their positive power, as I mentioned earlier, should not be exaggerated, but their power to frustrate or destroy is much greater.

Another factor in creating a reputation is performance, supported by a record of truthfulness and accuracy. And a third factor which, I believe was particularly relevant in this case, is that I had never hesitated to share my reputation with Victor, and could almost have been described as his PR man whilst, in earlier years, I had taken him on a ceaseles round of lunches and meetings to demonstrate our equality and his capabilities. This was not generosity on my part, nor was it calculation; of course I knew that if we were going to do all the things I wanted, he would have to have an adequate public reputation, but I had enough confidence in my own to feel secure in giving him all that he could get. Nowadays, particularly since the *Express*, he is better known than I am to the public at large, and my reputation, such as it is, is in the areas I have selected for myself. These thoughts are not digressive: they concern factors that were vital to our success with the Cunard offer. And, of course, we owed much to people like Jock Hunter and John Gillum – the fact that they trusted and respected us encouraged others to do so.

A sensitive area in our public relations concerned tax. Jim Slater has written that he decided to sell out of Cunard when they disclosed that they had an £80 million investment programme. My reaction was the reverse: we wanted to invest, and leading counsel confirmed my expectation that the tax allowances on this programme would become available to the whole of Trafalgar if we bought Cunard. The position was this: the Conservatives, who had abolished Labour's investment grants, substituted their own 'free depreciation' tax allowances. This means that UK tax relief on the whole cost of an investment programme in new equipment is available to cover revenue and capital gains anywhere within a group whose subsidiaries incur the expenditure. Perhaps it seems surprising that the significance of this was not generally understood at the time, but it was not. We had a delicate path to follow: to let it be known that these allowances would be of early significance to us, but not to seem to brag about it. This, in its way, was another revolutionary facet of the concept which had to be handled with controlled modesty. These investment aids, of course, were of little assistance to an independent Cunard, because on their own their profits were too small for them to make significant use of them. We were also to benefit from their earlier expenditures, and found the total of available allowances to relate to the investment of over £100 million.

Our financial year ended in March, and I did not want to make the bid before our annual accounts had been published in July. We had a holding of almost 10 per cent in Cunard, we knew Jim Slater's position (in fact 11·6 per cent), so we asked a friendly broker, unconnected with Trafalgar, to secure Jim's holding at the moment when the three-week time limit the law then required for disclosure of a holding of over 10 per cent would extend beyond the publication date for the accounts.

The broker we chose was Bill Rawlings of James Capel & Co., whose senior partner I had met in the Caribbean. In his book *Return to Go*, Jim Slater describes how, at the end of Bill's visit, he said, 'Give my best wishes to Nigel.' Bill did his best to look blank and said, 'Nigel who?' So we now had over 21 per cent, and three weeks in which to perfect our preparations. The reason I wanted to get the accounts out of the way before we started the action was that, with all our other recent activity, Trafalgar was growing and changing rapidly, and I wanted investors to digest a clear statement of where we had got to before turning their minds to where we wanted to go next. This was important because the bid would amount to £27 million or so, a large sum, and much of it in shares; Cunard themselves were likely to resist, and might attack us as an aimless conglomerate. This in turn might weaken our share price at a crucial moment, devaluing the bid and making underwriting more difficult. Security during these three weeks was vital.

The Trafalgar board knew of our earlier share purchases, but not of the latest one: only Bill, Victor, Eric and I – and, of course, Ian Fowler – knew what we had bought from Jim. Nevertheless, there was a leak, and the shares began to rise on buying from another source. The market sensed that a bid was on the way, but only the *Daily Telegraph* guessed that it might be from us; a reporter put the question directly to me on the telephone, and I replied with a categorical denial; I had no choice, but the journalist deserved credit for his inspiration, and we did not want him as an enemy in the weeks that followed. Fortunately Kenneth Fleet, then City editor of the

Telegraph, was (and is) a good friend, and someone I trust completely; so I told Kenneth the whole story, and he respected my confidence. In fact we rather enjoyed ourselves, and as the mystery began to interest the general public, the story moved to the front page and Kenneth would phone to tell me of the latest rumours: 'P & O and Trust Houses Forte have just denied it,' he would say. 'Why not try the Rank Organization and Furness Withy?' I replied; and all four denials appeared in the paper the next day – but not ours. Coincidentally, the daily paper prepared electronically on the *QE2* used to be the *Telegraph*; another coincidence was that Cunard were our tenants, and Sir Basil Smallpiece had a fine suite of offices on the top floor of Cleveland House which had been fitted out at considerable expense by Trollope & Colls. But the most extraordinary coincidence of all was the code name they had chosen previously for their defence: *Trafalgar*.

On the morning of 30 June 1971 we convened a short board meeting, we told our colleagues of the recent addition to our holding, and it was agreed to proceed with the bid at once. At this stage our brokers and merchant bankers were informed: I telephoned Sir Basil Smallpiece, and his secretary said that he, too, was in a board meeting, and should she disturb him? I said I thought my message would interest all his colleagues; and we met. I have never known a bid where communications were so easy, and even during periods of hostility Basil would visit my room, or I his, for a chat, and occasionally a cup of tea or a drink. Cunard had known for some time that they were vulnerable to a bid (perhaps Basil secretly believed it would not necessarily be a bad thing) and some months earlier they had retained Henry Grunfeld of Warburg's to advise them. Warburg's assignment was most secret, hence the code name of *Trafalgar*.

Basil's next step, after receiving my announcement, was to phone Grunfeld. He was terse and secretive with his message: he wanted an urgent meeting about *Trafalgar*; what about *Trafalgar*? it was *Trafalgar*! what was? ... It is understandable that it took Grunfeld a moment to understand what on earth Sir Basil was trying to say. Our own security had been complete.

The public reaction was not unfavourable, and probably for

some time it had been assumed that eventually someone would take over Cunard; but more than one of our own larger shareholders were taken aback that it should be we who did it – and Messel's, our brokers, were ill-equipped to explain the rationale. Some sold (this had happened before with our earlier diversifications, and happened again at the time of Beaverbrook), whilst others were curious to know more. Two directors of Ivory and Sime, the investment managers, James Laurenson and Peter de Vinck, came down from Edinburgh to see us at Cleveland House; later they came for dinner to our house in London where Joyce made them welcome, and Justin, with other musical friends, played chamber music by Beethoven and Brahms. The next day they picked up a very large number of shares: for their part this was bold and decisive, from then on our shares moved upwards, and Ivory and Sime made a large profit.

There was no mud-slinging during the affair, and no counter-bid, but two people felt most strongly that even our final offer was grossly inadequate. These were Donald Forrester, a former director, and Max Joseph, who was on the board. Forrester announced publicly that, unless we paid more, they would make their own bid; but they did not. Mr Forrester was an elderly gentleman of considerable means who made something of a speciality of investing in the great names of British industry; Max Joseph had been recruited for the relevance of his hotel knowledge to the new concept of the *QE2*, and he told me later that never again would he join the board of a public company, unless he was chairman. The *QE2*, of course, had to compete with air travel, and this called for particular attention to hoteliers' skills, in addition to routine seamanship and transport.

The conclusive meeting took place in the South of France. Sir Basil Smallpiece chartered a jet to come to see me in a suite in the Hôtel Negresco (built by César Ritz) overlooking the Promenade des Anglais and the Mediterranean at Nice; he had a portfolio of threats combined with inducements for a better price; I added a few pennies per share, and we shook hands. We had paid Jim 175p per share and our first public offer was 198p, which I raised to 204p during Basil's visit. The majority of their board recommended our increased offer, but

Max Joseph and Mr Forrester still voted against it. I drove Basil on to La Violetta for lunch with Joyce and our three children, and then back to Nice Airport where he collected his McAlpine HS125 and flew back to London. I wrote the memorandum of our agreement in pencil on a notepad, we both initialled it, and Basil took it with him to get it typed. I was absolutely thrilled with the acquisition.

Soon we had control and declared the offer unconditional. I then returned to London to address the senior staff and to collect a mass of confidential documents, including the McKinsey report that stated that present trends would lead the *QE2* to annual losses of £3$\frac{1}{2}$ million, whereupon she would have to be laid up. Victor became the new chairman of Cunard, and began to sort it all out; I returned to France to concentrate on the records and statistics.

A few days later I was back in London again. Victor and I took the train to Southampton, drove to the docks, and visited the *QE2*. We had seen her only once before, when we were flying over the Clyde, and wondered how on earth such a huge vessel could be launched from the yard where she was being built with the help of government loans (not subsidies) at a us, and now the height, rising massively more than a hundred feet above the quay. But what impressed us most of all was the decor and the huge scale of the public rooms. This was an asset that *had* to be made to work profitably. She had been built with the help of government loans (not subsidies) at a cost of £33 million, and already the replacement cost would have been over £100 million, though she was only two years old. There would probably never be another, and it was vital to Trafalgar's reputation that the operation of this ship should be a success.

There were problems with layout and catering, and one of the first priorities was to rearrange things so that all passengers could have their meals when they wished, rather than being allocated to one of two regular sittings, as was the case for many of them previously. There were a thousand other things to do, seventy other ships to consider, and profound complexities to understand in our relationships with partners and customers in the two cargo container consortia; but the *QE2* came first, and Cunard's own staff quickly came to see that our takeover was probably the best thing that had happened to the company for very many years. Morale rose rapidly, and for more than a year Victor devoted himself to the *QE2* in particular, to ensure that food, service and sales were all put in good order. We added de luxe penthouses in unused space behind the bridge; we introduced an extra kitchen, and, above all, pressed every marketing device to fill the ship, and to keep it full.

After the acquisition we revalued the fleet, rather as one does with property from time to time. The *QE2* was written down to £15 million on that occasion, and since then we have spent nearly £7 million on improvements; but we provide every year for her depreciation as she becomes older, and now, halfway through her normal life, she is having a major refit, and after that will stand in our books at less than £15 million. In theory one can go on repairing and renewing fixtures, fittings, plant and machinery for ever, and the ship would never wear out; but in practice such things are overtaken by obsolescence, and perhaps she will expire in a decade or two. Nevertheless, she is the only vessel of her kind now left in the world, and nothing would surprise me! Since the acquisition we have built two new, smaller passenger ships, and the public demand for this sort of accommodation is growing at a time when there are only seventy liners left in the world. Half now belong to the Russians, and half are over twenty years old. We are examining plans for a new one, or to convert one or two fast cargo ships into passenger ships, but the cost projections are daunting, not to mention the fact that the construction facilities, here and elsewhere in the world, have largely dispersed.

My affection for the ship is clear from what I have written, and I am sorry to have seen her so infrequently. Apart from one or two more day visits, like the one with Victor in 1971, Joyce and I have had only two real voyages: once from Sri Lanka to Japan, via Singapore and Hong Kong, and once from Tahiti to Sydney, via New Zealand and Tasmania. The second of these demonstrated her full potential in terms of the entire Trafalgar group: at Wellington, Melbourne and Sydney, Cementation and the cargo division of Cunard could have parties of a hundred or more on board; we would select the leading politicians for a private lunch, and there can be no doubt that this is the most remarkable way in the world to capture the attention of important people. I wish we had time to do more of this sort of thing.

Cunard profits reached a peak of £17 million in 1976, largely earned from the cargo side, but pressures now are heavy due to the absence of growth in the economy of the free world, uneconomic competition from the Communist countries, and mindless determination from every quarter to build more new cargo ships than are required. This last point is particularly political: in the old days private shipyards would have closed if there was no demand, but now they are propped up by the governments which own them. Our future lies in the container trades and, curiously enough, in the passenger business – the 'no-hope' situation of 1971.

15

Life at the Time

For many years Joyce and I had spent quite a lot of time in sunnier places than England. She does not share my mild interest in skiing, and I soon get bored with nothing more than regular meals and a sandy beach. I am not gregarious, but time and again I have reached an important understanding with a busy man when I find him relaxed and off duty, so to speak. Most large companies need someone who, with authority, can meet others of all nationalities in a tranquil state of mind, which generally means when they are away from their offices. This is not just a matter of transactions, bids and deals: it concerns the exchange of opinions, impressions and expectations, and the chance to think. I do not work particularly hard, but I work all the time, and my only complete relaxations are silver work and design, periods at sea, and reading. I do not ride or shoot, or follow any of the conventional English outdoor recreations.

In 1970 we bought Mortimer House, a large private house in the Brompton Road ; Justin by now was at Eton, and we felt that Victoria and Simon would benefit from a period at day school in London before moving to their boarding schools. We did a lot of work to the place and built an enclosed swimming pool in the garden; it is unusual for central London, standing behind a long, tall, brick wall, and with all its reception rooms on the ground floor. It was a very good base for entertaining and for private business meetings, and served us well until the last of our children went to boarding school, after which it seemed rather large for two people, and we sold it in 1976 to a gentleman from Saudi Arabia. It was during this period that Wargrave became purely a weekend house, again too large for two of us: so in the summer of 1974 we bought the Deanery at Sonning and, late in 1975, after renovating the new house, sold Wargrave Manor to the Sultan of Oman.

Victoria had gone to Heathfield, and there she made friends

with a girl named Annabel Freyberg whose mother, Lady Freyberg, asked one day to see Wargrave Manor, because her husband's aunt, Gertrude Jekyll, had been born there. Miss Jekyll
was a famous gardener who worked closely with Sir Edwin
Lutyens, the architect, and our next house, the Deanery, was
the result of one of their earliest collaborations, built on an
ancient site for Mr Hudson, the founder and first editor of
Country Life. It is a most comfortable and agreeable house,
and we open the gardens to the public once or twice each year.
It stands next to the church, and beyond the church is the site
of a former bishop's palace. In about the year 920 Bishop Odo,
a Viking converted to Christianity, founded the place, and it
was from Sonning that Salisbury was established, as a satellite.
We enjoy it very much, and divide our time in England more
or less equally between there and our new London house in
Chelsea Square. My work revolves around our head office on
the corner of Berkeley Street and Piccadilly, where we moved
from Cleveland House to our development on the site of the
old Berkeley Hotel. I do relatively little business travelling
nowadays for Trafalgar, although until recently I did quite a
lot for the Government.

I first got to know Michael Heseltine in 1971 when he was
the Junior Minister responsible for Office Development Permits.
In the summer of 1972 he became Minister for Aerospace and
Shipping at the Department of Industry, and it was in that
capacity that he telephoned one afternoon to say, 'I know I
haven't done you any favours, but I'd like you to do me one:
will you become the chairman of our new Ship and Marine
Technology Requirements Board?'

I replied that at least I would not be disqualified by knowledge
of the industry, as had happened with the New Towns Commission, and I agreed to give him an answer after reading the
relevant papers that he agreed to send me. Eight of these boards
were being set up to give effect to Lord Rothschild's recom-
mendations that the 'customer/contractor' relationship should
be introduced to government-sponsored contracts at the
Ministry's industrial research establishments [IREs]. I took the
job on the basis of one day a month for three years, and did it
for four and a half years, sometimes spending as much as one

day a week on it. We were a board of fourteen, half from government departments and half from industry, and I enjoyed it. At the peak we were placing work at the rate of about £12 million a year, and were steadily increasing the proportion that was spent with the private sector.

Our job was to allocate government money, sometimes with financial support from industry, in the furtherance of research and development to improve the competitiveness of those sectors of industry with which we were concerned, and to support government departments with the equipment and information they needed to carry out their statutory functions in such areas as health, safety and so on. We operated in three distinct fields: shipbuilding, ship operation, and offshore oil and gas and, as I put it at the time, there is no doubt that we caused things to happen which would not have happened otherwise, and we made other things happen more quickly.

The four principal government research establishments where we placed work were the National Physical Laboratory at Feltham, the National Engineering Laboratory near Glasgow, the Warren Springs Laboratory at Stevenage, and the United Kingdom Atomic Energy Authority at Harwell. The industrial firms who worked with us or for us included such companies as Decca, Plessey, EMI and the British Aircraft Corporation. Some of our work was innovative, but for the most part it concerned the selection and evaluation of other people's ideas, the allocation of priorities to carry them out, and the monitoring of progress. The function was executive rather than advisory, and I had the unusual experience of not once having a proposal rejected by the Treasury.

I learned later that the civil servants had been apprehensive about my appointment, but later it generally came to be accepted that mine was the most successful of these boards. I found I had an easy authority with everyone in this work – easier than in Trafalgar, perhaps because to most of the people I dealt with, I was as novel as a creature from outer space. Michael Heseltine was the best and most effective of the young Ministers I met in this work, and the only one to take a proper interest. Lord Beswick, an older man who had the responsibility later on, must have had many other talents, but seemed unsuited to this particular task. Most of the others (I am including the Departments of Trade and Energy) always seemed to have other pre-occupations – these are observations rather than criticisms; the senior civil servants were very good.

The official representatives on my board came from Trade, Defence and Industry. I chose most of the men who joined us from the private sector – people at, or just below, main board level with such companies as British Petroleum, P & O, Marconi and Swan Hunter. It was interesting to be told that, although I was the youngest chairman of any of the boards, I had chosen members who gave us the highest average age of all. In the first two years we met every month, and during this time I visited all our principal contractors and got to know the directors of the IREs.

After that we reduced the frequency of our meetings to an eight-week cycle, but I would see the officials every week. I made friends with two in particular: Sir Ieuan Maddock, Chief Scientist at the Department of Industry, now retired; and Walter Marshall, director of Harwell and for a short time Chief Scientist at the Department of Energy. Walter is a large Welshman, a year or two older than I, and exceedingly clever – a Fellow of the Royal Society since his twenties, also un-usually gifted in administrative and commercial matters, and a regular visitor to the United States, where he could very easily earn ten times more than he does here. These men were outstanding, and at the level below them I found well-moti-vated, sincere and patriotic individuals who worked extremely hard; it was only as one descended in the hierarchy that signs of feebleness began to appear. As the numbers increased, the quality fell sharply away. At the lower levels, judged by com-mercial standards, one found idle and ineffective men, over-paid and too secure in their appointments.

I am glad I did this job; I found I had a lucid if unsophisti-cated fluency with ideas and equipment at this 'interface' be-tween scientific and material matters. To give some idea of what we did, I will describe what was presented to me, and what we made of it.

When I became chairman of the SMTRB in 1972, I found that over 200 individual projects of research and development where assigned to us. For the most part these were already under way, and my initial task was to categorize and allocate them between our members so as to be able to comprehend the scale and diversity of what was going on. We pressed hard to compress projects into comprehensible programmes so as to make it easier to take the necessary strategic view in each case. Only in the area of hovercraft research did we decline to undertake commitments beyond those already made by the Government. We were particularly concerned to limit the multiplicity of minor, random endeavours that could not be related directly to our strategic objectives (under the Rothschild doctrine the directors of the IREs were given their own discretionary budgets for these smaller projects). In particular we selected a number of major developments for priority treatment, and these I named Star Projects. There were more than a dozen of them and, during my four and a half years as chairman, it was gratifying to see most of them reach fruition in terms of tangible equipment and apparatus, by then in practical operation in the field.

One of the first was the Side Scan Sonar for use by Royal Navy hydrographers. This was one of several items of equipment for which an obvious need existed. No alternative was available on the open market, and financial stringency or departmental indecision had delayed production for some years.

The Side Scar Sonar, mounted underneath a ship, prepares what is virtually a photographic image of the sea bed beneath the track of the ship. I had been surprised when I took up this SMTRB work to learn that most of the Admiralty Charts of our coastlines, which are universally used by mariners, are those that were originally prepared during the last century with lead lines. In those days it was unusual for a ship to have a draught of more than thirty feet, but by now it is not uncommon for a large oil tanker to draw sixty-five feet, and considerably greater draughts were in prospect for very large crude carriers ('VLCCs'). We backed this work on the condition that it should lead to operational equipment within a specific period of time, and this it did.

Another example concerns the Nocturnal Ship Handling Simulator. This was built into two interconnecting caravans within which were reproduced a captain's cabin and a ship's bridge, beyond which appeared in facsimile the bow of the vessel and a night-time landscape in which different-coloured points of light represented other vessels and the navigation marks of a real marine seascape – in the first place, Southampton and the Isle of Wight. The apparatus was of course based upon a computer which, in addition to plotting the relative movement of other vessels to the simulated ship, would relate all this to the chart of the area and the characteristics of the particular ship that was being simulated. This last point was particularly important, because the computer reproduced the handling characteristics of anything from a small trawler to a 250,000-ton VLCC, and this comprised an invaluable aid for training masters who might have been experienced with small ships, but had no practical experience with large ones. It was a weird sensation to stand on the 'bridge', to feel the simulated vibrations of the vessel beneath my feet, and experience the different time delays as one changed speed or course according to the vessel one was 'master' of.

The requirement for this simulator was first expressed by the industry, and our initial concern was to examine what was available elsewhere in the world, and to assess its usefulness. A major engineering company from the North of England put proposals to us for a full daylight simulator, the cost of which would have run well into seven figures; but I suggested that we went to Decca, where I had already seen something superficially similar which they had set up to demonstrate to customers the extent of their marine radar and electronic devices. This proved a good route to follow, and Decca carried out the work for not much more than a quarter of what would have been the cost of the original proposal for a daylight simulator.

Other work included support for the British Aircraft Corporation's unmanned submersible, an ocean data buoy, and a fundamental study of fluid loadings of offshore structures. This, of course, was before the Arab/Israeli war, but offshore production rigs for oil and gas in the North Sea were already being installed, although the engineering industry had relatively little knowledge of how the steelwork would withstand such a hostile environment. The Americans had many years' experience from the Gulf of Mexico, where the occasional hurricane would batter these massive structures, but the lower temperatures of the North Sea, combined with the unique and sustained hostility of the climate, made this unchartered territory. This work later passed to the Department of Energy's Offshore Energy Technology Board, of which I became deputy chairman. But during the period 1972–4 the SMTRB was the only active government agency in this field, and I found the work absorbing.

By mid-1976 I had served half as long again as my original appointment, I felt it was time to give more time to my other work, and I was succeeded by Sir Frederick (Tim) Bolton, previously chairman of the General Council of British Shipping. It was interesting to have this minor involvement with the British government machine, particularly in a non-controversial, non-political, quasi-scientific role. I saw over-manning at the lower levels, overworking at the top, and realized how extremely difficult it will be to secure the essential reductions in government spending that must occur. The key to this is not indiscriminate redundancies; it is to reduce the brief, so to speak: worthy people throughout Whitehall are doing their best to cope with a lot of work that is not always really necessary.

Six years earlier, when I retired from the various charitable housing trusts with which I had been associated, I had a comparable sensation: bureaucracy was creeping in, and natural economic forces were gently being eased aside. With the Ship and Marine Board, things gradually became more complicated and less productive. With housing, as the legislative burden increased, the economics decayed: in 1963 the charity would buy a house, convert it into three or four decent flats, let them at reasonable rents, and service the cost without subsidy. By 1969 the same work called for a subsidy of £3,000 or £4,000 per dwelling; this required assistance from central or local government; this needed legislation; this called for administration; and so on. . . . A reasonable test of fairness in a sensible society is that the craftsman who builds a house should be able to buy a house, and that is not an area of progress today.

Generally, in Trafalgar, people are far too busy to take up outside appointments, but in my case I nearly always have one or two. It is refreshing and instructive. At present I have two: I am a director of the Tote and a trustee of the Royal Opera House. I cannot claim to be much help to Covent Garden, but I was glad to be able to lend them money for a few months to help with the purchase of adjacent property; and I give advice when required on the subject of their proposed rebuilding. They will get any profits or royalties that are earned by this book. Lord Weidenfeld, the publisher of this book, is also a trustee. Sir Claus Moser is chairman of the Royal Opera House and, apart from being the Government's former Chief Statistician, is a profoundly sensitive and musical man. I was impressed to find that our son, Justin, who by then had won a music scholarship to Oxford, could keep up when Claus asked him to take part in an hour of Schumann piano duets at a musical evening given by Rosemary and Freddy Fisher. Claus is soon to join Rothschilds as deputy chairman.

The chairman of the Royal Opera House Trust is Lord Kissin, a most subtle and cultured individual who came to this country from Russia via Poland, and demonstrates our extraordinary ability to welcome and take full advantage of emigrés who in turn develop more respect for English virtues than we have ourselves. Harry, with vigour and imagination, does much more than merely raise money for Covent Garden. And behind it all is the languid, willowy and winsome figure of Lord Drogheda, the previous chairman, and author of Covent Garden as it is today. Garrett has a will of iron, expressed with resolute courtesy. He comes from a *Financial Times* background, as does Lord Robbins, now eighty years old, who heads the redevelopment committee.

The Tote is quite a big business – with a turnover of £75 million and profits of well over £1 million, compared with virtually nil when the present chairman, Woodrow Wyatt, took over. When Woodrow asked me to join, I explained that I knew nothing about horses and had no interest in racing. 'That's splendid, you're just the man I want,' he replied, and I give them what guidance I can on financial and administrative matters. The Tote is responsible to the Home Secretary, and its profits, apart from considerable sums paid in levy and sponsorship, are for the benefit of racing, though for the time being a fair part is pre-empted by the cost of the large computerization programme for terminals and displays to replace the 1930s equipment currently in use at race-courses. Woodrow has been clever in choosing the members of his board, who range from the Duke of Devonshire to Frank Chappel, General Secretary of the Electrical, Electronic, Telecommunications and Plumbing Union; we meet once or twice a month for a morning session followed by lunch: the food is not very good, but in all other respects it rates as one of the best lunches of the month!

I mentioned earlier that I sold quite a lot of shares in Trafalgar during the late sixties and early seventies. This was not to reinvest in other businesses – Victor, Eric and I have no outside business interests, and that is how it should be (and perhaps goes some way to explain why Trafalgar itself contains such a variety of activities). My diversification was mainly into works of art. Joyce and I have no formal education in this area, but it gives us sustained satisfaction, and she has good appreciation and a keen eye. Our tastes are very similar and cover a wide spectrum: in pictures, ranging from Brueghel and Dürer to Graham Sutherland, and in *objets d'art* and sculpture, everything from Fabergé to Elizabeth Frink – readers may have noticed the bronze horse and rider which Trafalgar commissioned from her to stand beside our offices in Piccadilly, opposite the Ritz. This is an important part of our lives. We do not specialize in, or pursue, any one category or artist; what we tend to do is assemble a small collection of one particular kind, keep it, and move on to something else. Domestic insurance of these things is costly, and burglar alarms are a nuisance, but well worth putting up with.

I have explained how, after becoming chairman of Trafalgar in 1969, I planned to broaden my life. I have described some of my non-company activities and the pleasure and interest they give or gave me. From these sources I developed an ambition to design and to make things; I wanted a more active and creative hobby as well as the passive satisfactions of observation, judgement and purchase. Boyd Gibbins, the rough, tough, polo-playing builder whom I described in connection with Buckhurst Park, astonished me one evening in 1968 when he told me of his secret desire to be a silversmith. He never became one, but intermittently I would ponder on the idea. . . . We had bought various articles of modern silver and silver-gilt from Gerald Benney, the designer and silversmith, and it must have been in 1973, one evening at a party, that I surprised Gerald by asking him if he would give me a lesson. He agreed, and one Saturday I went to his house, where he works near to us in the country. We spent all day together, completing a rather graceless mug by the evening. Gerald had hit his thumb with a hammer; I was tired, uninjured and elated, and gave him a cheque for £100 for a charity in which he was interested.

Gerald is a part-time professor at the Royal College of Art and at that time also had a London workshop. I am sure he was still sceptical about the degree of my interest, but when the economic collapse began in 1974, he decided to close his London workshop, and asked me if I would like to buy any of the plant. I agreed with alacrity, leaving it to him to decide what I needed. Without going into technicalities, let me try to explain how important this was: lathes, drills, hammers, files, polishing equipment and a forge can all be bought from dealers, though it would be a slow and frustrating process, but the silversmith also has to make his own steel tools of all shapes and sizes against which the work is hammered. These are ground from steel, filed and then polished, and if I had had to make my own, I would still be doing it, or else my repertoire would be distinctly limited. As it was, I was able to purchase from Gerald not only the routine equipment mentioned earlier, but also several hundredweight of assorted tools: an instant, complete workshop.

I had no time for the hobby during the worrying years of 1974/75, but as the builder's work proceeded at our new house at Sonning, we converted what had been a cloakroom in the courtyard into a small workshop, and there the plant was installed. I started work in the spring of 1976 and ever since, when we are in England, I have spent about six hours a week at this hobby. I enjoy the designing just as much as the physical work–perhaps even more so, because I find the two are interconnected, and as I make something, I become more aware of shapes, planes and reflections.

I realize, of course, that this topic is of greater interest to me than it is likely to be to the general reader, but I have illustrated some of the work amongst the photographs. The candelabra weighs about twenty-two pounds, and the wires round the candle-holders are of four colours of gold: green, red, yellow and white. In the flower vase, all but one of the flowers are Vincennes, about 1750; the stems and foliage were cast from real flowers in our garden at Sonning by Johnson Matthey in Birmingham; and the bowl is my own abstraction from the eighteenth-century basketwork in which such flowers used to be displayed. The metalwork is all gilded silver. I do not hesitate to use my commercial connections to get what help I need for my hobby, and I started the flower project (the casting was crucial) by asking Lord Robens to lunch. Alf is chairman of Johnson Matthey and must have been amused by my request – but he has a great capacity for taking pains, and his people at their Birmingham premises were most helpful and co-operative about this small order.

The limitations are physical as much as a question of time: businessmen have soft, smooth hands, and to make one arm of the candelabra called for about eight hours' hot forging with a seven-pound hammer on a blacksmith's anvil; I must admit that I have subsequently accepted help to sub-contract this sort of thing. I find six hours a week at silver and gold work suits me well; I would not want to do more. It is a good hobby for thinking about: by this I mean one can muse in bed, or else, if one has nothing else to do, visualize shapes and techniques for production.

This chapter brings up to date all that I have to say about non-Trafalgar activities in this decade, apart from one event which springs to mind: the Queen's Silver Jubilee. I was surprised to find how patriotic we felt. Sonning staged a small pageant and the High Street was illuminated with a full set of ships' flags and pennants which we had borrowed from Cunard. Victoria was home from Heathfield and Simon from the Dragon School, and we all had a picnic on the local recreation ground. It was sad that Justin had to stay and study at Oxford, where, by this time, he was working hard at philosophy.

With the acquisition of Cunard we had arrived in the 'big time' in terms of public awareness of our existence. This was the moment when the credit-based boom of the Conservative Government was beginning to accelerate and, as I have said, we were unhappy about it. We were starting to generate cash at a higher rate than hitherto; we were deliberately abstaining from the excessive commitment to property that attracted others, and by a combination of direct investment and calculated takeovers we had established the complete substructure for the strategy described on pages 164–5 – particularly the central services that gave us our own resources (in everything from pension fund management to purchasing) of a higher quality than any of our constituent divisions could have supported on its own: we were equipped financially and administratively to take on fresh challenges. In a moment I will explain our top-management structure. We spent weeks and months examining possible extensions to our existing activities, but concluded that in each case we would grow as far as we wished from internal momentum, so we sought no further acquisitions in similar trades; monopoly restrictions might, in any case, have frustrated us. We examined every form of lateral or vertical integration, buying competitors, customers or suppliers, and found nothing large that attracted us.

Up to this point we had adhered to the 'accommodation concept' which I have explained earlier, and were fearful of assuming the 'conglomerate' image. These were the days of Jim Slater and his satellites, John Bentley (Vava-who?) and so on; we were quite different, and determined to remain so. We rejected opportunities – and there were many – to acquire companies which it would be profitable to 'break-up'; we only wanted Trafalgar to develop with enterprises which we would cherish and retain. Victor's personality and nature coloured this paternalistic attitude; Eric had installed systems to service enterprises which would be integrated and improved, and I was concerned with a ratchet-like concept to build, brick by brick, a structure that would endure. I say all this not to appear virtuous, but to record a concurrence of temperaments which characterizes what we did, what we do, and what we did not do. So we faced a choice: carry on as we were, and do well; or acknowledge that we would become a conglomerate, and add something quite different to our range of activities. Cosmetic considerations affected the procedure, but the answer was quite clear: we were ready, able and willing to enter another industry.

At this time the board consisted of Francis Sandilands,

D'Arcy Biss, Henry Longden, Victor Matthews, Eric Parker and myself. The first two were our non-executive directors, and the last three comprised what for some years had been known as the executive committee. Today we have a larger board and more directors of both kinds; but the same basic system still applies and, although there may be nothing particularly unusual about it, I will explain how it works. For clarity I will describe it in terms of our present activities: there are now two consolidated profit centres for printing and publishing – Express and Morgan Grampian – and nine for the earlier constituents of Trafalgar:

UK Building,
Cementation International,
Civil Structural and Offshore Engineering,
Specialist Engineering,
Housebuilding,
Passenger Shipping and Hotels,
Cargo shipping, Aviation and Offshore Marine,
Property,
Investment Activities.

The divisional managing directors of the last nine each meet Eric formally once a week, and their proceedings are minuted. Victor deals with the first two, and the minutes are less frequent; the minutes of all these meetings, plus papers on matters of concern to the holding company, reach the three members of the executive committee on Friday evenings for discussion the following Tuesday at a weekly meeting which typically lasts from 1 p.m. to 7.30 p.m. The minutes of this last meeting are circulated regularly to the full board, which meets once a month. Sometimes people ask me how we keep track of all our activities, and this is part of the explanation; the other part is that every divisional managing director has a financial controller with a direct reporting function to the group finance director. Obviously the system occasionally breaks down, but the requirement is for this fail-safe device in the form of parallel reporting. The divisions themselves all, of course, have their own boards of directors, as do all the operating subsidiaries, and the monthly board meetings of the divisions consider the proceedings of all their subsidiaries under the chairmanship of either Victor or Eric, and their minutes go to the main Trafalgar board once a month. I am not a director of any of these divisional holding companies, but from time to time I join their meetings to get a first-hand impression of the individuals and their activities.

It will be clear from what I have said that Eric in particular has too much to do, and I hope that by the time this book is published there will be fewer people reporting directly to him. Apart from the operating functions, whose reporting I have described, there are regular weekly meetings on finance and banking, and monthly and quarterly meetings on such subjects as taxation, audit, and pension funds. The minutes of all these come to the executive committee, of which I am chairman, and that is how the three of us, with the help of Ian Fowler, the secretary of the holding company, have kept in touch with all that has been going on for the last ten years.

Apart from the monthly meetings of the full board, the non-executives join the executive committee when necessary to consider questions that are beyond the scope of the other executive directors – their terms of employment, for example.

It will be apparent from the way I am writing this book that the reason I mention Victor, Eric and Ian Fowler so frequently is that I see them so often; the only person I see more of is my secretary, Miss O'Dell, who is typing this book. She is an attractive and efficient lady, a few years younger than I, and does much to help me preserve this simple, uncluttered life. She joined me in 1970 at D'Arcy Biss's suggestion, and Victor interviewed her for me, as I was abroad at the time.

Obviously I am not a recluse, but I may be more reclusive than most: Victor, for example, is always eager to see people who approach him, but I nearly always want them to see someone else, at least in the first place. Perhaps my vitality is lower, or perhaps I want to preserve it for a small number of major events – I really do not know, but it may be that I am mildly eccentric in this respect. If so, it is nothing new. I like peace and quiet, music but not crowds, and the company of people I trust and understand. I am amiable, but not extrovert. I observe important men who fill their diaries and their days with meetings and with journeys, and are always looking at their watches. I rarely visit other people's offices, and usually manage a half-hour's walk in one of the London parks during the day.

Generally I know what the time is without looking at my watch. I enjoy my routines, and in the case of Trafalgar they relate as much to the fact of my having founded the company as to being its chairman. The same thing applies at home: we are not energetic or aggressive socially, rather the reverse. And where private and commercial life overlap, with business visitors from abroad, for example, we do less domestic entertaining than others seem to do. Eric and I might exchange family visits once a year, but I have never seen Victor's farm, which he bought eight years ago. We are not unsociable, but we do not socialize. In other large companies the directors and their wives might encounter their colleagues regularly, but with us that is not the case. Our race day at Sandown Park is our only major corporate entertainment. We built the grandstand where our annual party consists of about 1,600 people.

I see from my records that since our foundation twenty-three years ago, twenty-four people have been at one time directors of Trafalgar; currently there are thirteen, and I will speak first about those who are no longer on the board. David Fremantle left us ten years ago, as I have explained. Frank Woodward, the director of Eastern International, who introduced Geoffrey Crowther, left the board in 1963 and later retired to York, where he lives happily with his wife and family. Geoffrey died. Leonard Cooper left when he retired from the Commercial Union in December 1967, and his present life is only marred by a slight inflexibility of the fingers, which inhibits his piano-playing; Leonard's successor at the CU, Horace Frost, joined us on 1 January 1968, stayed until his retirement in 1971, and died suddenly not long after. Henry Longden, Cementation's former chairman, served as an executive from 1970 until the end of 1975, when he retired; Basil Smallpiece was a director for only a few months from August 1971, but continued as chairman of ACT(A), the Australian shipping consortium; he lost his wife, but is married again, to Rita, and is the most vigorous septuagenarian I have ever met. Ted Brian and Norman Thompson, who were two of the first four divisional managing directors appointed in July 1973 as part of our endeavours to make the main board more representative of our detailed activities, left in 1975 and 1974, each in different ways to improve themselves. John Mitchell, who had started with housebuilding and moved on to look after passenger ships and hotels, resigned a few months ago. And Sir Max Aitken served for precisely a year as a non-executive director before health considerations caused him to retire; I never knew him well, but I admire and respect him, particularly for the way he bore his recent afflictions.

I will now describe the present composition of our board of thirteen. D'Arcy Biss was one of the originals, and will be hard to replace when he retires at the age of seventy next year. Francis Sandilands, chairman of the Commercial Union, joined just before our public issue in 1963 and, quite apart from his knowledge of our affairs that results from fifteen years' involvement, demonstrates with us the best qualities of a non-executive director, which I am sure he does elsewhere with other companies like ICI and Plessey, where he performs a similar role. Francis, of course, is the author of the Sandilands Report on the effects of inflation on business, a profound study of great importance. Our other non-executive director, the Marquess of Tavistock, joined the board in April 1977. He is a numerate, alert man, at present a partner in an excellent firm of stockbrokers, and one of his attractions to us is that he is young – six years younger than myself; another is that his connections (I am not referring to the aristocratic ones) are quite different to ours: for example, his elder son's godfather was Walt Disney.

The executive team, apart from the executive committee, comprises Geoff Carter, an old-Stoic chartered surveyor who, as I have explained, came in via Marsh & Parsons and the KHT. He runs the property side. Bill Slater, a sound man in his early fifties, looks after our cargo shipping, and has been with Cunard since he left the Royal Marines at the end of the last war; Vincent Grundy, another sound man, whose father had been managing director of Cementation, now runs our specialist division; Brian Hill, also a Cementation man, is likely to be the 1979 president of the Institution of Civil Engineers – the profession he follows with us. Peter Howell came to us with Willett's, the civil engineering business that

Harold Samuel sold to us after Land Securities bought the Westminster Trust; Peter runs general contracting for us in the UK. Bill Francis, formerly with Tarmac, joined us last year to take charge of Cementation International. The most recent appointment, and the only other executive to come 'from outside', so to speak, is Dennis Groom, who now looks after the passenger ships. He is an Englishman, but recently was president of the Churchill Falls hydro-electric project in Canada. We recruited him when Victor became chief executive and Eric, formerly finance director, became managing director of the whole group, apart from the printing and publishing section.

I have explained how the reporting system filters upwards from operating levels to the main board. Decision-making is delegated downwards in the reverse order; levels are generally defined in terms of money, and it is all set out in a manual. Individuals sometimes complain that the rules are too strict, but generally the decision-making process is swift, and the system usually works well.

16

New Ideas

I have described our 1971 financial condition, our state of mind at the time, and the reasons for it; I have not described the multitude of routine matters and concerns which clearly dominated our proceedings because this book is concerned with strategy and major events. The Cunard story, for example, and particularly the renaissance of the passenger side, could be the subject of a book rather than a few paragraphs, and perhaps one day someone will bring it up to date; but the point of my narrative is to explain that the 'accommodation concept' was more or less complete; it would continue to serve us well, but we had by now the resources, the systems and the personnel to do more.

This was the time of denationalization, and we tendered unsuccessfully for Thomas Cook and for Rolls-Royce Motors. The attraction of Thomas Cook was to start an international credit card business unrelated to a bank. The Wagon-Lits Cook name was as strong in Continental Europe as it was at home, and this would have been a major new enterprise – and an exceptional characteristic of the business was that rarely did they have less than £30 million in the bank, representing travellers' cheques which they had sold, but which had not yet been cashed. The highest bid came from a consortium of the Midland Bank, the Automobile Association and Trust Houses Forte, and subsequent figures were poor, resulting in the Midland buying out its partners. The bank, of course, had no desire to develop another credit card.

We tendered £33 million cash for the Rolls-Royce company; Rothschilds were advising the Government on the sale, and their advice was that a public offer-for-sale would produce more – it did, but after fees and brokerage the difference was small.

I must not give the impression that we were casting about at random. The reverse was the case: we had eschewed purely financial opportunism, the business which we had assembled was doing well and showed more promise than most others; but we were in all respects ready for something extra. Cunard had bought a major travel and package tour business just before our takeover – Sun Air and Lunn Poly, which might have seemed a logical base for development, but we found the business (and other parts of the industry) in such a mess that we decided promptly that it must be sold. It took a year to get it into intelligible shape for disposal, and then we paid the Thomson Organization over four million pounds to take it from us.

The business we eventually selected was Bowater, paper, packaging and newsprint. But before I describe how close we came to success I must set the scene with a few words about official attitudes to mergers and monopolies, and about Jim Slater, whose role was important.

The Monopolies Commission was becoming tougher, and refining its standards, a process which has continued ever since. Our state of mind within Trafalgar was influenced by the Commission's recent rejections of two proposed bids for Glaxo, one from Boots and the other by Beecham: it was conceded in the report that in conventional terms there were no significant monopoly considerations, but the Commission decided that it was preferable for Glaxo to remain independent so that its research facilities should be so. Here was something altogether more sophisticated than crude calculations of market share which was already a potential constraint on aggressive takeovers in existing industries. Later the concept of financial dominance was added: it might be accepted in a proposed merger that there were no monopoly issues involved, but if, through an acquisition, a group of great financial strength was seeking to enter an industry where there were no strong competitors, that too would be rejected. I will not moralize here about the Commission – I could list persuasive arguments for and against all of these sanctions: the point is that things were not what they used to be; the boundaries were closing in.

Jim Slater is an interesting man, never a close friend, but a friendly acquaintance since 1966 when his company occupied a small building in Hertford Street. We would meet for lunch once or twice a year, but never developed any durable association, and I saw, and reflected on, his meteoric career whilst it was going on. He was certainly the most able stock market operator of the period. It is beyond the scope of this book for me to analyse or moralize about the different phases of his career and the changing philosophies which he pursued, but let no one doubt that he is a kind and considerate man. He fascinated the financial press, and believed his own press cuttings; finance to him was a game of chess, and he claimed the role of knight grand master; shares in companies, and companies themselves, were pawns; his involvement was intellectual, not emotional, and much of the game was played with himself and the satellites which he created to join him. His machine thrived on press support, and the image became self-breeding as his powers of patronage grew with the scale of his ability to buy and sell shares, and with the volume of commissions earned by the stockbrokers who were chosen to carry out his business His creation was already pregnant with the seeds of its own destruction when he attempted the mergers of his own organization with what I can only describe as *real* bankers – and it is surprising how near he came to what would, viewed from today, have been the most brilliant coup of them all.

It must have been in 1970 that Victor and I were having lunch with him in his dining room in the windowless basement of his offices by St Paul's Churchyard. Jim was in an expansive mood and, when the coffee arrived, he leaned back and said, 'Let's face it: none of us here are interested in management!' Victor nearly choked, and we left soon afterwards. Five years later Patrick Sergeant, City editor of the *Daily Mail*, asked me what I thought about the latest collapse, and I mentioned John Donne's 'No man is an island . . . ask not for whom the bell tolls, it tolls for thee'. Henry Berens, better educated than I, was able to confirm that Donne wrote those words three hundred years earlier in St Paul's Churchyard. Patrick Sergeant, of course, got the point. I was not referring to him, but to the fact that we were all by then uncomfortably close to what could conceivably become a universal disaster.

In April 1972 Jim offered us his shares in Bowater, nearly 10 per cent of the company. His practice at the time was to assemble and 'warehouse' what were known as 'strategic stakes' in a very wide range of companies, which he would then pass on for a profit to someone who would make a bid; indeed this activity had become more of a retailing operation than the word 'warehouse' suggests. I have mentioned the cases of Cunard and Costain, and there were many others. We liked the idea of Bowater, but rejected it because at the time it seemed that, although we knew of certain weaknesses within the company, Bowater was too much of an establishment concern, with no serious credibility problem with the general public such as we had noted in other cases where successful bids were made.

Evidently there was no one else willing to buy the shares, so Jim temporarily adopted what, for him, was an entirely new approach: he would join with others to buy more shares, join the board, and help to improve the company by his counsel from within. Rothschilds were to be his partners and Jacob his co-director of Bowater. Jim was in touch with Hill Samuel, the company's financial advisers, and if he had stuck to his plan it might have worked well: Bowater would probably have benefited, and so would Jim's image. But then he had another idea; he was always having ideas, and had no close colleague of similar status to try them out on: perhaps the whole Slater story would have turned out differently if Peter Walker had been at St Paul's Churchyard instead of heading a huge department of government. The new idea was this: let Bowater take over Ralli, giving Jim a profit on the value of his shares in Ralli, and giving Bowater his able former lieutenant, Malcolm Horsman, who ran Ralli and wanted independence and recognition. Bowater accepted the plan and, when its £80 million offer for Ralli was announced, the press understandably reported the proposal in terms of the company paying a premium to diversify and, through Jim's good offices, to acquire entrepreneurial top management for itself. The scheme required the approval of the Bowater shareholders.

Malcolm Horsman had spent several years with Jim before embarking on his own, Slater-backed leadership of Ralli, which Jim had acquired in 1969, after he bought Drages from Sir Isaac Wolfson and associates to help to solve the problems of the day. By this time Ralli was involved in a multiplicity of operations, banking and commodities in particular. Its record was good, but certainly one could question the quality of the earnings, and in particular the price placed upon it for this purpose.

Bowater's acceptance of the Slater proposal had the effect of putting up the 'For Sale' signs on its own business, and at this moment Bill Rawlings (the stockbroker who had bought Jim's Cunard holding for us) reappeared with a colleague who knew a great deal about newspapers, newsprint, paper in general, and Bowater in particular. The research and consideration were rapid; perhaps now we could acquire the company; it was worth trying, and would suit us. So we decided to proceed. We asked Rothschilds to act jointly with Kleinwort's for us in the bid because of Jacob's familiarity with the situation. The plan was to make a bid for Bowater that was conditional on the Ralli deal being rejected.

We had found from earlier experience that covert negotiations before a bid were usually unhelpful and often led to personal commitments to individuals that soon became inappropriate. So we arranged to see Jim at 5 p.m. on the afternoon of 31 October 1972, to see J. Martin Ritchie, the chairman of Bowater, at 6 p.m. that day, and then to make a public announcement. The meeting with Jim was illustrative.

Victor and I met Jacob in Jim's waiting room and then proceeded to his office, where several large canvases were resting on the carpet or leaning against the wall (Jim by now was 'into' paintings as he was 'into' wine, not for the product, but for the market). Jacob began a courteous conversation about pictures, for he was the owner of Colnaghi, the Bond Street art dealer's; then we explained the purpose of our visit. Jim began, and finished, with expressions of regret that Victor and I had rejected the idea of Bowater when he offered us his interest six months earlier; but in the meantime he and Jacob had a personal argument that I can only say we felt privileged to witness at first hand: how, in view of their partnership, could Jacob appear acting for Trafalgar with a plan to sabotage Jim's Ralli plans? And how, in view of their partnership, could Jim have launched this plan for Ralli, which Jacob learned of first from the daily papers? Victor and I had not realized previously that Jim had failed to inform Jacob when he decided to terminate their partnership and do something else. This was vintage stuff, and a pleasure to recall.

We concluded with a firm statement from Jim that, whilst he found our intervention most unwelcome, he would be realistic and, after giving Malcolm Horsman the chance to make amendments so that the Ralli deal would look better for Bowater, which he acknowledged would be difficult, he would either sell his shares in Bowater to us, sell on the market, or accept our bid, thereby becoming a Trafalgar shareholder. That is what he said, but not what he did.

Jacob left us then, and Victor came with me to the Bowater headquarters at the top of Sloane Street. This building was one of Harold Samuel's successes from the early fifties, and Bob Chapman had designed it with his colleagues when they were at Guy Morgan & Partners. A private lift took us to the penthouse where Martin Ritchie was most comfortably ensconced with footmen and butler in the extensive accommodation that had been created for his predecessor, Sir Eric Bowater, surrounded by good furniture and fine plasterwork carried out by Italian craftsmen.

Our bid was a good one, £125 million, and the Ralli idea was less good, but our conversation with Martin Ritchie was purposeless. Victor told me as we left that I had diminished our chances by telling Ritchie that his personal future with us would be limited. He was right, but so was I: by this time we were too large and busy for compromise, and it was more important to preserve the integrity of Trafalgar than it was to acquire companies with the complication of prior personal commitments, the point I made earlier.

As I said, the Bowater/Ralli scheme called for approval by the former's shareholders. Because of Bill Rawling's introduction we used his firm as well as Messel's, our own brokers, to analyse the register and divide between them the work of checking with all the major holders, the pension funds and insurance companies, to establish their loyalties. So Capel's and Messel's embarked on a long series of telephone calls to institutional shareholders to classify them as pro-Trafalgar, undecided, or pro-Ralli. There was no longer the option of leaving Bowater as there had been before they accepted Jim's plan, and Victor and I would visit the waverers to help them in their decisions. Shareholders were to vote on the Ralli proposal and, if this was accepted by the majority, Trafalgar's alternative would lapse; if the Ralli proposal was rejected, Trafalgar's formal offer for Bowater (without Ralli) would then be considered by shareholders – and possibly by the Monopolies Commission. Jim, incidentally, did nothing to improve Ralli's terms, and continued to support them.

Victor is a great workmaster, and he would acknowledge today that, if his personal commitment to the Bowater bid had been greater at the time, he might have got from one of our two firms of stockbrokers that extra ounce of effort that can be conclusive. As it was, the Prudential and the Norwich Union were included on the pro-Trafalgar list by one of the brokers, and if either had voted against the Ralli plan or not voted at all, we would have won the vote. We place large insurances with the Norwich Union and, had we known, might have influenced them; and it was two or three years later that I learned that the pro-Ralli vote of the Prudential had been determined by the fact that the Pru felt an understandable loyalty to Bowater's proposal, because they managed their pension fund. But the Pru is our third-largest shareholder.

I was at Wargrave when the meeting took place. Victor went there and graciously thanked Martin Ritchie for his statesmanlike conduct; and then the counting of the proxies began. But I already knew the outcome, because Ian Fowler, who had seated himself beside the representative of the Pru, telephoned me as soon as he observed this investment manager, behind his cupped hand, place his tick in the box that favoured Ralli on the blank proxy he had brought to the meeting. Jim's 20 per cent was voted for the Ralli proposal, and the fact that 49 per cent voted against it meant that nearly two-thirds of the non-Slater holdings were opposed to the idea.

We could so easily have won. I have not disclosed the details of our appreciation of the company, but, reverting to page 164, it will be clear that one of the attractions was that its debt was mainly in sterling, whereas its assets and revenues were mostly in dollars. This was a balance sheet and profit-and-loss-account selection, as well as being an engrossing idea for our operations. We knew that sterling must decline against the dollar, though we did not realize how much further it would drop against the major European currencies.

There were two lessons that I learned: that for a specific

project, one merchant bank or one broker is more effective than two, irrespective of their individual merits; and that Victor's special ability (which he withheld on this occasion) to extract that extra ounce of endeavour from someone, can be of decisive importance. We lost nothing (except Bowater) by the experience, and as with MEPC, it was their shareholders who would have gained; it was only later that I learned that it had already been decided by others that Martin Ritchie would soon leave Bowater irrespective of who achieved effective control of the company: and so he did in December 1972, although he may not have realized when we met that this was inevitable. Malcolm Horsman was soon to recede, and the Ralli idea proved a disappointing dilution to the equity of the shareholders in Bowater.

I must not allow this section of my story to depress readers, or to let it sound as if it depressed me. We were beginning to win in our areas of greatest difficulty, such as the *QE2*. Victor, who did most of the work, questioned whether we wanted more, and I knew quite well that, although we could welcome what was worthwhile, we now had an equilibrium with potential that meant we had no further dependence on takeovers for their own sake.

Some time before the Bowater incident the idea of newspapers had crossed my mind, not as a corporate objective, more a glimpse of something which might one day come our way. I mention the point here because, had we been in the newsprint business in 1977, we probably would not have been allowed by the Monopolies Commission to buy newspapers. This was at the back of my mind in 1972, first a hazy premonition, nothing more; an image of panelled rooms, private lifts, thick carpets and male secretaries; perhaps a film or a novel or a play had provoked the vision. Victor assures me that the black, glass building in Fleet Street possesses none of these comforts. It is odd to recall that Martin Ritchie did – but only for another month.

There is only one other activity of the 1971–4 period that I want to record in my attempt to give the reader the feeling of what it was like to be in my position within Trafalgar at the time. Most human progress involves fumbling and groping for ideas, and in the case of offshore oil and gas we were lucky rather than successful, but the story is quite an interesting one.

Cunard had a fleet of twenty-eight offshore supply vessels, boats that look rather like large tugs and which are used to carry provisions, machinery, anchors, piping and so on to and from offshore drilling and production rigs. This they do all over the world. Cementation were involved with drilling for water in various parts of the Middle East, and in the servicing of oil wells and drilling equipment. Cleveland Bridge and Engineering had ideas for their own design of steel production platforms. So even before the Middle East war it seemed a good idea to draw these threads together and set up a division to enter the offshore oil industry more purposefully. We recruited George Williams, a geologist who had just retired from Shell at the age of fifty-five. He is a nice man, and now runs the Offshore Operators' Association, but probably was not the best choice for our particular entrepreneurial requirement. Now, six years later, we are back where we started, apart from the new plant we built at Port Clarence where we construct giant steel modules for North Sea platforms, and apart from our engineering design services, which are growing fast; but two events in the meantime were engaging and instructive. One was the purchase of 40 per cent of the capital of an American company involved in offshore drilling and supply, and the other concerned the development in Scotland of a complete village and dock on virgin land to build production platforms in concrete. These ventures were both components of our plans to become a major force in this particular industry.

The first episode, the American one, arose from our analysis of the exploratory drilling business. We went through the usual process of considering the alternatives of direct investment in new plant and people, or the purchase of an existing company. This was one of those cases where a company purchase was preferable, partly because the required skills and know-how were quite remote from our own, and partly because the oil companies, who would be our employers, have a very strong resistance to employing contractors who are inexperienced or untried. Only in America were suitable drilling companies to be found, and the first step was for Henry Berens to identify them and examine their accounts. This led to the discovery of a rather strange company, the Dearborn-Storm Corporation. On 17 July 1973 Henry and George Williams went to see them, and on 31 July Victor addressed their full board in Chicago and persuaded them to recommend our tender offer for 40 per cent of their capital. This was successful, and cost about $33 million. The reasons we went for only 40 per cent included the preferences of certain of their large shareholders, and our own preference to move cautiously, in contemplation of 100 per cent ownership at a later date, if we liked what we found.

Dearborn was originally a computer-leasing company, founded by a group of Chicago businessmen who had bought Storm Drilling & Marine of Houston, Texas, as a diversification when their original business began to fade. Storm had jack-ups, drill ships and semi-submersibles, and a fleet of thirty supply boats; in some respects they had more in common with Trafalgar than with these shrewd investors from Chicago. The Chicago group were predominantly small Jewish professional men, accountants and the like, and the Texans were just as one imagines them: giants with large hats, who drank phenomenal volumes of beer and Jack Daniels whisky. On one occasion I arrived by air from London, three hours late for a board meeting at Houston, to find members of both groups so paralytic that I left them arguing amongst themselves, and went to a cinema. It was interesting to visit New Orleans, the nearby Bethlehem shipyard where we placed large orders, and some of the rigs in the Gulf of Mexico. Transport was by helicopter or in the company's Dakota, which had once been Howard Hughes's, and carried a heavy load of liquor for the regular hunting trips during which the company's executives would entertain their oil company customers.

One might have thought that the sudden increase in the price of oil in October 1973, only a few months after we made our investment, would have benefited this particular industry; but the subsequent world depression exposed a situation in which too many rigs had been ordered for the reduced demand for oil. Apart from this, the American authorities became sensitive to foreign interests in their energy industry, and seemed inclined to classify rigs as ships, which have to be American-owned to trade in US waters. There was no longer any possibility of being allowed to buy full ownership, and to run the business with 40 per cent was difficult and time-consuming. So in October 1974 we sold to a larger drilling concern called Odeco who paid us nearly $38 million and took over, and absorbed, the whole company. Their shares fell subsequently.

This, and the next story, show how we had been trying to expand into a market which, although we did not yet understand it, had received a severe set-back.

In the case of the platform building plant in Scotland, we were just as much misled as the Government had been by its own statistics and forecasts of the number of platforms that would be required in the North Sea. In 1974 the official estimate was that between fifty-five and eighty new platforms would be required over the next fifteen years. It seems now that the demand was very considerably exaggerated. Several contractors have lost a lot of money in consequence, and we had a narrow escape.

We were attracted by the idea of these huge orders, ranging from £30 million to £80 million for a single platform, and in 1973 formed a partnership with a consortium which included Marples Ridgway and the Dutch civil engineering firm of Royal Netherlands Harbour Works Company. We selected a site at Portavadie on Loch Fyne 80 miles west of Glasgow, and we bought part of it, relying on an understanding with the Forestry Commission for the rest. But by the time the Labour Government returned in February 1974 it became hard to get planning permission; there were special Scottish considerations, and a specific Socialist commitment that the means of production of these enormous structures should be in the hands of the State. Our design by this time was for a concrete platform, and we were eager to get a move on.

Quite by chance Victor and I both found ourselves one evening in May 1974 at the Park Lane Hilton Hotel where Lockheed, the US aircraft builders, were giving a party in connection with their plans to license or sell rights to build or operate the midget submarine they had developed. Several Ministers were there, and so was Sir Trevor Lloyd-Hughes, formerly Harold Wilson's press secretary, and now an independent, public relations consultant. I mentioned to Trevor that Portavadie was proving a frustration, and he offered to help;

some of the help took place at the party, and some, subsequently, at a higher level.

The result, a few weeks later, was agreement that the Government would buy the land, place contracts with us to build accommodation for five hundred workers, carry out all the civil engineering works, and license us to use the place when we got our orders. I am not in favour of State ownership, but there is no point in resisting offers of this kind. So the Government got a state-owned yard and we got a £15 million contract to build it. But unfortunately there were no orders. We still speculate in my office as to whether, if Mr Heath had won the 1974 election, we would have built Portavadie at our own expense. Victor thinks we would, Eric thinks not: I am not sure, and, of course, a decision of that magnitude would have been for the main board.

17

General Crisis

It is strange to recall how slowly the events of the depression were to manifest themselves. We were busy with all the details of our work, but knew at the time that a crisis was inevitable. What I had realized after the dinner at Chequers at the start of 1972 was that the Conservative Government still wanted simultaneously to pursue policies of full employment and to apply harsh 'lame-duck' standards to employers; it wanted to encourage an investment boom with an abundance of easy credit, and this flow of money was soon to be increased. It had abolished investment grants; but the free depreciation system that I have described in the Cunard context gave us one of the more benign Corporation Tax systems in the free world; nevertheless industrialists lacked the confidence to invest. It is odd to reflect that today we regard as inevitable an unemployment level of twice the amount that so concerned Mr Heath and his colleagues. We were not the only ones to be worried, but the stock market continued to rise for another few months.

The notable U-turn came in April 1972 and I felt from then onwards that the Government, for all its appearance of firmness and inflexibility, was really more akin to a weather-cock responding promptly, but without mental preparation or deep thought, to every brief change in the direction of the wind of popular opinion and international influence.

At the same time we were beginning to see the results of the Bank of England's new policy of competition and credit control. The former predominated, and little was seen of the latter. The policy was announced in a short consultative document issued by the Bank in May 1971, and it introduced what was, by the standards of the time, a revolutionary doctrine: that the principal banks should compete with each other. Over the previous fifteen years, lending had been subject to direct controls, and the clearing banks had been accustomed to operating as a benign, non-competing cartel; interest rates for depositors and for borrowers were almost identical wherever one went, and what came to be termed 'fringe' banks were of minor importance, operating mainly in the fields of hire purchase finance and second mortgage lending.

Competition and credit control changed everything at a time when the Government was deliberately increasing the liquidity of the financial system; and this coincided, for a variety of unrelated reasons, with an influx of foreign banks to London. The whole system was awash with money, including that created by a Conservative Government for virtuous investment in industry, plant and machinery; industrialists remained hesitant with their investment plans and the banks, old and new, competed with one another to lend and borrow money. Quite simply, what happened was that a lot of this money found its way to the property sector and fuelled, if not created, an astonishing boom. In December 1971 the clearing banks paid $4\frac{1}{2}$ per cent for three months' deposits. Two years later the rate was 16 per cent. Stock market prices had risen 80 per cent in eighteen months, and by the summer of 1972 the writing was on the wall, as high interest rates began to sap the confidence of speculators.

In the first two years of the new regime the UK money supply rose by over 50 per cent, bank rates more than doubled, personal advances trebled, and loans to the property sector quadrupled. Perhaps it was increasing competition among the major banks that triggered off this phenomenon; certainly it was most clearly evidenced by the associated boom in property values. But the oddest characteristic of all, now that I look back to those heady years of groundless euphoria, is that the fringe banks – known as Section 123 banks – were licensed by the Department of Trade, but were not supervised by the Bank of England. Huge funds were transferred from the traditional banking sector into the peripheral and less supervised sector, which burgeoned enormously as individuals with their own or other people's money sought out the areas where they anticipated the most profit and activity.

Having described the background, and before I come to the narrative of my own experiences and observations during the period, let me quote the case of a specific property which, in a series of transactions, gives a not untypical illustration of what was taking place. When we bought Ideal Building Corporation in 1967, we examined all its assets and had all its properties valued. Some were worth more than the figures at which they stood in the books, some less, and in every case we adopted current values. One of the assets was a site of just over an acre in the centre of Epsom which we used as a builder's yard. IBC had bought it a few years earlier in the expectation that one day it would feature in the redevelopment of the centre of the town; it had paid £60,000 for it and in 1967 we placed a value of £67,000 on it. We kept an eye on local prospects at Epsom, and if conditions had been more favourable we would ourselves have taken part in the proposed development. As it was, we regularly re-appraised the value of our site, but did not write it up in our books. These were three professional valuations:

May 1971:	£135,000
September 1971:	£460,000
January 1972:	£500,000

By the 1970s William Stern, as well as adding to his interests in residential property, was making an ambitious start in commercial development, for which he had little former experience. As the credit-fuelled boom accelerated we began a cautious programme of property disposals, and the Epsom site, for which there were no early foreseeable prospects, was an obvious candidate for sale. Stern, in his enthusiasm to accelerate his commercial development programme, approached us through an associate who agreed to buy it from us for £1·5 million. Contracts were exchanged in September 1973 for completion the following March. William Stern, who had guaranteed the contract personally, came to see me a few days before the completion date to ask for extra time to pay; I said I must consult with colleagues, and it was with real regret that I had subsequently to inform him that we would give no extension whatsoever. In fact we were paid in full on the due date – and I suspect we must have been amongst the last people to be paid. Stern had become London's largest residential landlord, and was soon to become Britain's biggest bankrupt, with liabilities of more than £100 million and assets of less than £11,000. Today, five years later, the Epsom scheme has still not started, but it shows signs of life; if it goes ahead, our former site might by now be worth £1 million.

I liked William Stern, and in our periodic dealings with him since 1962 his conduct was impeccable. When we acquired groups of flats, as with W & K, he would buy from us the blocks least suited to our improvement techniques, and, of course, one of his main vehicles was Metropolitan Properties, one of the Three Companies described in Chapter 8, which we were not willing to buy on the terms Hill Samuel would recommend. We sold our shares to Stern and he bid successfully for the rest. He was a residential expert, and the only 'operator' of the day who kept flats to rent, when other would buy whole blocks in order to sell the individual flats.

In contrast to his father-in-law, Osias Freshwater, Stern wanted to go places in a tremendous hurry. He had become joint managing director of the Freshwater Group in 1964, but his horizons were not restricted to running 20,000 flats in London. It is a measure of his achievement that, when he split from Freshwater in 1971, his main concern, Metropolitan Properties, had audited net assets of £28 million. It is a measure of his ambition that, by the time he crashed three years later, he had expanded his Wilstar Securities empire to gross assets of more than £200 million.

By the summer of 1972 we at Trafalgar were already in a state of resigned apprehension, but we did not anticipate the depth or duration of the depression that was going to follow the feared collapse. Our shares had reached their peak value of about 165p in the spring of 1972, and by December 1974 they were, for a moment, below 20p. Our spirits tended to follow this performance.

We made sales, as in the case of the Epsom site, but not enough. We were protected from the much greater pressures that affected others by two things, apart from Victor's temperament. Firstly, our main property holdings were of exceptional quality, well located and assembled in the 1960s; and, secondly, we had resisted very strong temptations to get much bigger in property during the early 1970s. In those days we would revalue our properties for our published accounts every three years, and for the year to September 1973 we reported a £70 million revaluation surplus. The following January I acknowledged to shareholders at our annual general meeting that values had fallen, and this attracted quite a lot of more general notice because I was the first person to make this admission in public. In our accounts a year later we simply reverted to 1970 figures, and I contented myself with the statement that 'the entire portfolio is worth substantially more than the book figures now re-adopted'. We still had capital and reserves of £66 million.

I think I can claim fairly that our judgement in the early 1970s was ahead of most other people's, but that is no cause for self-congratulation: the truth is that we could have been more decisive. In mid-1973 we considered selling the whole of our property portfolio, then worth about £125 million, either to a single buyer or as a new company to be sold to the general public. But we hesitated, partly from concern about staff considerations, and partly because I was still getting letters from shareholders (and exhortations from stockbrokers), who wondered why we, one of the brightest property stars from the sixties, were being overtaken in the seventies by so many more audacious operators. And I was hesitant to 'rock the boat' by telling them the reason.

Then came the October 1973 Arab/Israeli war, when the price of oil quadrupled. It is surprising how long it took to realize the full consquences of this, but the gradual decline of sterling against the dollar, and of the dollar against most other currencies, presented us with a host of fresh problems which were only gradually to be resolved with the resigned appreciation that the long-term upward trend of growth that had been going on almost everywhere since I was ten or twelve years old might have come to an end, rather than merely suffered a temporary interruption.

After this came the first of the fringe bank collapses, really quite a minor concern, but worth describing because of the surrounding circumstances, and what they led to. This was 'a cloud no bigger than a man's hand', and is interesting because of what was to follow. It was, I read later, in the small hours of Friday, 29 November 1973, that the National Westminster Bank's chief executive, Alex Dibbs, was woken up by his wife.

'There's a Mr Keogh on the telephone,' she said, 'and it sounds urgent.' James Keogh, head of the Discount Office at the Bank of England, had been called to a late-night meeting hastily summoned by the Eagle Star insurance group at the Knightsbridge office of merchant bankers Keyser Ullman. London & County Securities was going bust – the next day.

London & County was one of the newer City banks that had mushroomed in the early 1970s. It was run by barrister Gerald Caplan, who had graduated to banking via Christmas clubs and a family rag-picking business; L & C borrowed from everyone with money and lent (at steepish rates) to almost anyone who wanted money: optimistic property developers, hardpressed second mortgagors – and even to directors of London & County keen to speculate in their own shares. On paper, its profits looked good. In practice, its bad debts were horrendous. And it could no longer keep borrowing to stay afloat.

The meeting reconvened in Dibbs's office at eight o'clock that morning. London & County opened for business, although its share quote had been suspended after plummeting ominously from 305p to 40p in less than a month. (Bad publicity and desperate bidding for cash had left their mark.) Small depositors queued up to get their money out. Natwest and Keyser moved in to go through the accounts. James Keogh, official monitor of City banking, seemed relatively unruffled. His friend Pat Matthews of First National Finance Corporation would sort out L & C.

Keogh, a convivial Irishman familiar to 'secondary' bankers, could hardly have been more mistaken. London & County's crash, despite that reassuring rescue by FNFC, jolted public confidence and triggered off a domino effect. Large depositors began to withdraw funds wholesale from other fringe banks, just in case. Before long, Pat Matthews was finding it difficult to sort out his own problems. Cornhill Consolidated Group suddenly found itself insolvent; Cedar Holdings (second mortgage specialists) went bust. And as each collapsed, others teetered.

It was touch and go. Labour leader Harold Wilson described bank profits as 'obscene' in his February 1974 election campaign, Ted Heath had earlier referred to the 'unacceptable face of capitalism', Peter Walker had drafted a new Companies

Bill, and the Conservatives had introduced control of office rents. But all this was happening after the bubble had already burst, though people were reluctant to admit what had happened, or why. As whole property empires ran out of credit and reeled into liquidation, Barclays, Lloyds, Midland and National Westminster (prompted by Gordon Richardson, Governor of the Bank of England) found themselves having to devote money and manpower to supporting their former upstart competitors, not so much out of charity as self-interest. If the Big Four had allowed fringe banks to crash on regardless, what the Governor of the Bank later called 'the contagion of fear' could have infected them as well.

To understand how the collapse of one aggressive, but not particularly significant, finance house in November 1973 could (almost) have brought down the entire UK banking system, it is necessary to recall three points. Firstly, increasing competition among the major banks. Secondly, the credit-assisted boom in property values. Thirdly, the super-rapid growth of Section 123 banks that borrowed excessively to maximize profits while the going was very good indeed. Far too much credit had been extended to minor figures in the property business, who by now were major debtors to banks of every description. It was significant that the Bank of England had hardly recognized the Section 123 banks and did little to monitor their activities, pointing out (as was formally correct) that this was the responsibility of the Department of Trade. It was also significant that the Department of Trade, though entrusted with the power to confer banking status, previously reserved exclusively to the Bank of England, had neither the staff nor the expertise to control what 'their' banks did afterwards. In the circumstances, it is perhaps not altogether surprising that some comelately deposit-taking institutions developed unorthodox banking techniques.

I never met him and Caplan, per se, really was not very important; but because of what he represented in this extraordinary period, let me describe a little more of his operations.

He had been confident that his London & County shares could only move upwards, and he borrowed from his bank to buy more, which (in a bull market) had the affect of boosting the share price. He started to do this on the quiet in 1970, running up his *interest-free* personal overdraft with London & County (Foreign) to more than £109,000. But in June 1971 auditor Matthew Patient of Harmood Banner found out, and argued forcefully that these purchases 'had been made to influence the L & C share price during takeovers and acquisitions'. (It was not until much later that outside critics became aware of this practice.)

Gerald Caplan promised to behave himself, repaid the L & C loan *with* interest and the auditors were satisfied. And then Caplan did it again, this time buying through a private company known as Capebourne (without disclosing his interest) on the strength of loans from the Whiteley's store branch of London & County *Investments*. By June 1972 he had run up his new, no-interest, corporate overdraft to £180,000. Once more, Harmood Banner found out. Caplan again promised to conform, undertook to trim the Capebourne overdraft to £25,000 by June 30, and achieved this by borrowing £156,000 from yet another subsidiary, London & County (A & C).

Caplan was not just a conventional banker who borrowed from depositors and lent to clients with a profit margin in the middle. He saw himself more as a powerful tycoon, wheeling-and-dealing with the best of them. Share prices had been rising fast on the Stock Exchange and zesty investors were prepared to ignore conventional yardsticks like price/earnings ratios. What they wanted were 'hot stocks', previously underrated shares that would really motor when it was learnt that some dynamic entrepreneur had taken over and was about to transform prospects with a bid here or a deal there. Someone like himself – or Jim Slater.

Most of this only came to light much later. If old investors had been able to glance behind those new bank façades, they would certainly have wondered. From April 1972, for example, Gerald Caplan had stepped up his support for London & County shares. Colleagues, friends and even customers were persuaded to buy large blocks of shares financed on a 'warehousing' basis by the bank. By the year's end, L & C had lent a startling £3·7 million on the 'security' of its own paper. 'The chairman indicated that the recipients would not lose any money,' his manager subsequently told the Department of Trade, 'because he believed to the point of megalomania that the company was invincible, and the shares would rise to £5 or £6.'

The full extent of London & County's quite remarkable 'creative accounting' was not revealed until the Department of Trade report was published in January 1976. But by the summer of 1973, with the stock market off the boil, Gerald Caplan and other fringe bankers had to be creative to survive. 'Warehousing' deals, where blocks of shares were 'farmed out' (financed by bank loans), with the guarantee that they would be bought back at a profit when the takeover bid was launched, were looking distinctly sick. And overall security had not been helped by lending to each other back-to-back, mostly for personal speculation or corporate 'window-dressing'.

Even the promised reviver of British industry, Jim Slater, had encountered his problems. With one mighty bound, as I mentioned earlier, he had looked briefly like becoming a major pillar of the City establishment, when on 26 April 1973 it was announced that Slater Walker Securities was to merge with merchant bankers Hill Samuel. 'Together they will form a comprehensive international banking group with a market value of £250 million, capable of challenging the big American, Japanese and European banks,' the *Daily Telegraph* reported. 'It will be easily the biggest British merchant bank.' Most papers initially reacted in similar, enthusiastic fashion. But by 19 June, the merger was off. This was the twilight era of the phoney boom, and I have recounted our part in all this.

I have mentioned Jim Slater already, and he has given a clear account of his activities in his book, but no record of the period could be complete without further reference to his effect. He was far more important than Caplan. What may have torpedoed the Slater Walker–Hill Samuel merger was an embarrassing flashback to Christmas Past and an unnerving portent of Christmas Yet to Come. What made things more embarrassing was that Slater was obliged to spell out the extent to which his escalating profits depended on dealings on the Stock Exchange, many with, or between, satellites which he had created or controlled.

By 1966 Slater's avowed policy of taking over sleepy companies, ripping out (and selling off) the loss-making sectors to build up the profitable core, had become received wisdom among Conservative radicals. His keynote takeover of 1968 was the Crittall-Hope metal windows group, whose profits he reckoned to boost 150 per cent. (Whether this target was achieved is open to dispute between accountants. He offered us the company, but we declined.) Characteristically he used the cash and the quoted 'shell' of its South African offshoot to start a local go-go conglomerate, much the same as he had with the assets of Thomas Brown in Australia the previous year. By 1969, as I explained, he had bought through Sir Isaac Wolfson into Drakes, to Ralli Brothers and banking.

In 1967 his bright young men began to be launched into orbit, semi-independently, as 'satellites' revolving around Slater Walker finance, and paying them fees. First John Bentley with Barclay Securities (pharmaceuticals to toys), then Malcolm Horsman with Ralli International (cotton trading and carpet dealing, then Bowater – the best of the lot). . . . Deals came thick and fast, deals within deals, and the shares went up. Insiders did best, but other punters did quite nicely. Somewhere along the line, industrial rationalization turned into pass-the-parcel. Even a mention of the magic name would galvanize any share. Never mind the earnings, watch the price! By the time Slater moved late into property, he had an imperial image to support. 'When do we stop buying farm land?' an agent asked. 'When you reach the sea,' he replied.

Though by the time of the Hill Samuel proposal the details had become extremely complex, the basic facts were quite simple. Slater Walker Securities had made profits of £22,977,000 in 1972. Its *dealing* profits account for no less than £9,205,000 or 40 per cent of the total, though for accounting purposes £5,385,000 had been transferred to 'inner (banking) reserves'. Furthermore, some £33 million of £123 million loans to companies outside the group had also been for share dealing. The company therefore was vulnerable to a stock market downturn. More than £8 million of those dealings' profits had been made in the first half of 1972, whereas the first half of 1973 produced only £4·8 million.

What had made Jim's position more sensitive was that Slater Walker generated much of its profits not by open-market operations but by dealing 'in-house' or with his satellites. In 1972, for example, he had floated off Dual Trust to allow the public to invest in 'young financially-oriented aggressive companies'. Critics swiftly pointed out that this would enable SW to unload stakes in satellites like Allied Polymer, Barclay Securities, Crittall-Hope Engineering, Drakes, Hanson Trust and Ralli International. Dual was promptly nicknamed the 'Dustbin Trust' in the City. It nevertheless produced an overall capital profit of £4·6 million for the 'house'.

As early as May 1972, Graham Searjeant of the *Sunday Times* had commented perceptively: 'The whole circus has become a machine that earns a lot of its profits by generating the premiums that boost its own income – a seething pyramid of escalating paper.' Slater Walker had recently thrown the Hong Kong stock market into profitable confusion by announcing several deals based on Haw Par, which Slater had taken over less than a year earlier – stripping out the bank, the newspaper and Tiger Balm to reinvest the cash. Haw Par was now taking control of the quoted Kwan Loong pharmaceuticals business and the King Fung property concern, 'reversing into' Southern Pacific Properties.

Such was the magic of Jim Slater's name in March 1972 that the market value of Southern Pacific, incorporating a Fijian holiday resort project set up by his associate Simon Pendock, and still very much in the early stage of development, jumped from less than £14 million to £21 million in a single day. By June 1973 when Searjeant's colleague Lorana Sullivan made a flying visit to Hong Kong, Fiji and Australia to see what was actually happening out there, the gilt on his entrepreneurial gingerbread was wearing thin. Slater Walker shares fell faster than the market and Slater announced his conversion to the merits of hard cash.

Something had to give and, as I have explained, it was Gerald Caplan's 'invincible' London & County Securities bank (which had made a last abortive attempt to window-dress the half-year accounts with £4 million's worth of fast-moving cheques in September, and finally passed £5 million through a private account to pay off investors 'warehousing' its own shares). Amazingly, this overdraft was paid off by siphoning matching loans through a £2 property company called Avon Land Securities. Among the bank's top senior management this convoluted scheme was known as 'the total arrangement'. It left L & C unable to withstand the slightest puff of wind.

When L & C collapsed, others quickly felt the knock-on effect. John Morris of Cornhill Consolidated, for example, who had built up a top-heavy group in everything from banking to taxis on a (debatable) capital base of only £2·5 million. With share prices and property values falling as interest rates rose, Morris had cut back on short-term borrowings. (At one stage, he was taking in £12 million of 'overnight' money every day.) He was too late. 'We went from a position of liquidity to a position of illiquidity in about six hours,' he recalled. 'At that time, we had approximately £3 or £4 million of "short money". . . . It was all pulled out in one day.'

Morris kept Cornhill going for a week before appealing for help to the Bank of England. And by that time, James Keogh already had a bigger headache. Cedar Holdings, which had made the most of second mortgages with backing from Prudential Assurance and three pension funds, was bleeding to death, losing deposits at the rate of £10 million a week. (It took the promise of up to £80 million of standby credits from institutions like Barclays Bank and the National Coal Board Pension Fund to stem the outflow.) Suddenly, every fringe bank had problems. Cornhill went down in January 1974 with an estimated £7½ million deficit, leaving Cannon Street Investments short of £2·5 million. . . .

Politicians had already woken up to the fact that some City operators had done some very odd things with shares and were making (or at least had made) rather large profits from dealing in properties. In a belated reaction against the free play of unruly market forces, Secretary of State for Trade Peter Walker introduced a reformist Companies Bill, and Chancellor of the Exchequer Anthony Barber announced a new property Development Gains Tax in December 1973. I have mentioned these moves earlier, and it is ironic that both these well-intentioned measures did little to correct excesses in either market, but contributed in some measure to their collapse.

Uneasily aware that his Bill was designed in part to meet criticism of his erstwhile business partner Jim Slater and his former political colleague Duncan Sandys (whose £130,000 tax-free compensation before taking the chair at Tiny Rowland's freewheeling conglomerate Lonrho had prompted an even bigger City row in the spring of 1973), Peter Walker proposed to make 'insider dealing' a criminal offence, to tighten regulations on takeovers, to debar businessmen from being directors of companies with subsidiaries in which they had personal interest and to ban company loans to directors' families or private concerns.

While Peter was arguing for maximum disclosure, Tony Barber was more concerned about maximum avoidance. Betterment Levy had been a bad tax, he emphasized, because it centred on the physical disposal of land or buildings with development value. Development Land Tax would enable buildings, except for houses and flats, to be taxed for capital gains *when they are first let* (i.e. even without actual 'disposal'). 'In short,' as the *Financial Times* commented, 'the proposal is the latest in a long line of attempts to tap some of the increase in property values – windfall gains – made as a result of decisions by planning authorities acting on behalf of the whole community.'

If Barber and Walker hoped these moves would restore commercial order and political popularity, they were soon disappointed. Prime Minister Edward Heath stuck rigidly to his incomes policy, the miners' strike put the whole country on a three-day week and the snap 'Who Rules Britain?' election in February was won by Labour. Harold Wilson installed himself at 10 Downing Street and Denis Healey moved in next door as Chancellor of the Exchequer, apparently convinced that the new rich had had it far too good for far too long. 'We will squeeze property speculators until the pips squeak,' he had declared beforehand, on February 17. Ironically, the money market had beaten him to it.

By this time the witch-hunt was an anachronism, and these targets for popular public distaste were, for the most part, insolvent, though many did not yet realize what had happened to them.

I have commented already on the inevitability of it all, and the inexorable slowness with which it developed. In the first half of 1974 people generally assumed that a few peripheral financial excesses had led to the usual consequences and that these had been contained by our political and financial masters and, although the stock market was in a dismal condition, it was generally thought that in due course our, and the free world's, economy would return to former trends, and in some way recover from the oil crisis.

The Conservatives, through a mixture of mismanagement and misfortune, had lost the February 1974 election by a small margin, and Labour's first preoccupation was to prepare for an autumn election, which they intended to win with a larger majority; as they did. But in the meantime things went from bad to worse.

It was on 8 May 1974 that Ronald Lyon came to see me; his companies had what he described as 'a slight, temporary, cash flow problem'. He wondered if we could help; and if it would have been worthwhile to do so, we would have. This was the case with so many of them: for a year or two they lived their lives without realizing that they had already suffered or invited a mortal and irreversible wound. Ronnie had some excellent industrial developments, and he left with me lists of assets and creditors. I took less than five minutes to decide that the case was hopeless, because I read the latter first, and it was clear that the lenders were mainly from the second échelon and, even if they had wanted to help, their own pressures from their own creditors would have precluded it. We then looked at the assets, and many were worth far less than they had cost. I had to tell him that there was nothing we could do.

Others came to us, some who had credit from Trollope & Colls for major building contracts, and the answer was always the same. I had known what was likely to happen, but only gradually came to realize the magnitude of the money that was involved. In a newspaper interview in December 1972 I see I made the mild remark: 'Traditionally in times of high inflation people have turned to bricks and mortar as the safest haven for their savings . . . [but] for new investors perhaps the time has come to wonder whether last year's growth has not compressed into the recent past all that might reasonably have been expected in the next four or five years.' This was an unfashionable remark, and had little impact: it was the understatement of the decade.

A fortnight after Ronnie Lyon's visit I met Roy Jenkins,

then Home Secretary, at a private dinner party in St John's Wood. Did the Cabinet, I asked late in the evening, realize that the property and fringe banking crisis was of a magnitude that might come to bear heavily on our whole financial fabric and structure? He, and presumably they, did not.

Fringe banks had been the first to feel the pinch, desperately calling in outstanding loans as they were themselves 'called' by creditors. This meant that over-stretched property concerns were next in line, as higher interest rates and lower investment ratings combined to throw their financial gearing horrifically into reverse. 'There has never been such a sudden drop in values as that between January and May 1974,' William Stern remarked later, 'when the market effectively stopped.' By 17 May, his Wilstar Securities empire was finished and Kenneth (now Sir Kenneth) Cork of Cork Gully & Co. took over as receiver. Ronnie Lyon was another to hand over his problems to Kenneth.

By the middle of June 1974, the first publicly-quoted property company had also called for Kenneth Cork (today Lord Mayor of London). Guardian Properties, run in go-go fashion by Harvey Soning, had emerged from obscurity in 1969 by investing everywhere from Anglesey to Vitry near Paris. (It was symptomatic of the times that one 1969 acquisition where the return did not cover interest costs was described as a 'killing', on the grounds that rent reviews would do the trick 'after a few inflationary years'.) By the middle of 1973, Guardian had bought 1,600 UK shop properties from Cavenham for £17·5 million, was buying its third block in the fashionable Avenue Louise in Brussels, and had bounced into Spain.

In March 1974, Guardian had begun to suffer from over-expansive indigestion. Soning, who came to see us, later admitted publicly to 'liquidity problems' and announced a series of disposals. Altogether ninety-six of the Cavenham shops had been sold for £6·8 million, for example, to show a 'substantial profit'. Two months later, Guardian was reported to be having 'talks' with First National Finance Corporation, whose own problems had not yet been disclosed. Nobody believed that 'they' would let a public company go to the wall. On 7 June, Barclays Bank and Drayton Corporation secured a floating charge. Five days later, Guardian went to the wall with a deficiency of £9·9 million.

Guardian was to prove an exceptional case. 'With every smart operator hocking himself to the eyeballs, rolling over unsecured loans and stacking up paper profits, it seemed to make sense to borrow short and lend long or see how many commitments could be balanced on a pin-head,' Richard Milner commented in the *Sunday Times* in September 1974. 'Now that the hectic party is over, deflated City swingers and their embarrassed financial hosts are clinging on to each other in the cold grey dawn. Because if they all tried to stand on their own feet, several would fall flat on their faces.' We had been thinking these thoughts, but not expressing them, for nearly four years. Mr Milner came to see me in the autumn of 1974, and even he must have been surprised when I told him that, when we received the $38 million from the sale of our interest in Storm Drilling and Marine Inc., the syndicate which had lent us money for the purchase would not allow us to deposit the proceeds with any English bank – there were only three banks in the world, US banks, where they would agree for us to place it, pending repayment at Christmas.

Nobody could say that the Bank of England was well prepared to cope with a secondary banking crisis. The realization that the fringe banks had been guilty of reckless lending may have come as no great surprise, but the size of their liabilities and the extent to which they had meshed themselves into the regular money market to obtain funds was an appalling shock. When a section of personnel was split off from the Bank's Discount Office, specifically to monitor banks, the new Head of Banking Supervision, George Blunden, had a staff of fifteen. It was September 1974 before they accepted responsibility for checking the affairs of more than forty secondary institutions, mostly Section 123 banks. Supervision now had seventy staff.

Perhaps the most remarkable aspect of what was very nearly the Great Crash of 1974 is that so few saw it coming; and even fewer appreciated the full magnitude of the potential threat to the UK financial system. Yet the City of London somehow muddled through to emerge battered, but more or less intact. In the public mind, the Bank of England simply mobilized a City life-boat with a mission to rescue some 'bankers in distress'.

That prime lenders were briskly instructed to sustain the prime offenders in a series of impromptu lash-ups, to avoid their own collapse, may seem a less tidy scenario, but might be closer to the truth.

This is easily forgotten, but supporting no fewer than twenty-nine secondary banks (including super-dealer Slater Walker, property-financing Keyser Ullman, ship mortgagee Edward Bates and hire purchase giant United Dominions Trust) involved even more money than anyone had expected. At the start, the Bank of England budgeted for a maximum of £1,000 million's worth of organized support. At the peak of the storm, life-boat members laid out £1,300 million. Even that would not have been enough if liquidator-in-chief Kenneth Cork had dumped the £500 million of property at his disposal on the market, driving down prices still further and undermining their already fragile collateral. Prudently, he waited for calmer conditions.

And now for rather a long postscript to this chapter of astonishing events: no other organization threw itself into the lending spree with quite the zest of our Government's Crown Agents, who had previously acted autonomously in rather staid fashion for overseas governments, and were to lose £236 million – the most, in this strange period. Their demeanour had changed when Alan Challis took over as director of finance in 1968. In a bid to expand the Agents' own reserves, he decided to expand its dealing offshoot Finvest from £50 million to £200 million within nine months. It had traditionally borrowed from banks to relend at a profit or invest in property. Now with Bernard Wheatley as its money market maestro, Finvest embarked on a remarkable period of speculative enterprise.

In 1969 the Crown Agents backed the formation of Sterling Industrial Securities as an investment bank, lent its first £1 million to Stern, and started financing its biggest single loser. It went into majority partnership (56 per cent) with Jack Walker and Ramon Greene in English & Continental Property Co., swiftly providing the new operation with £8 million of debenture money. Much of its own property portfolio was moved to English & Continental, Challis became chairman and it began buying office blocks. Lending to E & C shot up to £23 million before they started borrowing from commercial sources, supported by 'comfort letters' from the Agents.

By 1972 English & Continental Propery had nearly £100 million capital employed and, following a critical article by Charles Raw in the *Guardian*, a private enquiry headed by Sir Matthew Stevenson decided that this was a bit much for one investment. Eventually, the company was sold to the Post Office Staff Pension Fund for £34 million. This made Walker and Greene (temporary) multi-millionaires and looked quite nice business for the Crown Agents, too. And from the left-over assets, including three 'white elephant' development sites, another English and Continental started to grow. By the end of 1974, the Agents had lent it £35 million. It lost them £42·8 million.

As early as 1971, internal accountant Peter Nowers had written to former Senior Crown Agent Sir Stephen Luke: 'All that has happened seems to me to be evidence that the office has lost its sense of direction. From money being needed as reserves against hazards of traditional activities we are becom-ing geared to money-making as an end to itself.' (Among other things, Nowers was disturbed at proposals to cover up the fact that its clients' account fund was technically insolvent.) Nobody listened to him. But by the time Challis resigned from the Crown Agents in November 1973 to join Wheatley on the board of First National Finance Corporation (another custo-mer), the game was almost over.

Several financiers who had taken advantage of Competition and Credit Control to compete with maximum credit and mini-mum control could not afford to be so brutally straightforward. Labour minister-turned-banker John Stonehouse, whom I met on one of the proving flights of the Concorde, had set up British Bangladesh Trust in 1972 and used its money not wisely or well, but too much. He disappeared from Miami only to be extradited from Australia and sentenced in 1976 to seven years in prison for fraud. Gerald Caplan of London & County is fighting extradition from Los Angeles for alleged grand larceny, after quietly teaching judo in Monte Carlo. Bernard Wheatley of the Crown Agents was charged with corruption, but died last year.

Meanwhile Mr Justice Croom-Johnson is presiding over the

Crown Agents tribunal, where witnesses have been granted immunity from criminal prosecution. The City of London Fraud Squad is still wrestling with the tangled affairs of Cornhill Consolidated. The Department of Trade is trying to decide what to do about its report on Peachey Property under the late Sir Eric Miller, who shot himself. William Stern is bankrupt and living happily in Hampstead. Jim Slater, having fought off extradition to Singapore, explains that he is no longer a 'minus millionaire': he is back in the property-dealing business and writes children's books. And Ronnie Lyon, the last time I saw him, was involved with some huge transaction to fly cows from Argentina to Iran. I really do not know about the others. We were busy, and we had to get on with our work.

The events I have described concerned property people, fringe banks, and banks; but (as it turned out) the lowest of these low points coincided with the announcement by an establishment oil company, Burmah, in late December 1974, that they were in breach of the terms of a huge US loan agreement. The Bank of England, which by then had mobilized the so-called 'life-boat' through which the joint stock banks together put up their huge fund to protect depositors in the fringe banks, guaranteed this $480 million debt of Burmah's, but it seemed at the time that the rot might spread further. In fact it did not, and although there were a few more scandals and failures to come, the stock market began to recover at an astonishing rate and business returned to normal – though it took a year or two to come to terms with the fact that 'normal' did not mean the barely interrupted pattern of growth that we had all enjoyed for nearly thirty years. That was concluded for the foreseeable future.

It is said that the stock market recovery was triggered off by a select group of our most respectable institutions investing no more than £20 or £30 million in buying a wide range of shares in December 1974, having bought very little during the previous months. This action was wise and timely, because by then stocks and shares had fallen in value so far that the liquidity ratios of some major insurance companies were in jeopardy. Whatever the facts and the motives, shares doubled in price within a few weeks, and people's spirits recovered. The true turning-point, largely unnoticed at the time, had occurred two months earlier when Chancellor Healey announced several uncharacteristic aids to industry, including stock appreciation relief.

The market had fallen indiscriminately and far too far. In our own case the value of Trafalgar dropped from £200 million to £20 million, and I had begun seriously to consider making a public offer for it. An outlay of £50 million could still have been financed, and matched within a few months by the sale of high-quality, uncharged assets to leave a business making, at the most pessimistic estimate, £20 million a year. Probably such an offer would have failed, producing merely an earlier recovery than in fact occurred.

I am a faintly superstitious person, and my morale was reinforced when a few weeks later I was having lunch with Douglas Porcas at the Ritz and found a pearl in an oyster I was eating. This was a highly unusual thing to discover in an English oyster and Marcel, the restaurant manager, placed it in a small envelope which he inscribed 'Pearl at the Ritz 14.1.75'. I have it still: it is rather small, and a curious memento of a weird period in all our lives.

In March Edward Erdman, the estate agent, came to see me to ask if we would like to buy the Ritz, or rather the company that owned it. My first question was to ask why he had come to Trafalgar when there were at least two well-known hoteliers whom he must have thought of first; the answer was that he had already seen Charles Forte and Maxwell Joseph, and neither was buying anything for the time being. The financial crisis had passed, but a long period of convalescence was to follow.

Eddie made it clear that as the Ritz was a public company, and because the major shareholders were not necessarily unanimous in their desire to sell, one could not be quite sure what price, if any, would be acceptable; but he had received indications that £1·8 million would do the trick. I was keen, and at first Victor was neutral to the idea and Eric was hostile; then Victor became keen and Eric began to warm towards the idea. We offered what was asked, but got no clear answer, and the matter dragged on indecisively for the rest of the year. Charles Clore owned about 15 per cent of the company, an investment he had made in the 1950s when Harold Samuel was trying to buy the Savoy.

18

Beaverbrook and the Ritz

In February 1976 Joyce and I spent ten days in Barbados. Joyce had had some trouble with her back, and a splendid masseuse called Mrs Easy would come at eight o'clock each morning to our suite to give treament; and at this time I would take a long walk on the beach. I would think about all sorts of things during these walks, generally business topics, and one day I began to reflect on the Ritz: in 1958, when I was an estate agent, we had tried to buy it for a lady hotelier named Mrs Amy Rose, who had backing from Max Joseph. We had gone carefully into prospects for introducing shops to the ground floor; and we looked at the structural considerations that might restrict the addition of an extra floor. This was the first steel-framed building in London, and with what is known as breeze concrete one sometimes encounters erosion of the steel. Friendly engineers found us the original plans.

Now, eighteen years later, we were in the hotel business; we were getting nowhere with the Savoy; we had offered what was asked for the Ritz in the first place, then we had offered more, and for all that the transaction seemed to have petered out. Clore behaved as if he owned the place, which he did not, but his instinct not to sell was correct. I had been going there two or three times a month for lunch since the late sixties, and the establisment was gently deteriorating. The food was mediocre, but the staff never changed and the ambience was enchanting – to me, *la belle époque*.

Control was in the hands of Sir Guy Bracewell Smith through the Park Lane Hotel Company, the majority of whose capital belonged to him. His family came from Yorkshire, and his father had at one time been Lord Mayor of London; strangely enough, my father had been concerned with setting up the Park Lane Hotel Company when he was a young solicitor.

I do not know who was the original developer of the Park

Lane, but I had been told that it remained an unfinished steel skeleton during and after the First World War, standing on part of the Sutton Estate, and then was taken over by Sir Guy's father some time later. I never met Sir Guy, but a friend in Yorkshire had told me of recent sorrows in his family, including the death of his wife. He was to die soon after.

One of the attractions of the Ritz was that it had never been modernized. Most hotels, in seventy years, would have been 'done over' two or three times, and any original charm would have disappeared beyond recall, as one contemporary style after another had been applied in successive layers of current tastes in décor. But this one, particularly so far as the ground floor was concerned, was a magnificent, original artefact, needing only to be restored. What a pity, I thought: the Ritz Company had not the resources in talent or cash to carry out the work; we were uniquely qualified, with Trollope & Colls, to do the job; and reasonably qualified to run the hotel; but it seemed that this was not to be.

As I returned to our sitting room, still musing with regrets about the Ritz, the phone rang. Miss Colebrook said, 'Hello, Mr Broackes, Mr Matthews for you,' and Victor said: 'We can have it for seven pounds a share.' He did not say what he was referring to, and I did not have to ask; I just said, 'Well done.' By this time it was probably 3 p.m. in London. What had happened was this: Victor had gone to the Ritz that day for lunch and in the course of a friendly chat with Mr Grahame, the general manager, he said how sorry he was that our negotiations to buy the place had failed. 'One moment,' said Mr Grahame. 'Have you ever met Sir Guy? He is sitting over there.' This took place in what people now call the Palm Court, and was originally called the Winter Garden. Sir Guy was sitting alone, tired and dispirited, and Victor joined him. So far as he, Sir Guy, was concerned, the place would have to be sold, and he had no objection to Trafalgar. So the deal was done.

My only executive role in the transaction was to help Victor choose the carpet for the Winter Garden. At eleven one morning the furniture was removed, and one carpet after another was spread out before us; it was surprising what a variety of forty- and fifty-foot long carpets were instantly available in

London. There was one which we both liked, and I asked the price.

'Fourteen thousand pounds, Sir!'

'Offer him twelve,' said Victor, and we left. Oddly enough, Joyce does not like it very much – she prefers French carpets.

The price for the company was £2·7 million in cash. We soon let the former grill room in the basement to Max Joseph for £180,000 per annum, and his company has spent £1 million (with us) on restoring the place and establishing there what is already an outstandingly successful casino. (It was there that Max fed us with caviar and asked for our shares in Savoy; see page 182. We have put shops into the arcade to let for another £80,000 per annum. So in a sense we got the place for nothing, or rather for the £5 million it will have cost to restore and extend the establishment by the time the extra floor is finished. It is curious that for seventy years the shopping opportunity was overlooked. The shops do not intrude at all within the ground floor.

Only two senior staff left after the takeover, and a few months ago I was glad to see that one, a wine waiter, had returned. Victor did a clever thing when he addressed them after the transaction had been completed: when asked the usual question about pay, he replied: 'There's no more money for the time being, but you can all have a new suit.'

For the restoration of the ground floor, Victor for a while reverted to his former role of contracts manager, and the whole thing was accomplished with very little disturbance to the hotel and its customers.

I have described this transaction at greater length than its financial significance warrants because, as I said at the beginning of the book, I am giving relative weight to things according to their significance to me.

Late one evening in the summer of 1976 I was sitting alone in the drawing room of our house at Sonning, reading a book about Victorian and Edwardian architecture. I was not surprised to come across a full-page photograph of the Winter Garden at the Ritz; but I was astonished by what I read in the text: the architect was a young man called Davis of the Anglo / French partnership of Mèwes and Davis; he was twenty-six when he built the Ritz; he went on to build Cunard's offices in London and Liverpool; and later to design the interiors of the *Queen Mary*. César Ritz, incidentally, was never much involved with the hotel; by the time it was finished he had begun to suffer from the mental troubles that plagued the rest of his long life.

It was in May 1977 at lunch at the Ritz that I persuaded Victor that we could, and should, buy Beaverbrook. There is no better place in the world than the Ritz dining room in which to persuade someone to do something he is uncertain about. I have mentioned earlier indistinct and hazy images concerning newspapers. My thoughts revived when a publishing business was offered to us. It was on 16 September 1975 that Philip Sober, the partner of Stoy Hayward & Co., who has looked after my private accounts for the last twenty years, came to see us with his friend Graham Sherren, who runs the magazine publishing business of Morgan Grampian. Graham is some years younger than I, but had an eighty-year-old partner who wanted to sell his shares and, for a variety of reasons, Graham was not averse to the idea of a bid for the whole company. Our shares were still fragile and convalescent after the great bear market; we could quite easily have afforded Morgan Grampian, though reluctantly we decided against it because at the time we were apprehensive that our shareholders would react badly to such a diversification. But – and this is important – we examined the proposition with enough care to elicit from Graham his forecasts for the future. Morgan Grampian and Graham Sherren will re-appear at the end of this chapter.

Beaverbrook had for decades used Trollope & Colls for all their building work – indeed, there was hardly ever a time when we were not working there, though less goes on today than in the past. Victor knew Sir Max Aitken slightly, and at one point the latter asked us to examine the development potential of one of their properties, but at the time this came to nothing. I would read their annual accounts, and my first contact with one of their directors occurred at a dinner party at Claridge's in April 1975, where Healey & Baker, the estate agents, were entertaining a hundred or more of their major clients, who included Beaverbrook and Trafalgar. There I met Peter Hetherington. Peter is a chartered accountant in private practice, but at that time he had agreed to join the newspaper group for a period as deputy chairman. He had qualities and qualifications in areas where Beaverbrook were deficient. After dinner we chatted, mainly about National Service, of all things – he had been in the Royal Tank Regiment – and I mentioned that in my view Beaverbrook had financial and management problems which would in due course prove to be beyond their ability to solve. If, I said, they ever needed rescue from the unwelcome attentions of another company, please bear us in mind. Two years later, things came to a head.

Lord Beaverbrook had created a successful group with the *Daily Express*, the *Sunday Express* and the *Evening Standard*; but his objectives concerned power and politics; the company was overmanned, bereft in several areas of normal management, and undercapitalized. His son Max came from a most distinguished war-time background, and a successful record in major sailing events, but he was not a businessman. A large block of shares had moved from Rupert Murdoch to Max Rayne, then back to Murdoch, and then to Jimmy Goldsmith. But voting control was divided between Max and various of the trusts which his father had established in New Brunswick, Canada. Unlike the Savoy, there can be a case for non-voting shares with newspapers, television contractors, and the like. But here the trusts were precluded from adding to their investment, and the company was becoming critically short of money. Max had had more than one stroke, and some of the directors were at odds with one another. A struggle for power was under way between people who were none of them completely qualified to exercise it.

The active part of this story lasted from January to July 1977, and the main action only took eight days. But before I describe the acquisition itself, let me revert to Victor and his state of mind at the time. He was morbid and morose, and yearned for the days when we had both run individual operations. He had bought a house on the Isle of Man, and sometimes would talk of retirement to a place of moderate taxation; his horses, which were costly to maintain, were not winning races; admittedly his son was doing well at golf, but not at school; and his wife was unwell, and had been for some time. I had heard of these problems before, but this time it was more serious, and I had to face the possibility that we might lose Victor altogether. I do not want to sound flippant, and there were several other good reasons to want to buy a newspaper group which, whatever its problems, sold more than twenty million papers per week; but I must admit that at the forefront of my mind was the desire to see Victor once again engrossed in a challenge – something that would gratify and occupy him, leaving free part of his time for all the rest of Trafalgar where we would have missed his wisdom, experience and judgement. And, as I pointed out, it simply was not possible to go back to the personal management of individual segments of Trafalgar: it might even have transpired that we had subordinates who did it better!

The fact was that we needed another activity. With the exception of shipping, all our divisions were in good shape: they were growing spontaneously, and we had no large acquisitions in mind. Cargo shipping was a worry for two reasons: profits were under pressure, and because of our uncertainty about the future, our planned investment in further new tonnage was unlikely to take place. This second point is important, because it seemed likely that where previously we had been expecting to invest a fair part of our increasing cash flows in ships, there would now probably be no further investment, and perhaps even a dis-investment. Our cash flows were growing and the prospects of putting them to gainful use were receding. So in terms of strategy we were faced with the choice of adding another division to Trafalgar or merely resting on our laurels, collecting our revenues but under-using our resources.

Beaverbrook was not the whole answer by any means, but it was a step in the right direction, and when we decided to take this step it was not just to acquire three newspapers: it was to establish a new division of Trafalgar, of which the papers would form part. Other publishing ventures were to follow, creating a division of worthwhile size to cover a widening definition of what we termed the 'communications concept', sectors of which we judged to be good growth prospects for the years ahead. Having acquired Beaverbrook we would proceed rapidly with the kind of diversification they themselves should have pursued in the past, and perhaps would have done if they had had the resources to do so.

Victor knew perfectly well that the labour problems in Fleet Street were amongst the worst in the country; and that Beaverbrook, as one of the weakest members of the Newspaper Publishers Association, was as guilty as any of the proprietors for allowing this situation to develop. I had to convince him that he had better qualifications than anyone else to overcome these and other problems; that he would be successful; and that Trafalgar would not suffer in the process. This procedure covered many months, and sometimes my absence from particular meetings may have been helpful – if I am present at a meeting, then in our subsequent conversations he dwells on the problems; but if I am not there, he later gives me a more balanced narrative. I am not being boastful in this story – the person with the best chance to sell something to Victor is himself.

It is not necessary to own the Ritz in order to enjoy there an atmosphere of calm self-confidence and well-being, but I must admit that on this occasion it helped. He agreed that we should proceed, but only on the basis that he would have independence to run it as an individual; he would take only one or two key people from Trafalgar to help him; and it would *not* be integrated in the way our other acquisitions had been, for fear of what I can only (politely) call cross-infection. Another good reason for this approach was that Beaverbrook personnel were used to the idea of working for one dominant personality. Personalization would be better than vague, corporate ownership.

Now for a short account of how it came to happen. Jocelyn Stevens, managing director of the Beaverbrook Press, had made a tentative approach to Victor in January; Simon Jenkins, then editor of the *Evening Standard*, came to see me in March; there were well-publicized disagreements within the board of the company; they were short of cash and were losing money, and Max, the chairman, was seriously ill. It was fairly common knowledge that talks were taking place between Beaverbrook and Vere Harmsworth, now Lord Rothermere, who controlled the *Daily Mail* and the *Evening News*. A full merger

I

was improbable, but Lord Goodman was involved in their negotiations, which might have resulted in the sale and subsequent closure of the *Standard*.

Rupert Murdoch had expressed an interest in the whole of Beaverbrook, as had Tiny Rowland and Jimmy Goldsmith; and there were other approaches, some of which were described to me as 'by stealth rather than by wealth'. The bulk of the company's capital carried no votes, and voting control was shared between Max and two trusts set up by his father.

Evelyn de Rothschild, Jacob's cousin and chairman of the bank, was a non-executive director of Beaverbrook, well placed to understand what was going on and to influence the outcome. In the course of lunch at Rothschild's early in May I commented on Beaverbrook's evident travails and said we might be interested if the company would like us to help – but we would not take part in a Dutch auction; a fortnight later Victor saw Evelyn at Sandown Park where the latter is a steward and we were having our annual race-day. Evelyn said now was the time to decide if we were interested; the next few weeks would be critical.

June 1 was Derby Day, and that evening Evelyn came to see us with two colleagues at my offices. I remember the day particularly, because he wore formal dress and carried the print of the photo-finish. By now I had sounded out senior colleagues and was able to state that, subject to terms, and provided Max and the trusts would commit their shares to us irrevocably, we were prepared to proceed to the next stage. This involved, amongst other things, the exchange of certain financial details, agreement with the Takeover Panel about how the consideration would be split between the voting and non-voting shares, and government clearance in the form of an assurance that the proposal would not be referred to the Monopolies Commission. In fact the Aitken commitment was not forthcoming until the last minute, but the other procedures commenced the following day.

I met Max for the first time on the afternoon of Monday, 20 June. Victor and I went to his flat in Victoria where he received us in a small, warm sitting room, wearing a dressing gown. Speech was difficult for him at that time, but his brain was clear and after half an hour he told us that he had made up his mind, though he emphasized that we should not necessarily assume that the trustees would agree with him. By this time three merchant banks were involved – one for the trustees, one for us, and one for the company. Speculation in the press had fluctuated between Harmsworth, Murdoch, Goldsmith and Rowland, and it was not until the Thursday of that week that our name was first mentioned. All had indeed been negotiating with one faction or another, and some made assertive statements to the newspapers. Pressures mounted abruptly.

Within Trafalgar we had two thorough discussions at the main board and fixed our maximum price, at about £15 million. This was telephoned to a meeting of the Aitken trustees from our boardroom in Berkeley Street at 11 a.m. on the morning of Thursday, 30 June. A few minutes later Evelyn phoned to say he was coming to see us at noon. We met in Victor's room; the decision was still uncertain, but all were determined to settle the matter one way or another by the end of the day.

After half an hour of detailed and determined discussion, we parted: Evelyn would return to the trustees meeting. I left for lunch with a director of the British Aircraft Corporation, who had invited me to hear about developments that had taken place with the unmanned submersible since I left the Ship and Marine Technology Requirements Board. Things were going well there, and it was nice to have this change of subject for an hour or two.

I returned to my office shortly before 3 o'clock to give an interview to a journalist named Taylor from the *Sunday Telegraph*. As we sat down there was a discreet buzz from the private telephone which connects Victor's office to mine. 'We've got it,' he said; and Mr Taylor got an exclusive interview which filled half a page of the next Sunday's paper.

Because the affair was central to Fleet Street itself the story got wide coverage, and in no time at all Victor was on television and radio, and giving interviews to writers and journalists from all over the world. Politicians take newspapers very seriously, and soon he was accepting invitations to visit the Prime Minister, the Chancellor of the Exchequer, Mrs Thatcher and so on. He enjoys it; he says (and I believe him) that he likes it because these are things he could never have expected to do, and he is as much curious as committed; he enjoys much of it on a once-only basis and he looks forward to coming back to spend more of his time at our head office; but for the time being this is deferred, because we now find that printing and publishing is an even bigger growth prospect than had been expected, and it must be pursued to another stage. Consequently he spends nearly half his time in Fleet Street.

We do not delude ourselves regarding the ability to manipulate public opinion, and that was never the objective. Politicians, as I said, take the press very seriously, but sometimes, with a print of millions, I think that we are addressing only a few hundred politicians who are extraordinarily sensitive to what they and their colleagues read about themselves in the papers. The man-in-the-street in this country has a profound individuality of judgement; we give him information and news, and we offer what I hope are thought-provoking opinions, but his conclusions are his own. Each day's leading articles come in draft to Victor, and sometimes if Eric or I are there we might say, 'Why don't you put in something about . . . ?' But beyond that, we do not interfere. Victor's judgement is good, and so far the only editorial errors have concerned matters about which he was not consulted in the first place.

We would not have chosen to have our first industrial dispute so soon after the purchase, but a trial of strength was predictable . . . and it occurred when some engineers removed from the premises certain vital parts of machinery, thereby suspending production of the *Daily Express*.

When he is ready, Victor must tell the whole story, because it is his. Jocelyn Stevens, now deputy chairman of *Express*, displayed great vigour and energy; Peter Coles, Trafalgar's director of personnel, played a leading role in terms of technical advice, and even went to Blackpool where certain prominent figures were then at the TUC Annual Conference; and Victor produced a list of eighteen conditions without accepting which these men, who had been sacked, would not be re-engaged. The crisis reached its peak on a Saturday, by which time we had lost several hundred thousand pounds. Victor telephoned me four times; the third call was just after lunch, and I asked him where he was: 'At home, doing the washing

up,' he told me. This was wise. Coffee and sandwiches at
Number Ten never seemed to me the way to deal with these
things.

'They seem to have agreed to everything,' he said, in dole-
ful tones.

'Then why do you sound so depressed?' I asked.

'Because it's been too easy,' he replied. He sounded more
cheerful when he rang at tea-time to say the matter was settled,
but after consideration one more issue remained to be
negotiated.

The problems continue, but currently the *Express* has fewer
troubles than other papers. Victor wants to produce more
papers rather than to have fewer people. Several plans have
been examined and rejected, and, at the time of writing, the
proposal for a new national daily, the *Star*, seems the best. It
will give gainful employment to people who already work for
us, and give full employment for the modern plant and
machinery which we already possess. I will not say more at the
moment (October 1978) because, by the time this book is
published, the destiny of the *Star* will be clear.

Just before the leak about the Beaverbrook acquisition
Joyce and I had been to lunch at Hinton Manor near Oxford
where Nicholas Davenport was entertaining Peter Jay before
the latter's departure as Ambassador to Washington. One of
the guests was the solicitor Ellis Birk, and Ellis said to me,
'Lew [Lord Grade] wants to meet you.' We made a date for
Victor and myself to go to ATV for lunch, and this took place
on the Monday following the Beaverbrook announcement.
Beaverbrook held about 8 per cent of ATV (now Associated
Communications Corporation), but the reason for Lew's invitation was that he knew that the Reed shareholding in ATV
(over 20 per cent of the voting capital) might soon be sold
and, having considered hundreds of possible buyers, thought
that Trafalgar might be preferable. Ownership of newspapers,
of course, by now disqualified us in terms of the Annan
Report's proposed shareholding ceiling, but we became friendly,
and Victor joined the board of ATV. Lew treats us kindly and,
at his party after the 1977 Royal Command Performance, Joyce
and I found ourselves seated at a table for ten with Prince
Charles, Shirley McLaine, Bob Hope and Harry Belafonte.

I had little to say to these people, but it was nice to be there.

Soon after Beaverbrook, Morgan Grampian came back into our lives. Graham Sherren explained that the fears which had prompted his visit two years earlier had been well founded; he was a substantial shareholder himself, but now another group was gaining ground and he found this unwelcome. We knew that we wanted a magazine business, but that was for 1978 or 1979. The choice of the timing, however, was not ours, and we announced a £21 million cash offer for Morgan Grampian in December 1977. This gave us thirty-six UK periodicals and another twelve in the USA. Last year the business made more than £3 million, and this year will make over £6 million; we agreed to make the bid, although we were not ready for it, because there would not have been another chance and because Graham's forecasts from 1975 were all being fulfilled.

When we bought Beaverbrook, just as when we bought the Ritz, there was a certain amount of cynical comment from the City and elsewhere about 'ego trips' and 'self-aggrandisement'. There is no doubt that the ownership of newspapers gives us greater weight and influence than we had before, but what I have written will make it clear that in newspapers, printing and publishing we have put together a unit which is likely in a year or two to be one of the largest of its kind in the country.

The next chapter is the last, and readers should not expect too much of it in terms of forecasts. Let me explain why with an example from the past: I remember lunch at the Ritz in the summer of 1971 when Douglas Porcas, the senior partner of Hampton & Sons, asked me to meet Geoffrey James, a young property developer who was to be one of the few survivors of the 1974–75 depression. 'You must be terribly bored, Nigel. What on earth are you going to do next?' Douglas has asked this question on more than one occasion, and hardly ever have I been free to give an answer. That morning Trafalgar had passed the formal board resolution to bid for Cunard, but the public announcement was not to be made until late in the afternoon, after the Stock Exchange had closed. I enjoyed my lunch, but was not free to tell them what, if anything, I was going to do next.

19

Conclusion

One of my reasons for writing the book is to describe twenty-five years of adult life in an environment which it may be difficult for people to recall in a few years' time. If I now had the chance to set out on a similar course, I would be surprised to get as far as I have in terms of creating a business and making money – two things which generally go together. Money is needed for growth and it is an index of success; and, from a personal point of view, money contributes to privacy, service, pleasant surroundings and leisure to think, all things which I value.

The story makes it clear that I am interested in what I do, and that I enjoy it; in fact, I am probably luckier than most men because much of it fascinates me. This raises two obvious questions: given the chance, would I try to do it all over again? and would I recommend someone else to? The answer to the first question is 'yes', and the second causes me to reflect on current trends that would make me hesitate to give the same advice to someone else. The acceleration of my career paralleled the extended post-war boom, but now, I think one must assume that the kind of sustained, universal growth to which we all became accustomed will not return in the foreseeable future. Of course there will always be entrepreneurs and mobile, even virtually stateless, businessmen, who make a lot of money from this or that. But the odds have changed, and readers may be surprised to hear that I would recommend young people seriously to consider working their way to the top of large, existing organizations rather than embarking on solitary enterprise. We need both kinds of ambition but 'life at the top' can be sweet, and if that is one of an aspirant's objectives, I suspect the chances now are better through the major, established corporation route. The trouble is that real returns on industrial investment have gradually been falling for fifteen years or so, and by now they are far too low. Our society, with such a large public sector, becomes increasingly dependant on the private sector, but there is not a great deal that can be done by politicians or anyone else to reverse a trend that is evident in many other countries as well as our own.

My simple plan for business life was to learn about property, to develop property to create surpluses of capital value, and to direct these capital surpluses into other fields that interested me and where they would be useful – often into areas where established companies had been able to earn moderate revenues in terms of routine trading, but not enough, allowing for the effect of inflation, to accumulate capital resources to invest in the future. Now, unfortunately, it is not enough to possess the resources, because less and less direct investment in ships, machinery, aircraft and so on, is worthwhile. Twenty years ago there were innumerable opportunities, and it was hard to raise the money from a staid, reactionary financial system; now the situation is the reverse. This describes a condition of the free world, not just of the United Kingdom. We need enterprising individuals to direct themselves towards industry, at least for the rest of this century; and I mention here some of the reasons that make this course relatively unattractive to those concerned.

But first let me illustrate my restricted-growth point with the example of my own company: our profit projections are encouraging but we worry about levels of activity elsewhere. Over the next five years Trafalgar would like to invest as much as £350 million in new plant and equipment, but on current forecasts no more than £150 million worth will be worthwhile, in which case the rest will not take place. Shipping is the main disappointment in this context, though I am still hopeful that, at the very least, we will be able to justify orders for one or two new cruise ships – but today this can only be done with the aid of very large subsidies from the governments of whatever countries they are built in. Ironically enough, property work in all its forms, most of which Trafalgar follows, has a reasonably promising future. Like any other occupation, property development should not be undertaken as a cold financial manoeuvre; it works best for those who are emotionally committed, and they have to be numerate people with an instinct for valuation.

Britain's post-war productivity record is lamentable, and one must remember that, in fact, we have been receding for more than a hundred years by comparison with other advanced countries. The management record is not good and education probably is one of the root causes; just as much as ever, we fail in technical education to enthuse or qualify young people to be innovative and productive. Perhaps it is even worse now than it used to be in this respect: a social premium applies to artistic, 'service' and financial pursuits by comparison with industrial ones. And in the past there must have been greater social mobility, at least from one group to another, between the two. Differentials are muted by high rates of personal taxation, and it is not surprising that for those who have the choice, a non-industrial, metropolitan life offers the best prospect of a satisfactory existence.

We must remember that many public schools were developed in the eighteenth and nineteenth centuries to produce the young men we needed then for an expanding empire. As we possess the system (whether or not we would have introduced it now), and as the state system gets worse, I chose public schools for our children, and they will probably make the same choice for theirs; but the system is not entirely relevant to today's requirements, and this creates problems of a degree we have not yet come to grips with. I fear that we educate too many people towards expectations they are unlikely to realize, and too few who are likely to prefer careers in industry. Employment prospects for a fair part of this population are not good.

It is traditional to use the epithets 'French' or 'Dutch' to traduce activities or articles for which these nations were not, in fact, responsible – but we really ought to study the way in which the French deal with higher education; and we should examine what now is called the 'Dutch disease'. This is something we have contracted here, and without infection from Holland. Natural gas from the North Sea came first to them, and in relatively larger quantities than it has to us. This leads to a temporary situation where industrial decline and rising unemployment are made worse by a strong currency, unsupported by real performance, and evidenced by an exchange rate whose firmness makes the underlying malady harder to correct. The recent revolution in Iran will exacerbate this problem. For us oil and gas will last for a decade or two on a scale that will mask some of the problems, and then, if we are not careful, we will find that we have 'deindustrialized' too far ahead of the 'post-industrial' era. We must manufacture and export in order to live, and these activities become profitless when an unrealistic exchange rate is bolstered for the time being by a temporary surplus of energy resources.

The 'English Disease' is another well-known malady, and it has been my belief for many years that we led the way with this affliction, rather than suffering it exclusively. There are now signs that in Continental Europe and in North America similar symptoms are to be found. We may well have been leaders in this respect, and we can lead the way out. If that is so, and I believe it is, we need general public recognition of the problem and a programme of solutions that requires more than the life of a single parliament to implement. Education and re-industrialization lie at the root of the solution, and we should be grateful that the North Sea gives us time to make and implement our plans.

The sort of general growth we were used to is unlikely to return in the meantime, and we must all get used to a different situation altogether. Many economic and political mistakes have been made in this country in the last few decades and, until recently, none seemed to matter too much because the world was growing: standards of living still rose at home, even if foreigners did better. I may be wrong, but I think we now have to plan for a situation entirely different to anything we have seen since the war.

When the world was growing, we were carried along with the tide; and Trafalgar benefited from spotting some of the anomalies exposed by Britain's isolated poor performance. Now we must all (not just Trafalgar) come to terms with the new situation: nationally we must encourage reindustrialization at home, investment overseas and the cross fertilization of mental attitudes that this should breed; educationally we must make young boys and girls aware of recent history and of what will most be needed in ten or twenty years time; and socially (at least) we must create the right differentials in terms of gross as well as net pay. In Trafalgar ... perhaps less centralization and more incentives. For our children? Foreign languages, open minds and, above all, an awareness of the best qualities that are English.

Appendix

Lecture given to the West London Branch of the Chartered Auctioneers' and Estate Agents' Institute on 7 February 1967

The Future of Property Companies

In the last five years, property companies' shares quoted on the Stock Exchange have fallen in value by nearly 45 per cent on average, although most property values are higher now than they were in 1962. This presents a sombre background against which to discuss the future of property companies. Every year since 1960, the Finance Act has introduced new provisions affecting property companies. Corporation Tax has dealt the most serious single blow to the conventional property company, but there are quite a number of other tax considerations which I must mention.

I think it will be agreed that inflation is likely to continue throughout the foreseeable future and that property values are likely at least to keep pace with it. If the owner of investment property is able to mortgage such property, the leverage effect results in his equity increasing in value at a greater rate than the rate of inflation. The arithmetic of this is that if inflation runs at $3\frac{1}{4}$ per cent per annum compound, the monetary value of an article which keeps pace with inflation will double every twenty-one years. If property follows this pattern and is purchased with the help of a two-thirds mortgage, the value doubles in twenty-one years, the debt remains constant and the value of the owner's equity increases fourfold, or twice as fast as inflation: in the meantime, the property has produced a reasonable income. This combination of property-owning, gearing and inflation represents a uniquely attractive investment medium. It seems safe to assume, therefore, that well-chosen and well-managed property investments will continue to be highly satisfactory investments. Very few individuals can find, buy or manage what they require, however, and I fear that mortgages will continue to be extremely hard to arrange for the private investor. Consequently, the ease, the convenience and the marketability of investments in quoted property companies are likely to attract a growing amount of private investment and I think that such investments will soon return to favour. No practical alternative exists in this country for the small investor who seeks a stake in good investment property.

Another background matter to be considered in this context is the future of property development. Here again I feel quite safe in stating that one can reasonably assume for this purpose that, despite the many controls and restrictions which seem to be stifling our business, a high level of profitable development will recommence in due course. There is certainly a mass of work which needs to be done and this is one of the reasons why I feel a rather unfashionable degree of confidence in the future of property companies. But this confidence applies only to companies whose managements are alert to fiscal considerations and who take all the appropriate steps to place themselves and their capital structures in the best posture for profitable operation under the law as it now stands. Companies which fail to respond to these factors will not have a very bright future, and this remark includes companies which may have outstanding management from a purely property point of view.

A Look at the Past

I expect you are all familiar with the Financial Times Actuaries' Index of property share values, which started in April, 1962, with the basis of 100. By May, 1962, the Index had risen to 112, but it has fallen fairly steadily ever since and, despite some recovery during 1966, it now stands at 61 points. This represents a fall of 45 per cent from the peak, but several well-known property companies have done even worse. This, apparently dismal, performance needs to be considered very carefully in the context of a longer period of time.

From 1957 to 1962, property shares enjoyed an extraordinary boom. The only index by which one can measure this boom is, so far as I know, that maintained by a firm of stockbrokers who specialize in property shares. Between January 1958, and January 1962, this index rose from 100 to 520 and although it has since slipped back to the 300 level, there remains a threefold gain. During the same period, the Financial Times Index of ordinary share values increased slightly less than twice.

This ten-year period from 1957 has, of course, been quite exceptional and one now suspects that a once-and-for-all adjustment was compressed into this short time to compensate for the decline, spread over 35 years or more, in the purchasing power of our currency.

Although statistics are scarce where property companies are concerned, movements since 1930 can be traced through them. In general terms one can say that in this period the purchasing power of money and the value of an investment in Government stock decreased by two-thirds and that ordinary shares, which rose in value nearly three times, just failed to keep pace with inflation. Property company shares, on the other hand, beat the cost of living by a useful margin, and the value of a private house did best of all, increasing by nearly ten times. In taking this brief look at the past it is important to recognize that many property company managements must have been more conditioned to deflation than to inflation, and their gains would have been more spectacular if they had been able to foresee so much long-term continuing inflation.

I should make it clear that much of what I am saying is based on the expectation of continuous, controlled inflation: if this assumption should prove false, some of the policies I am going to advocate will turn out to be unsound. At present we have the freeze and the threat of a more permanent control of prices and incomes to succeed it. The Government have deferred charging reversionary rent increases to which they may be entitled as landlords until the period of severe restraint comes to an end, and if everything was to be frozen indefinitely, one would need to make other plans. But it is interesting to see that under the Rent Act, 1965, reversionary increases on residential properties are being awarded without any deferment and that much of the concern for controlling wages and prices relates only to the rate at which they are to increase — not to the indefinite maintainance of present levels. In fact, part of the Government's policy has been to remove surplus purchasing power from the general public; landlords, by increasing rents to full market levels wherever possible, are helping to do this. Indeed, we must recognize that what the Government take from us with one hand, they often return with the other. We may complain of unfair taxes, but we must remember that the ever-increasing demand for space by central and local government is a vital factor affecting rental levels.

I have been trying to demonstrate that investments in property have done well in the past and can be expected to do well in the future, and that investments in the shares of a quoted property company will continue to be particularly attractive as the only property investment medium available to the general public. The combination of tax and other controls which has caused the 45 per cent decline in share values over the past five years may well present a very good jumping-off point from which these shares could become popular again within a year or two.

Corporation Tax

I will now try to deal with the main characteristics of Corporation Tax and the reasons why many respectable property companies' shares stand at discounts of as much as 40 per cent compared with the value of the underlying assets. Corporation Tax is a species of double taxation. If an individual owns a property producing a net income of £100 a year, he receives that amount and pays income tax and surtax in the normal way, as he would on any other form of income. If the same individual owns the property through the medium of a company, the company first pays 40 per cent Corporation Tax and all that remains for distribution as dividend is £60 gross. One can extend this illustration on a larger scale to describe how Corporation Tax affects a public property company. To take a simple example, assume the company has £1 million's worth of property producing a net income of £70,000 before tax. Corporation Tax absorbs £28,000, so the maximum dividend that could be paid is £42,000 gross. If the quality of the properties were good, one could reasonably expect the shares of this company to stand on a $5\frac{1}{2}$ per cent dividend yield and, in that case, the value of the company's shares on the Stock Exchange would be only £750,000. This simple example explains why no new property investment companies have been floated for some years.

The situation is very bad for the industry as a whole, for apart from ruling out new flotations, it limits the capacity of existing companies to grow, because to raise fresh equity, even by means of rights issues, presents a problem which can be solved only at the expense of existing stockholders. I would like to distinguish the problems which face companies, as I have described, from the investment merits of the shares in question. Once the discount on net asset value has been established, the shares are very attractive to a new investor.

Reasons Against Liquidation

My example of the £1 million company described a share with a break-up value of 20s which would stand in the market at only 15s, and many are, of course, worse than this. At first sight one would expect break-up arguments to be most attractive to shareholders, but, in fact, scarcely any liquidation of public property companies has taken place since the Chancellor of the Exchequer's announcement of the imminence of Corporation Tax in November,

1964, although wholesale movement towards liquidation was fore-
cast at that time by many financial commentators.

One impediment is section 22 of the Finance Act, 1960, which
provides that where companies dispose of properties which they
have developed within the previous six years, the whole of the
difference between cost and sale price is to be subject to tax. This
applies on liquidation and it applies irrespective of the April, 1965,
value of the property in question, which may well have been as great
as the sale price. There are many more restrictions such as this,
particularly those applying to companies under the control of five
or fewer people. Another obvious consideration is that some companies would find that a fair proportion of their assets would, in
fact, be difficult to sell. Additionally, there are all the costs of
liquidation to take into account, not to mention the consequences
in human terms where employees have to be considered. There is
also the question of Capital Gains Tax on the individual shareholders. The company would, at the very least, pay tax on any
increases in value realized since April, 1965, and then the individual stockholders would be liable on their ultimate gains over the
cost of the shares or their value in April, 1965, whichever basis
was appropriate. Thus the difference between 20s and 15s is
whittled down. These are just some of the negative reasons.

The positive reasons for staying in business vary widely from
case to case. One example is the medium-sized company built up
by a single individual who owns a large number of shares but does
not actually control the company. For estate duty purposes it may
suit him very well to have the investment stand at a large discount
on break-up, since estate duty would be payable on the value of
the shares as distinct from the value of the underlying assets. The
most important reason, in my view, however, is the fact that a
large and respectable property company can borrow large sums of
money quite readily whereas the individual property investor cannot. I mentioned earlier the example of a property doubling its
value in twenty-one years and being mortgaged by the owner in
such a way that his equity quadrupled in value over the period.
The questions of Capital Gains Tax and discount on break-up
become relatively unimportant when set against gains on this scale,
particularly when the discount is no more than maintained at the
level it had already reached.

One can only judge these matters in comparison with other forms
of investment, and the characteristics of being able to own a mass
of investment property and to finance it advantageously have not
been much affected by the new tax system. This, in fact, contains

the fundamental motive of the property investment business. The only vehicle to combine gearing with marketability so as to provide a convenient means of investment in property is the property company as we know it today.

Fixed-Interest Lending

Insurance companies are now the most important single investors in property. Their attitude is very important and must, I suppose, be determined by competitive conditions within their own industry. Their requirements vary from the short-term investment of straightforward insurance premiums to the very long-term programmes for endowment business, pension funds, and so forth. Up to now it seems that many institutions have been content to invest only the minority of their funds, even of their long-term funds, in property and equity investments. The bulk of their money is invested in fixed-interest securities ranging from Government stocks to the debentures and mortgages which are so important to property companies. There have been few years since the war when a year's interest on a loan, after tax, has been sufficient to outweigh the effects of inflation during that year. Therefore, the policy of fixed-interest lenders must be regarded as susceptible of change, and it has already changed to the point at which the small borrower can get a mortgage only for owner-occupation, the medium-sized property investor finds it extremely hard to get a mortgage at all and the only enterprises which can borrow really considerable sums in the open market are the large property companies which can issue debentures. This is the pattern: up to a certain size it is difficult, or impossible, to raise fixed-interest money, but beyond that size the large property company is in an extremely powerful position and I should like to emphasize just how remarkable this is. There are literally dozens of property companies which can quite readily raise millions of pounds of debenture money repayable over 35 years or so and bearing interest at $7\frac{1}{2}$ per cent. A surprising number of well-known industrial companies would find this hard to do and certainly they could not raise such a high proportion of the value of their assets.

I should now like to examine how it came about that the majority of developers operate as investment companies. Again, the reason is fundamentally a tax reason, because up to 1960 their position was certainly very favourable and many individuals who are now very rich were able, time and again, to develop a building, let it, and mortgage it, on terms which enabled them to retain the whole equity for a small, or even negative, cost in a tax climate which left them free to dispose of their shares whenever they chose as a capital transaction free of tax. Some of the attractions still remain, because the ultimate liability to Capital Gains Tax is a smaller penalty than would arise through any other medium, even though a measure of double taxation is involved. It is again necessary to consider the time scale, because the latent surplus earned on a development, *i.e.*, the difference between cost and value upon completion, is something which can remain unrealized for a very long time. The large investment company can add to its portfolio by development from year to year on the basis that none of the investments thereby created need be sold in the foreseeable future. The income produced by this latent profit is, admittedly, taxed very harshly, but this is not as severe as it seems, since one must remember that the initial motive for the transaction, the developer's profit, has not been taxed at all.

If tax rates were much lower and if surtax were abolished, I should expect individual developers gradually to return to what I understand was quite a common procedure before the war—developing, letting and then selling the completed investment. As things are, however, the developer, although he may well be dismayed by Corporation Tax, is likely to follow the current trend of keeping the completed investment indefinitely wherever he can. This brings me back to the question of mortgage money, and I hope I have made it clear that my comments about the difficulty of raising money in this form are not just related to the credit squeeze or anything of that sort. I am quite sure that, whatever happens to bank credit, mortgages for investment purposes will become more and more scarce. The lender can call the tune and he will certainly want an equity participation or a continuing interest expressed in the form of leaseback finance, although this will not apply in the case of the larger companies, which can float debenture issues on the Stock Exchange and, as a rule, need not part with equity in connection with the issue of a fixed-interest stock, except when problems sometimes arise in financing future development. This again emphasizes the difference between small operators and large operators and I think that the premium on largeness will become greater, just as the difficulties of the small operators are bound to increase quite apart from temporary credit squeeze considerations.

Diversification
Property companies almost by definition are expected to distribute their income in full and one must assume that if they did not their

shares would stand at an even greater discount on break-up value. At the present time, indeed, many large property companies are still unable to cover the dividends which they have maintained at levels established before the introduction of Corporation Tax. This, however, is only one detail of the situation created by Corporation Tax.

The old system of income tax and profits also involved a measure of double taxation and in this effect was roughly comparable with Corporation Tax—at 25 per cent as against 40 per cent today. So the change is only one of degree. Under the new system, on the other hand, retained profits are favoured and the value of £100 of trading profit which is retained and not paid out as dividend is now £60 compared with £43 under the old system: thus just as profits which are fully distributed have attracted a new penalty, so profits for retention attract a premium. This can be expressed in terms of the critical amount of dividend cover beyond which a company is better off under Corporation Tax than it was under the old system. At present tax rates this critical point is about 1·7 times cover. Thus, if a property investment company with an investment income after Corporation Tax of £100,000 can add to its income £70,000 from dealing and other sources, it will find itself better off than it could have been two or three years ago, and it can maintain its practice of distributing investment income in full without any net penalty. This is an incentive to property companies to use their strength to generate new income in addition to their income from net rentals, and I would expect more and more companies to examine their position on the lines which I have described. Some may get involved with full scale diversification into other fields, but I would not expect such operations to be completely satisfactory so far as shareholders are concerned, because anything approaching the appearance of an industrial holding company is sure to be regarded as suspect by the general public, in view of the bad record put up by so many of these concerns.

Successful diversification must be limited to one's own field, but for a property company this includes quite a wide range of activities—from housebuilding and general contracting at one extreme to the development of investments for re-sale at the other. Some large companies are already well embarked on this course and although no useful dividend covers are in evidence, I think they will be before very long. The point is to earn additional money from trading sources for retention, not for distribution; to refuse to do this is to bury one's head in the sand, because the Corporation Tax structure should be looked on as an incentive scheme designed to favour this form of activity. I need hardly point out, however, that it is only the larger companies, possessing or being able to acquire expert management, which can seriously contemplate the course I am proposing: for the smaller companies various other solutions will have to be found, or some will perish.

True Cost of Borrowing

Another matter to consider is the true cost of borrowing as against the real value of franked investment income. If a tax-paying company borrows at $7\frac{1}{2}$ per cent, it receives tax relief on the interest and the net cost is $4\frac{1}{2}$ per cent. If a company builds up an investment portfolio of ordinary shares to yield on average 6 per cent—and securities of the highest standing can be bought today on this basis —the dividend is franked income, i.e., it bears no further tax in the hands of the company and can be passed on intact to shareholders as dividend. In theory, it might be argued that the pure property investment company which will have nothing to do with trading should still borrow all it can by way of mortgage, even if the proceeds are used only for investment on the Stock Exchange to produce a diversified portfolio of quoted securities. Indeed, the property company is better placed in this respect than the orthodox investment trust, because tax relief on the cost of borrowing is granted only to the extent that the borrower would otherwise have paid tax. Thus, the property company gets Corporation Tax relief on the cost of borrowing, whereas the investment trust often does not, because orthodox policy would be to invest mainly in equities in order to produce franked income to pass on to its shareholders. Consequently, the orthodox investment trust usually has very little liability for Corporation Tax. There arises, therefore, the curious position that the effective net cost of borrowing at, say, $7\frac{1}{2}$ per cent is $4\frac{1}{2}$ per cent to a tax-paying property company but $7\frac{1}{2}$ per cent to an investment trust, which, in any case, pays no tax. The significance of this simple situation has not, I think, yet been appreciated very thoroughly, but when it becomes better understood it may prompt a number of significant moves.

One can extend this thesis in another direction by saying that the real incentive of the Corporation Tax system is to place oneself in the position of paying as little tax as possible. This sounds quite obvious, but very few people, I think, direct much strategic thought to it. Ideally, one might aim at the position where the whole of one's existing taxable or unfranked income should be committed to pay interest and so forth, so that the net profit distributable to shareholders could be backed by franked income. To put this proposition another way, I am saying that the limited company can best afford to own investment property if the cost is covered entirely by borrowing in one form or another. The shareholders' equity can then reflect sources of franked income and trading profit.

The old-fashioned companies which are proud to own large portfolios of uncharged property may indeed possess a most creditworthy and respectable structure, but this is pointless, because, from a taxation point of view, it is most wasteful unless the structure is used for the basis of borrowing on the largest possible scale to finance growth in their own chosen field and also in the other areas which I have described.

Understanding the Tax Position

The characteristics of our tax system penalize different classes of investors to different extents and this means that a source of unfranked income in the form of rent really has different values to different people. The example of a short-leasehold investment being worth much more to a pension fund than to a limited company is well known. The different values of income from a freehold are not, perhaps, appreciated so thoroughly. The income from a freehold investment returning 7 per cent on cost is worth 7 per cent to a gross fund, only about $5\frac{1}{4}$ per cent to several forms of endowment insurance company funds and less than $4\frac{1}{4}$ per cent to a property investment company. Investment by each of these three in the shares of ICI at the present Stock Exchange price would return 6·9 per cent and this would be franked income, the value of which to each of the three would be exactly the same—the full 6·9 per cent. The property company which uses shareholders' money to buy an investment property must seek a yield of $11\frac{1}{2}$ per cent to return the same net income for its shareholders.

It is not quite as simple as this, of course, but I hope I have said enough to illustrate how important it is for people to understand the tax position of others as well as the way it affects themselves. Property companies are not now the best buyers of completed property investments, and they have not been for some time. Any new tax system is designed to shift the burden of incentives and disincentives and it is foolish to persist with a rigid attitude. Low-yielding reversionary properties can be worth far more to an institution than to a property company and I expect more and more investment business to develop where companies will sell such properties in order to re-invest to better effect. Similarly, although one would like to retain every development after letting, it would now be better, in some cases, to sell and realize a taxable profit. The outlook for agents with really good investments departments is very bright.

Reports in the financial papers show that quite a number of property companies are reconstructing themselves so as to limit their Corporation Tax liability and to increase the income of existing shareholders. This is done by forming a new company which acquires the capital of the old company, partly for new ordinary shares and partly for loan stock. The interest on the loan stock is allowable for tax and, consequently, the new group pays that much less tax: if £1 million of 8 per cent loan stock is created in this way, the new group will pay £32,000 per annum less tax than was paid by the old group. Reconstructions of this nature are perfectly legitimate and are an understandable reaction to the Corporation Tax system. You will gather that I am saying that the limited company may not be perfect, but it is the best thing we have and its sensible operation requires a contemporary understanding of tax.

I should like to conclude with a reference to experience in the USA, where Corporation Tax is higher than it is in this country at present and where at one time the ownership of investment property in corporate form was so heavily penalized that the position became absurd. In 1960 the American Government introduced the Real Estate Investment Trust Act which allowed bona-fide investment companies representing small shareholders to operate free of Corporation Tax to the extent that they distributed their income to the stockholders. There is no doubt that Corporation Tax will go up rather than down in this country and it might not be premature for our industry to start to canvas along the same lines.

Just as tax rates will rise, so the rules will change, and it can be only a matter of time before the earned income of individuals is treated more favourably. If anyone feels particularly depressed about the current state of the rules, he should remember that everything is continually changing and it is a matter of timing to determine the best way of moulding the conduct of our affairs so as to fit the rules from year to year. I hope I have managed to convey the message that if we plan sensibly we can operate effectively under Corporation Tax and that to do this requires the best advice, a general knowledge of tax and an inquiring mind. We must avoid rigid concentration on our own problems and develop a wider understanding of the whole framework presented to us by the Government. If we do this sensibly, our businesses can be more successful than they are today.

Index